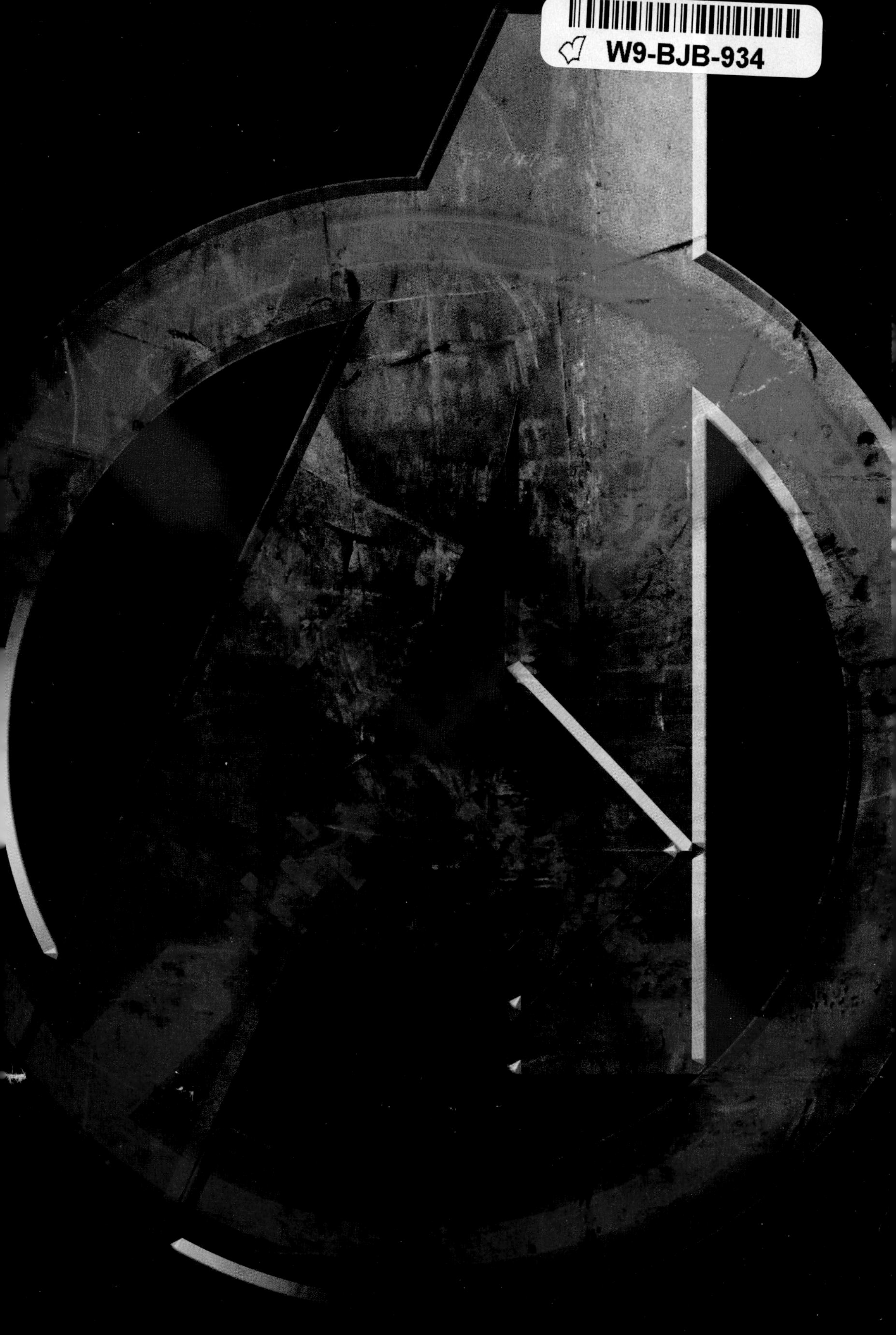

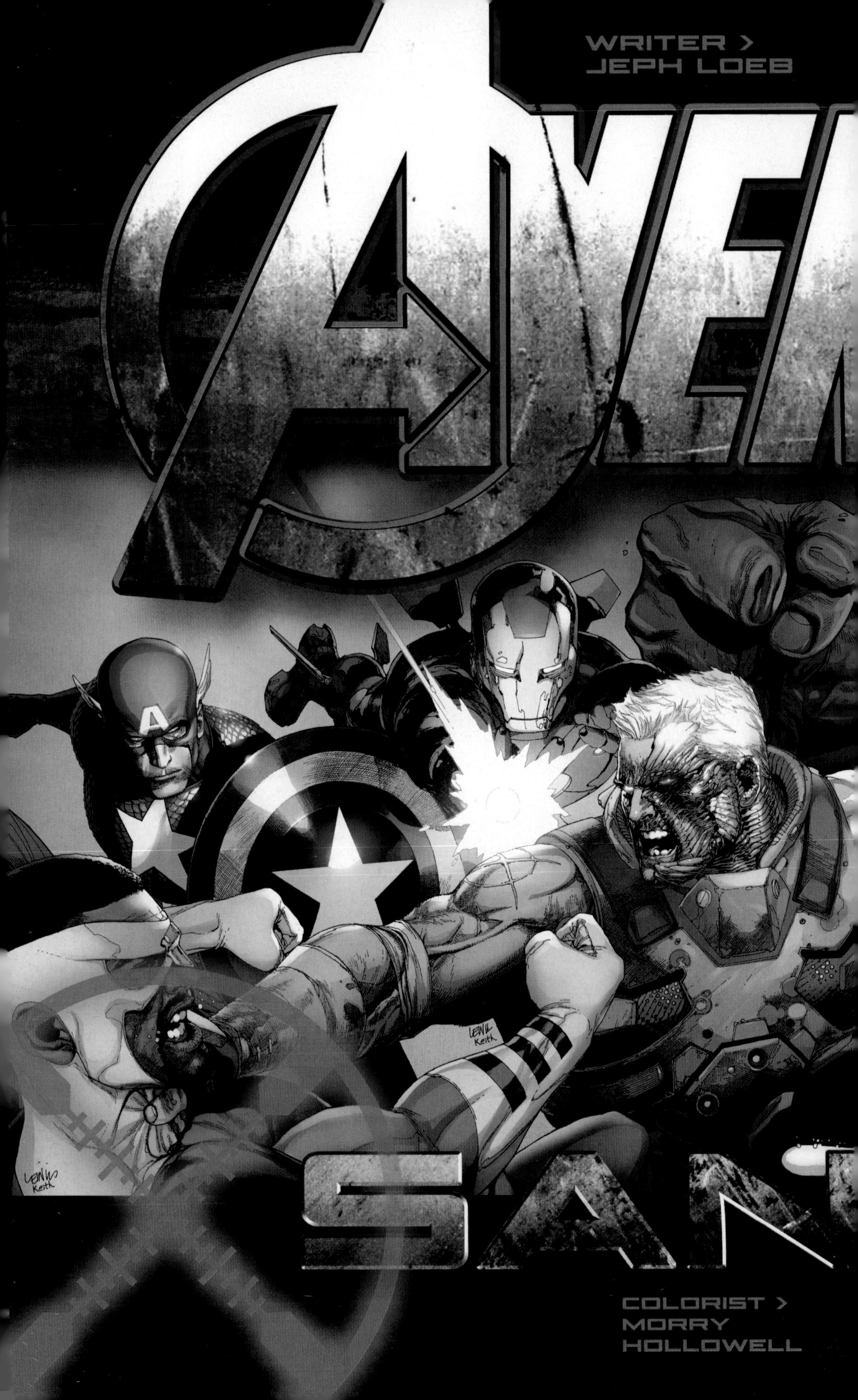
WRITER >
JEPH LOEB
COLORIST >
MORRY
HOLLOWELL

ED McGUINNESS DEXTER VINES

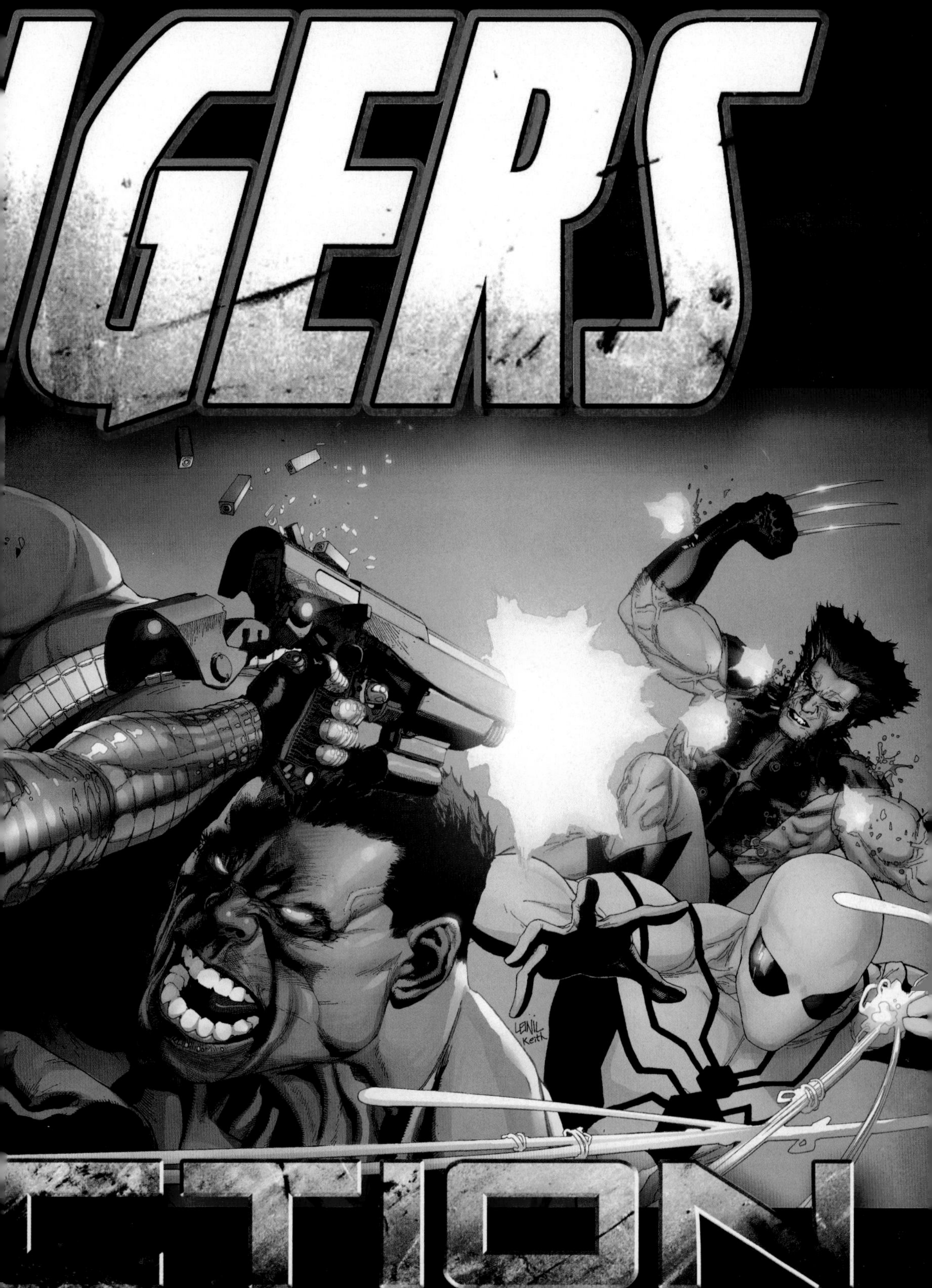

LETTERING >
COMICRAFT'S
ALBERT DESCHESNE

COVER ART >
ED McGUINNESS, DEXTER
VINES & MORRY HOLLOWELL

ASSISTANT EDITOR > JOHN DENNING
ASSOCIATE EDITOR > LAUREN SANKOVITCH
EDITOR > TOM BREVOORT

COLLECTION EDITOR > JENNIFER GRÜNWALD
ASSISTANT EDITORS > ALEX STARBUCK & NELSON RIBEIRO
EDITOR, SPECIAL PROJECTS > MARK D. BEAZLEY
SENIOR EDITOR, SPECIAL PROJECTS > JEFF YOUNGQUIST
SENIOR VICE PRESIDENT OF SALES > DAVID GABRIEL
SVP OF BRAND PLANNING & COMMUNICATIONS > MICHAEL PASCIULLO
BOOK DESIGNER > JOHN ROSHELL OF COMICRAFT

EDITOR IN CHIEF > AXEL ALONSO
CHIEF CREATIVE OFFICER > JOE QUESADA
PUBLISHER > DAN BUCKLEY
EXECUTIVE PRODUCER > ALAN FINE

AVENGERS: X-SANCTION. Contains material originally published in magazine form as AVENGERS: X-SANCTION #1-4. First printing 2012. ISBN# 978-0-7851-5863-9. Published by MARVEL WORLDWIDE, INC., a subsidiary of MARVEL ENTERTAINMENT, LLC. OFFICE OF PUBLICATION: 135 West 50th Street, New York, NY 10020. $19.99 per copy in the U.S. and $21.99 in Canada (GST #R127032852); Canadian Agreement #40668537. **Printed in the U.S.A.** ALAN FINE, EVP - Office of the President, Marvel Worldwide, Inc. and EVP & CMO Marvel Characters B.V.; DAN BUCKLEY, Publisher & President - Print, Animation & Digital Divisions; JOE QUESADA, Chief Creative Officer; TOM BREVOORT, SVP of Publishing; DAVID BOGART, SVP of Operations & Procurement, Publishing; RUWAN JAYATILLEKE, SVP & Associate Publisher, Publishing; C.B. CEBULSKI, SVP of Creator & Content Development; DAVID GABRIEL, SVP of Publishing Sales & Circulation; MICHAEL PASCIULLO, SVP of Brand Planning & Communications; JIM O'KEEFE, VP of Operations & Logistics; DAN CARR, Executive Director of Publishing Technology; SUSAN CRESPI, Editorial Operations Manager; ALEX MORALES, Publishing Operations Manager; STAN LEE, Chairman Emeritus. For information regarding advertising in Marvel Comics or on Marvel.com, please contact Niza Disla, Director of Marvel Partnerships, at ndisla@marvel.com. For Marvel subscription inquiries, please call 800-217-9158. **Manufactured between 10/17/2012 and 11/19/2012 by R.R. DONNELLEY, INC., SALEM, VA, USA.**

10 9 8 7 6 5 4 3 2 1

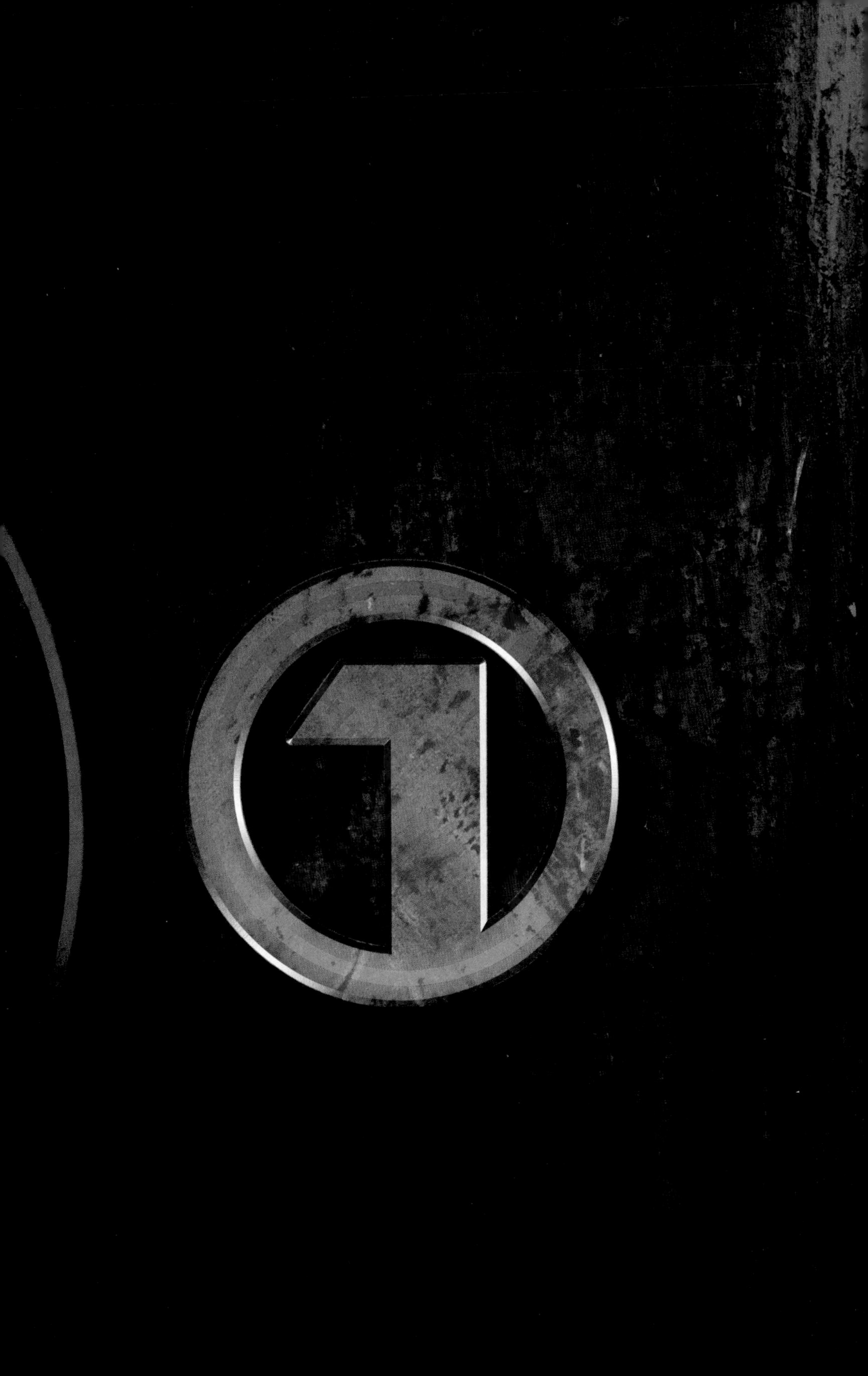
1

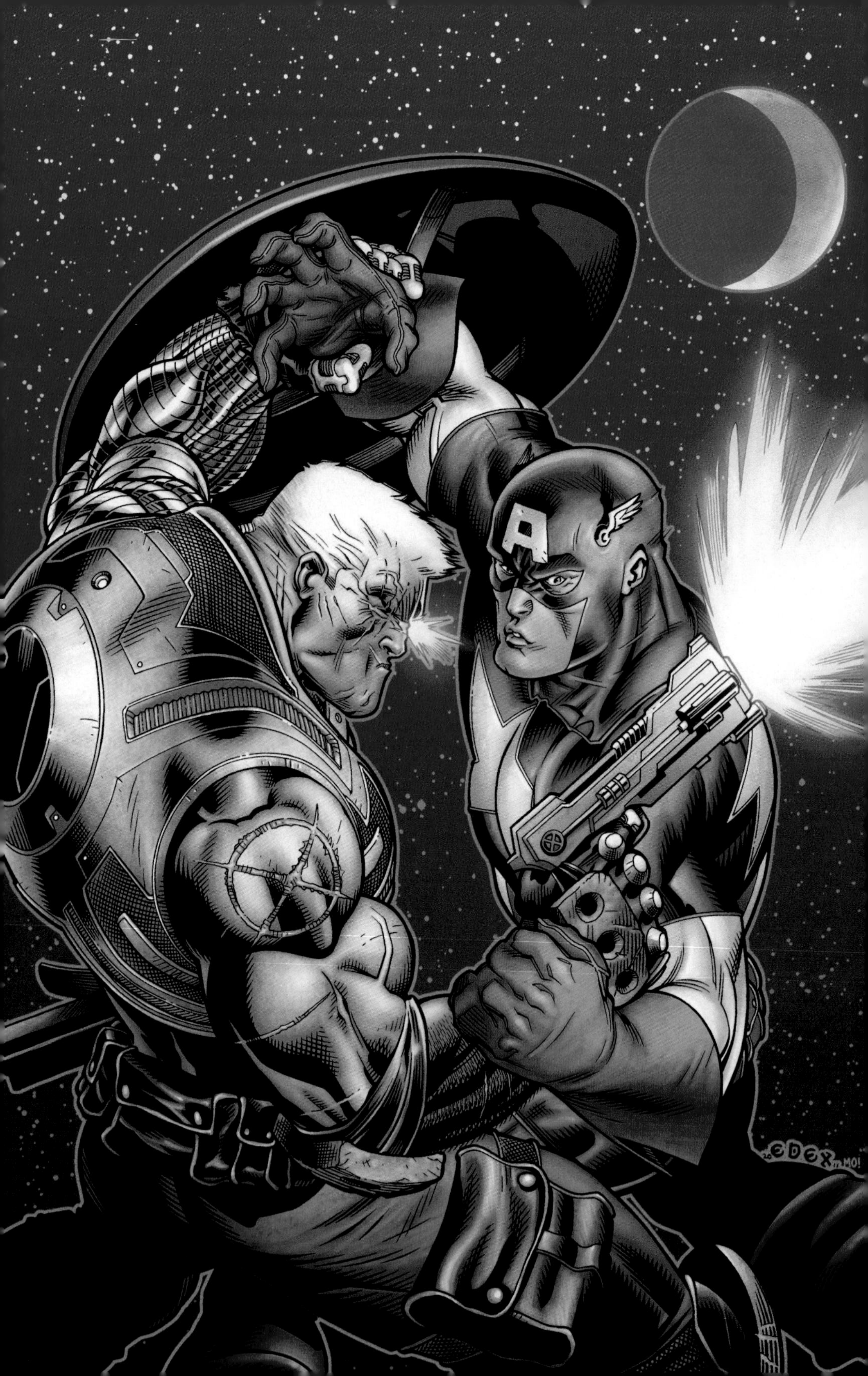

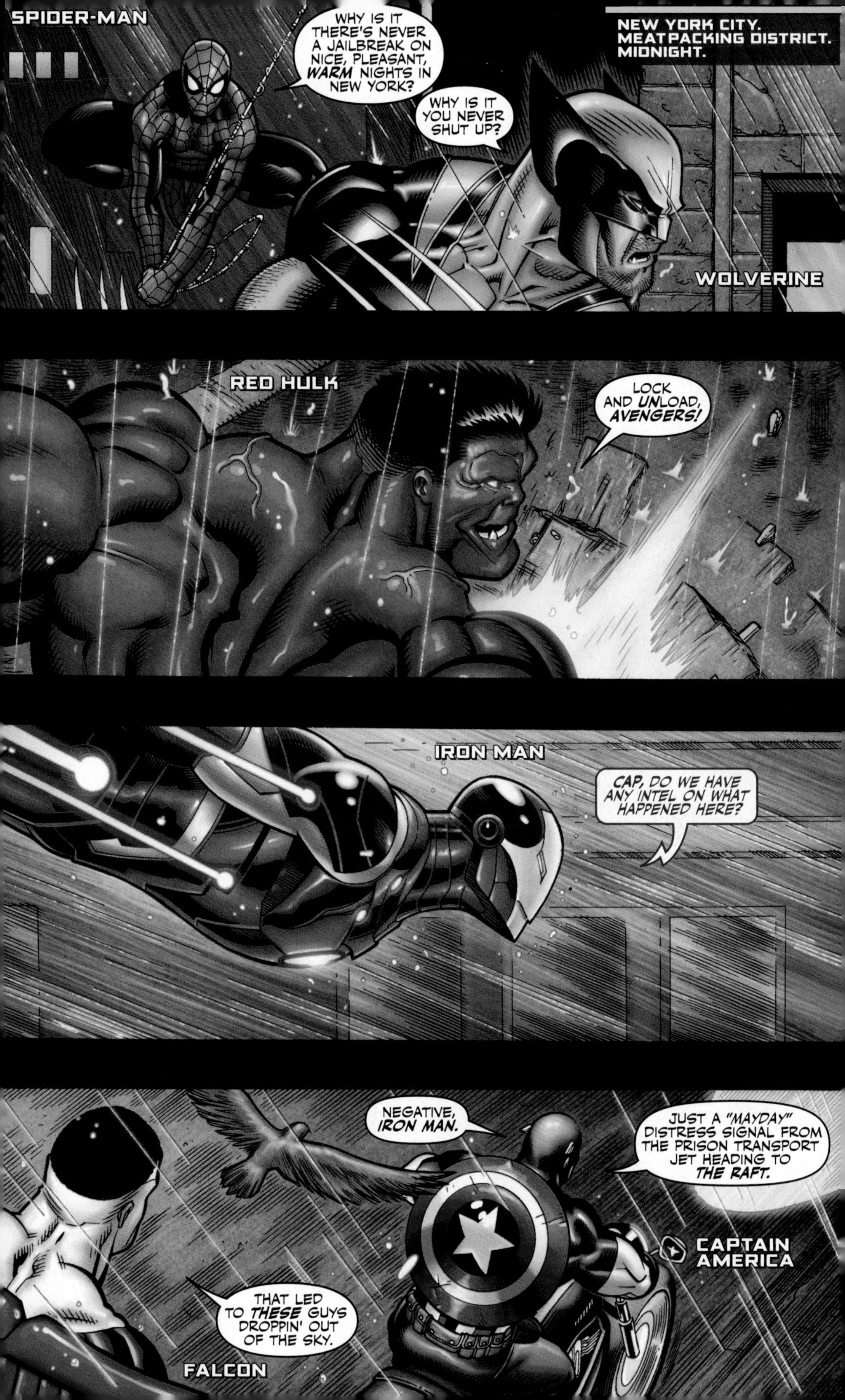

SPIDER-MAN
NEW YORK CITY. MEATPACKING DISTRICT. MIDNIGHT.
WHY IS IT THERE'S NEVER A JAILBREAK ON NICE, PLEASANT, WARM NIGHTS IN NEW YORK?
WHY IS IT YOU NEVER SHUT UP?
WOLVERINE
RED HULK
LOCK AND UNLOAD, AVENGERS!
IRON MAN
CAP, DO WE HAVE ANY INTEL ON WHAT HAPPENED HERE?
NEGATIVE, IRON MAN.
JUST A "MAYDAY" DISTRESS SIGNAL FROM THE PRISON TRANSPORT JET HEADING TO THE RAFT.
CAPTAIN AMERICA
THAT LED TO THESE GUYS DROPPIN' OUT OF THE SKY.
FALCON

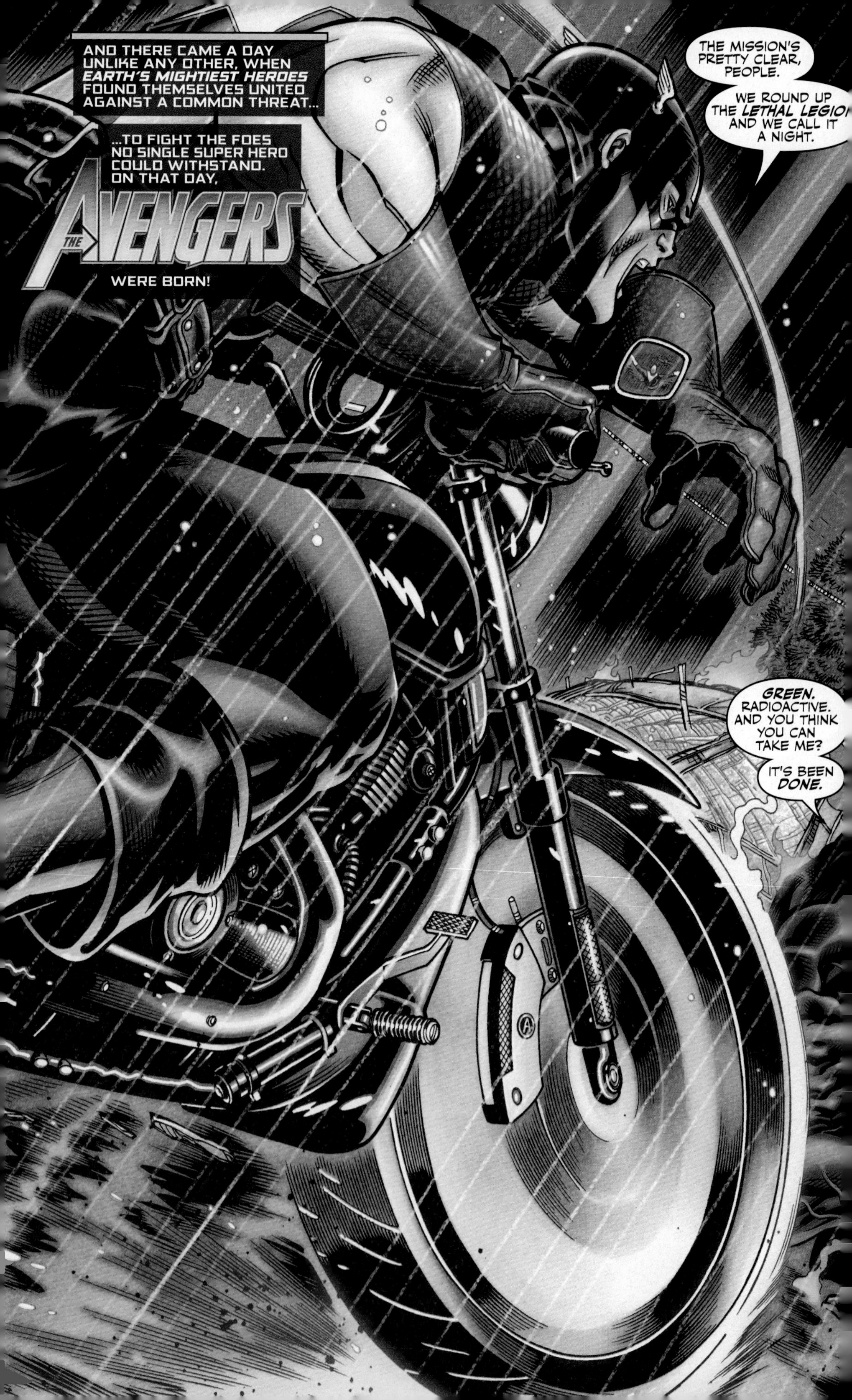
AND THERE CAME A DAY UNLIKE ANY OTHER, WHEN EARTH'S MIGHTIEST HEROES FOUND THEMSELVES UNITED AGAINST A COMMON THREAT...
...TO FIGHT THE FOES NO SINGLE SUPER HERO COULD WITHSTAND. ON THAT DAY,
THE AVENGERS
WERE BORN!
THE MISSION'S PRETTY CLEAR, PEOPLE.
WE ROUND UP THE LETHAL LEGION AND WE CALL IT A NIGHT.
GREEN. RADIOACTIVE. AND YOU THINK YOU CAN TAKE ME?
IT'S BEEN DONE.

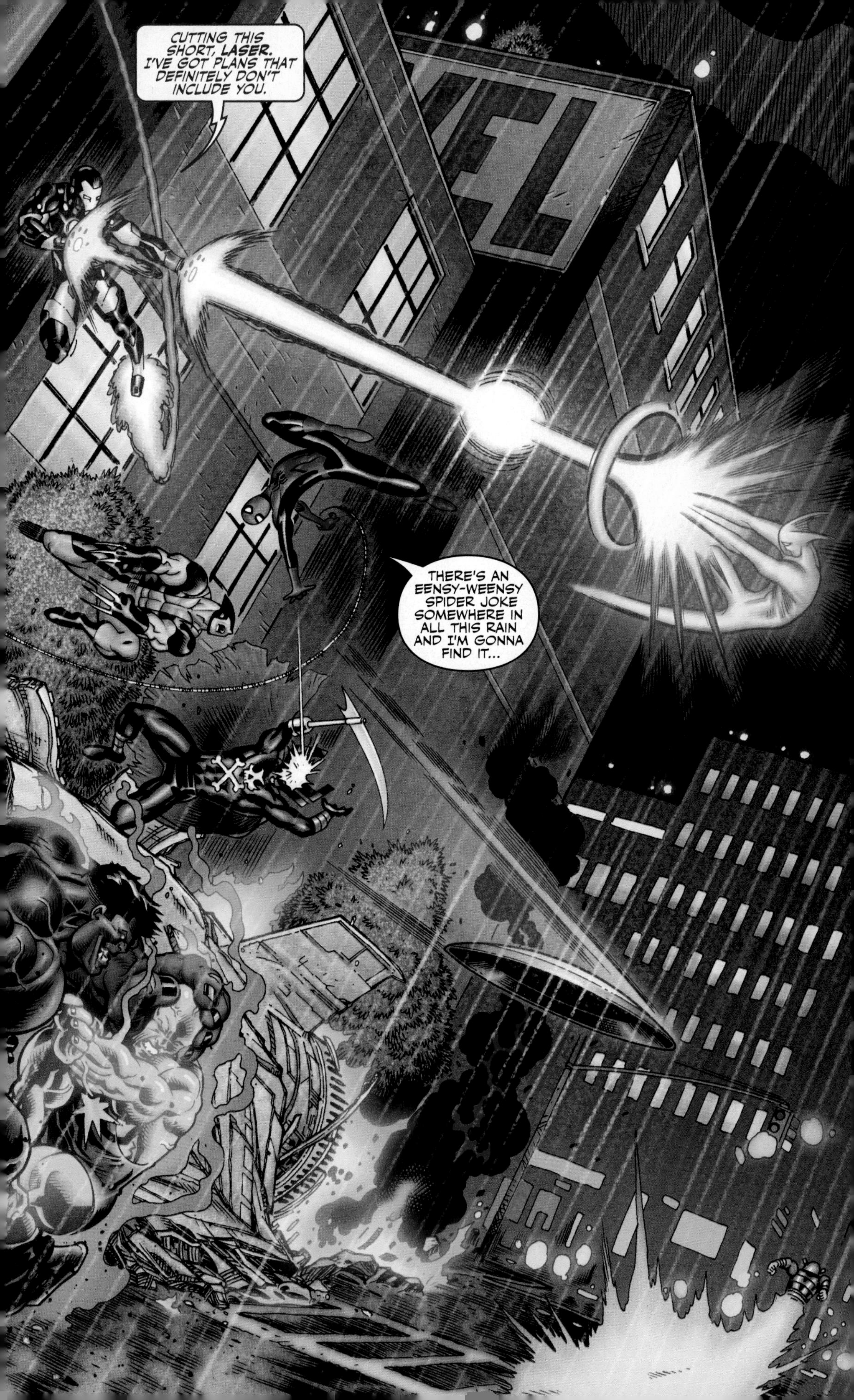
CUTTING THIS SHORT, LASER. I'VE GOT PLANS THAT DEFINITELY DON'T INCLUDE YOU.
THERE'S AN EENSY-WEENSY SPIDER JOKE SOMEWHERE IN ALL THIS RAIN AND I'M GONNA FIND IT...

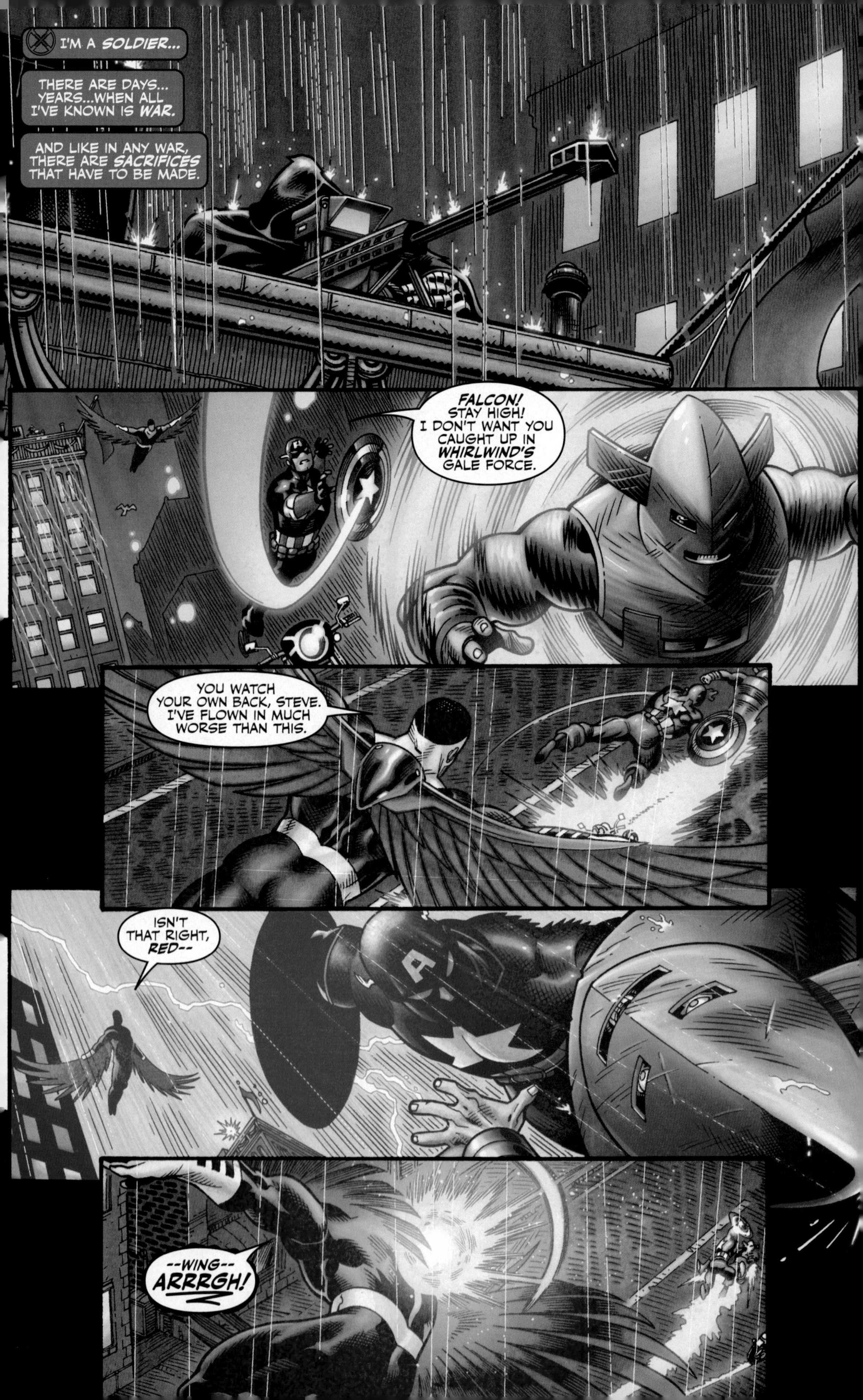
I'M A SOLDIER...
THERE ARE DAYS... YEARS...WHEN ALL I'VE KNOWN IS WAR.
AND LIKE IN ANY WAR, THERE ARE SACRIFICES THAT HAVE TO BE MADE.
FALCON! STAY HIGH! I DON'T WANT YOU CAUGHT UP IN WHIRLWIND'S GALE FORCE.
YOU WATCH YOUR OWN BACK, STEVE. I'VE FLOWN IN MUCH WORSE THAN THIS.
ISN'T THAT RIGHT, RED--
--WING--
ARRRGH!

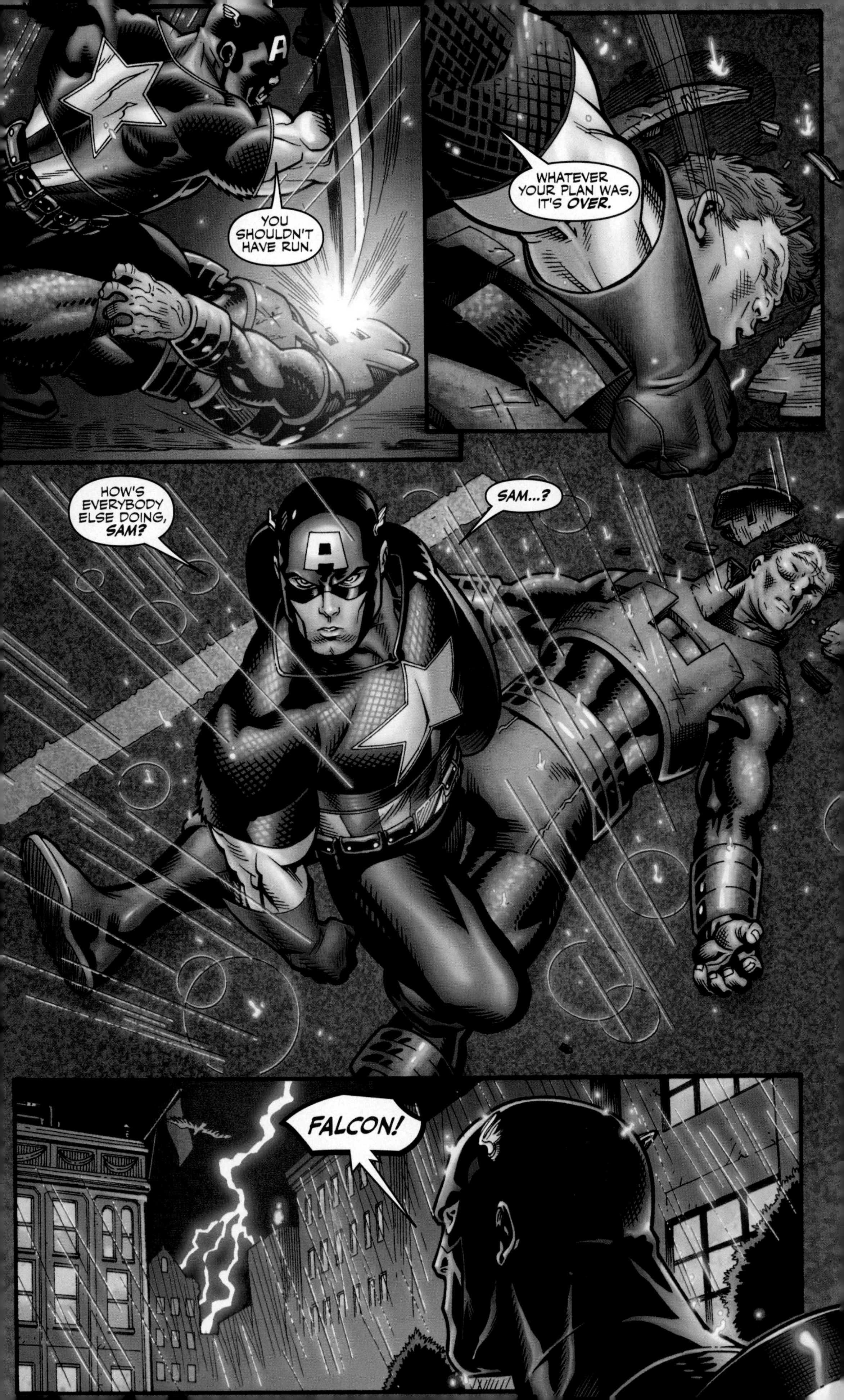
YOU SHOULDN'T HAVE RUN.
WHATEVER YOUR PLAN WAS, IT'S OVER.
HOW'S EVERYBODY ELSE DOING, SAM?
SAM...?
FALCON!

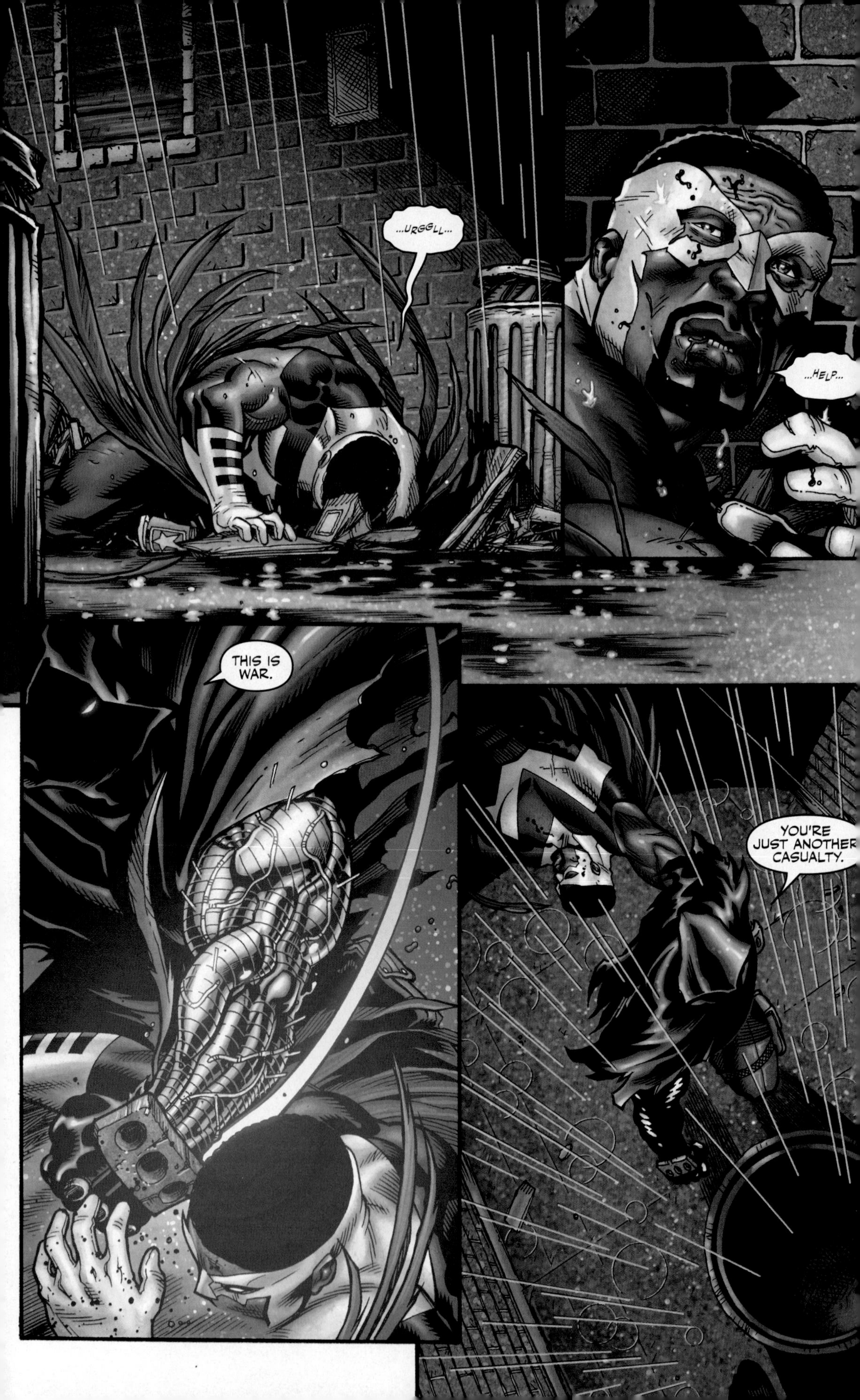
...URGGLL...
...HELP...
THIS IS WAR.
YOU'RE JUST ANOTHER CASUALTY.

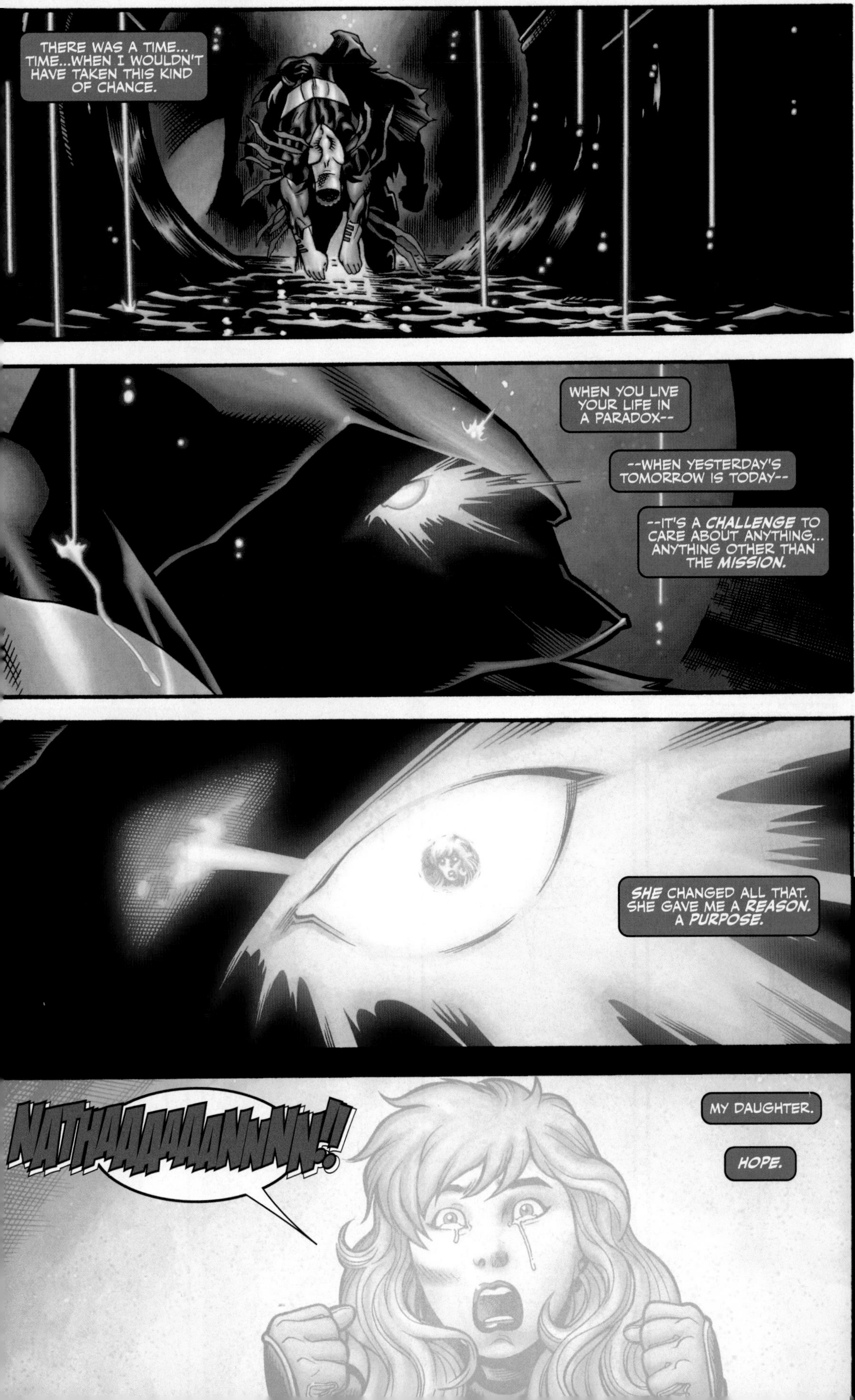

THERE WAS A TIME... TIME...WHEN I WOULDN'T HAVE TAKEN THIS KIND OF CHANCE.
WHEN YOU LIVE YOUR LIFE IN A PARADOX--
--WHEN YESTERDAY'S TOMORROW IS TODAY--
--IT'S A *CHALLENGE* TO CARE ABOUT ANYTHING... ANYTHING OTHER THAN THE *MISSION.*
SHE CHANGED ALL THAT. SHE GAVE ME A *REASON.* A *PURPOSE.*
NATHAAAAAANNNN!!
MY DAUGHTER.
HOPE.

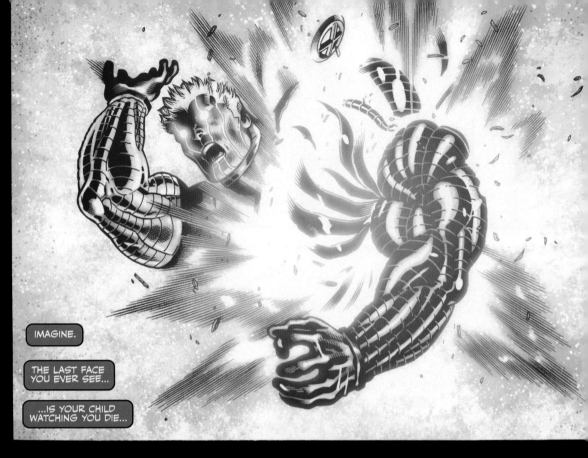

IMAGINE.

THE LAST FACE YOU EVER SEE...

...IS YOUR CHILD WATCHING YOU DIE...

TIMESLIDE. THE FAR FUTURE.

HELLO...?!

IS ANYBODY OUT THERE?!

HELLLLLLOOOO!

OH...

...HELL..

IT WAS A TIME...TIME... THE HEAT...OPPRESSIVE.

...NOTHING... BUT ASH...

...MAYBE I DID DIE...

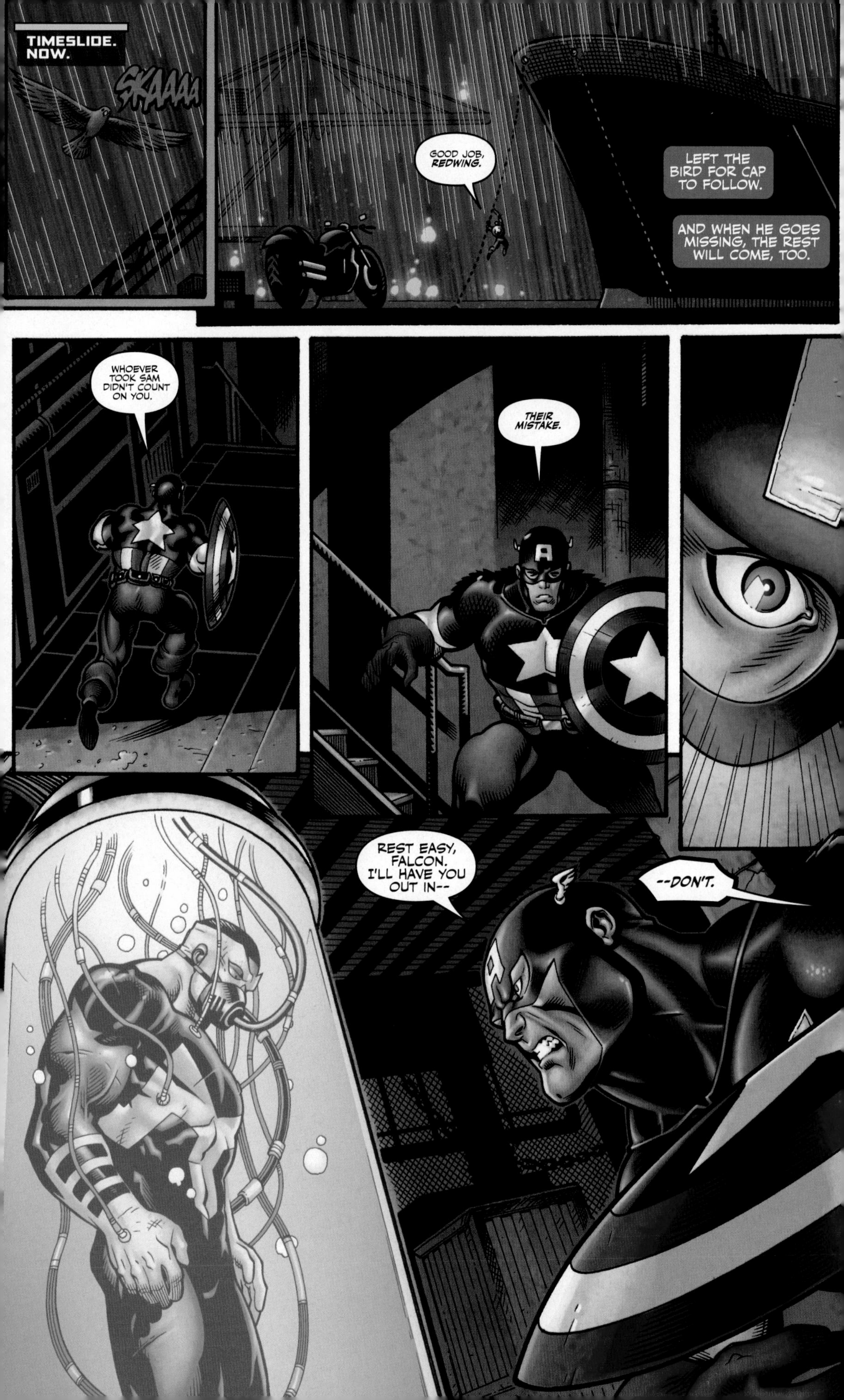

TIMESLIDE. NOW.
SKAAAA
GOOD JOB, REDWING.
LEFT THE BIRD FOR CAP TO FOLLOW.
AND WHEN HE GOES MISSING, THE REST WILL COME, TOO.
WHOEVER TOOK SAM DIDN'T COUNT ON YOU.
THEIR MISTAKE.
REST EASY, FALCON. I'LL HAVE YOU OUT IN--
--DON'T.

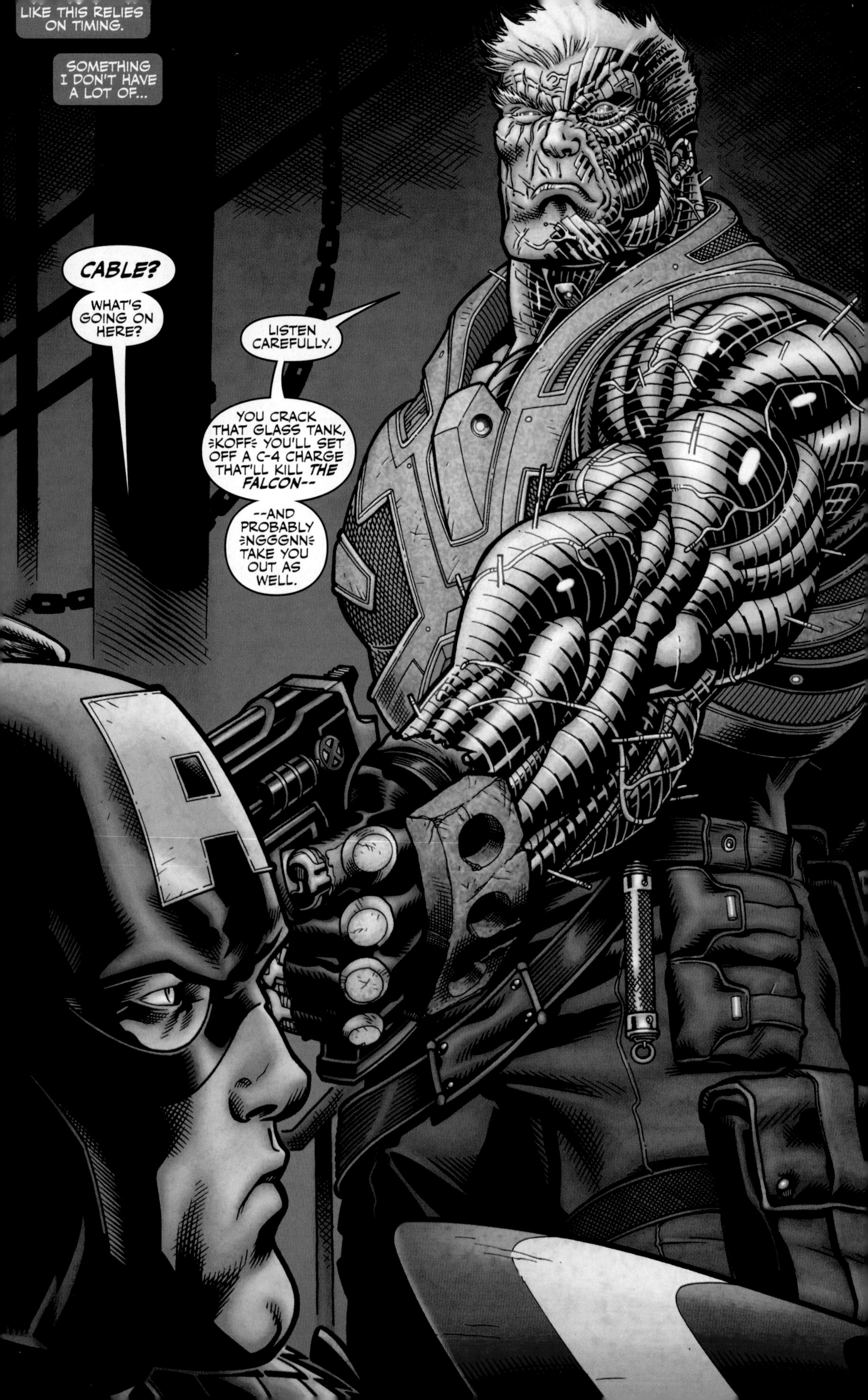
LIKE THIS RELIES ON TIMING.
SOMETHING I DON'T HAVE A LOT OF...
CABLE?
WHAT'S GOING ON HERE?
LISTEN CAREFULLY.
YOU CRACK THAT GLASS TANK, KOFF YOU'LL SET OFF A C-4 CHARGE THAT'LL KILL THE FALCON--
--AND PROBABLY NGGGNN TAKE YOU OUT AS WELL.

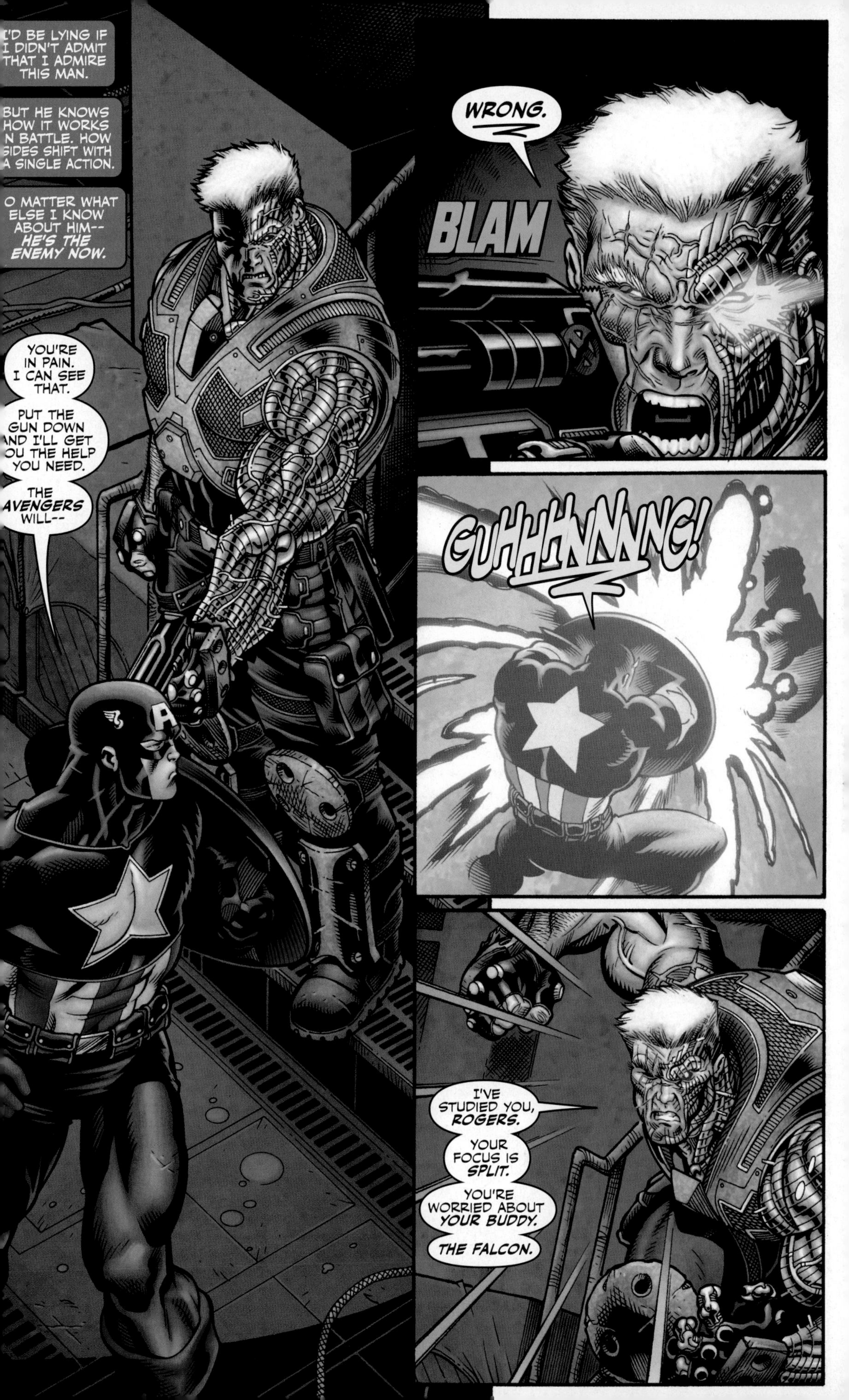
I'D BE LYING IF I DIDN'T ADMIT THAT I ADMIRE THIS MAN.
BUT HE KNOWS HOW IT WORKS N BATTLE. HOW SIDES SHIFT WITH A SINGLE ACTION.
O MATTER WHAT ELSE I KNOW ABOUT HIM-- HE'S THE ENEMY NOW.
YOU'RE IN PAIN. I CAN SEE THAT.
PUT THE GUN DOWN ND I'LL GET OU THE HELP YOU NEED.
THE AVENGERS WILL--
WRONG.
BLAM
GUHHHNNNNG!
I'VE STUDIED YOU, ROGERS.
YOUR FOCUS IS SPLIT.
YOU'RE WORRIED ABOUT YOUR BUDDY.
THE FALCON.

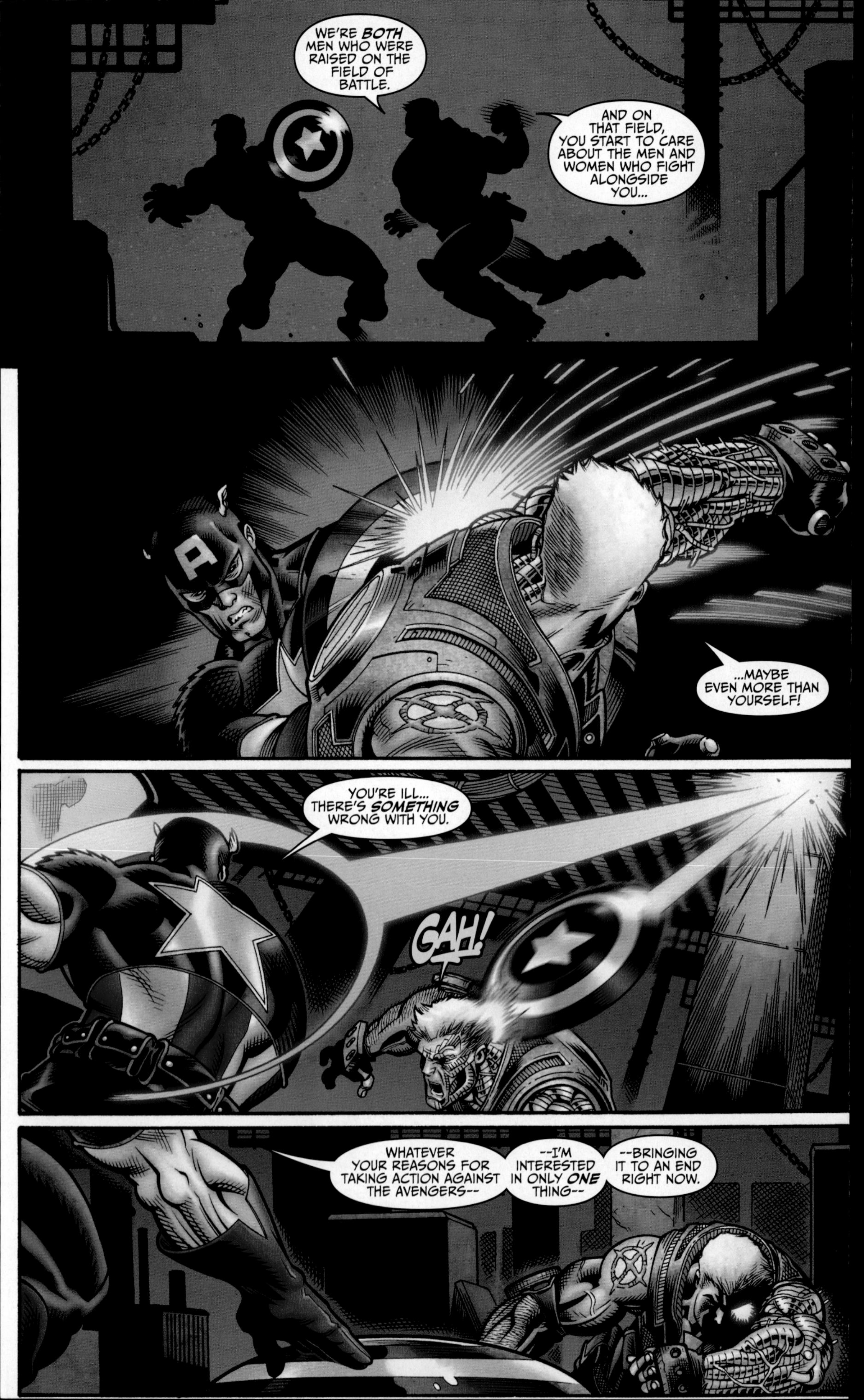
WE'RE BOTH MEN WHO WERE RAISED ON THE FIELD OF BATTLE.
AND ON THAT FIELD, YOU START TO CARE ABOUT THE MEN AND WOMEN WHO FIGHT ALONGSIDE YOU...
...MAYBE EVEN MORE THAN YOURSELF!
YOU'RE ILL... THERE'S SOMETHING WRONG WITH YOU.
GAH!
WHATEVER YOUR REASONS FOR TAKING ACTION AGAINST THE AVENGERS--
--I'M INTERESTED IN ONLY ONE THING--
--BRINGING IT TO AN END RIGHT NOW.

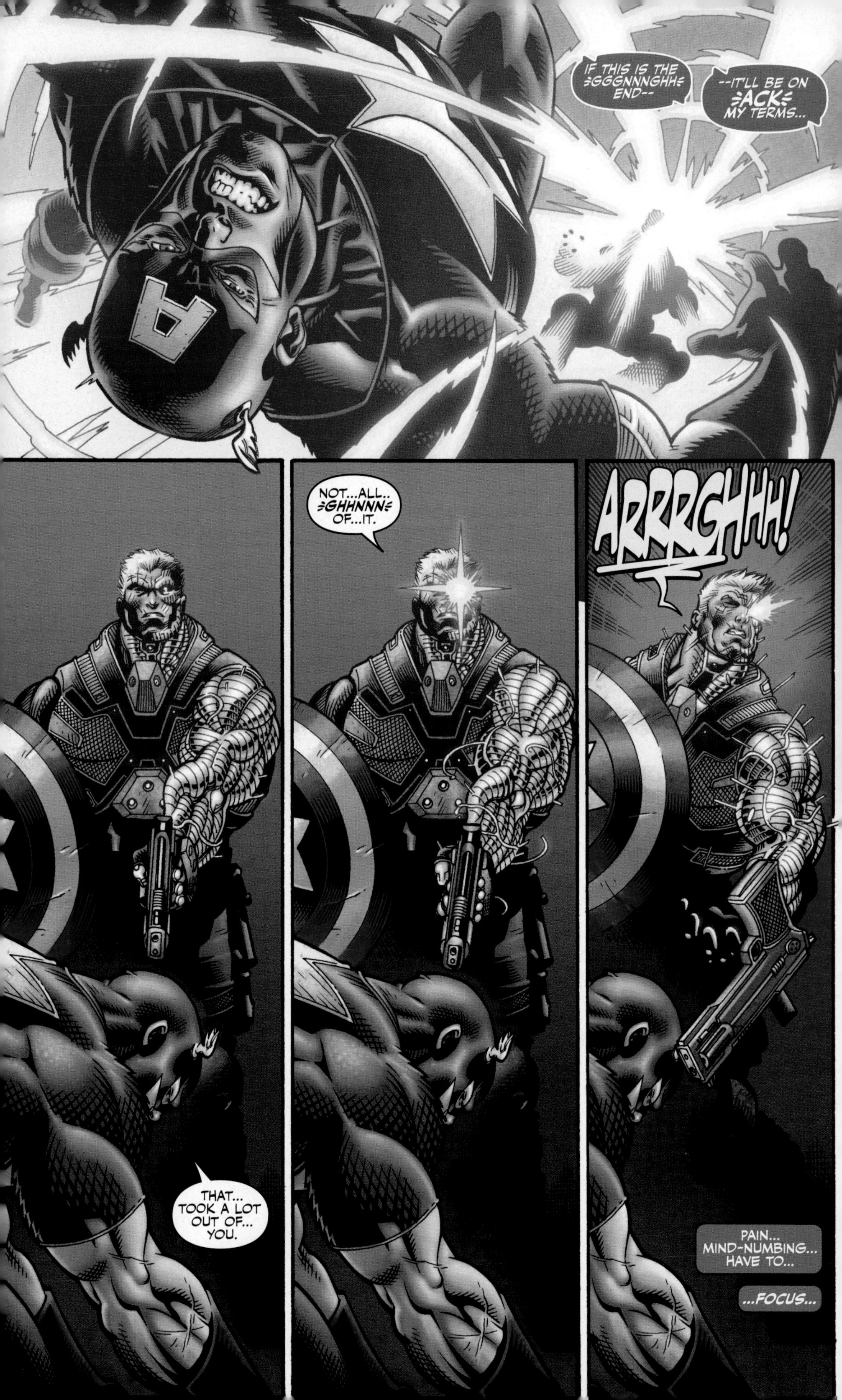
IF THIS IS THE GGGNNNGHH END--
--IT'LL BE ON ACK MY TERMS...
THAT... TOOK A LOT OUT OF... YOU.
NOT...ALL.. GHHNNN OF...IT.
ARRRGHHH!
PAIN... MIND-NUMBING... HAVE TO...
...FOCUS...

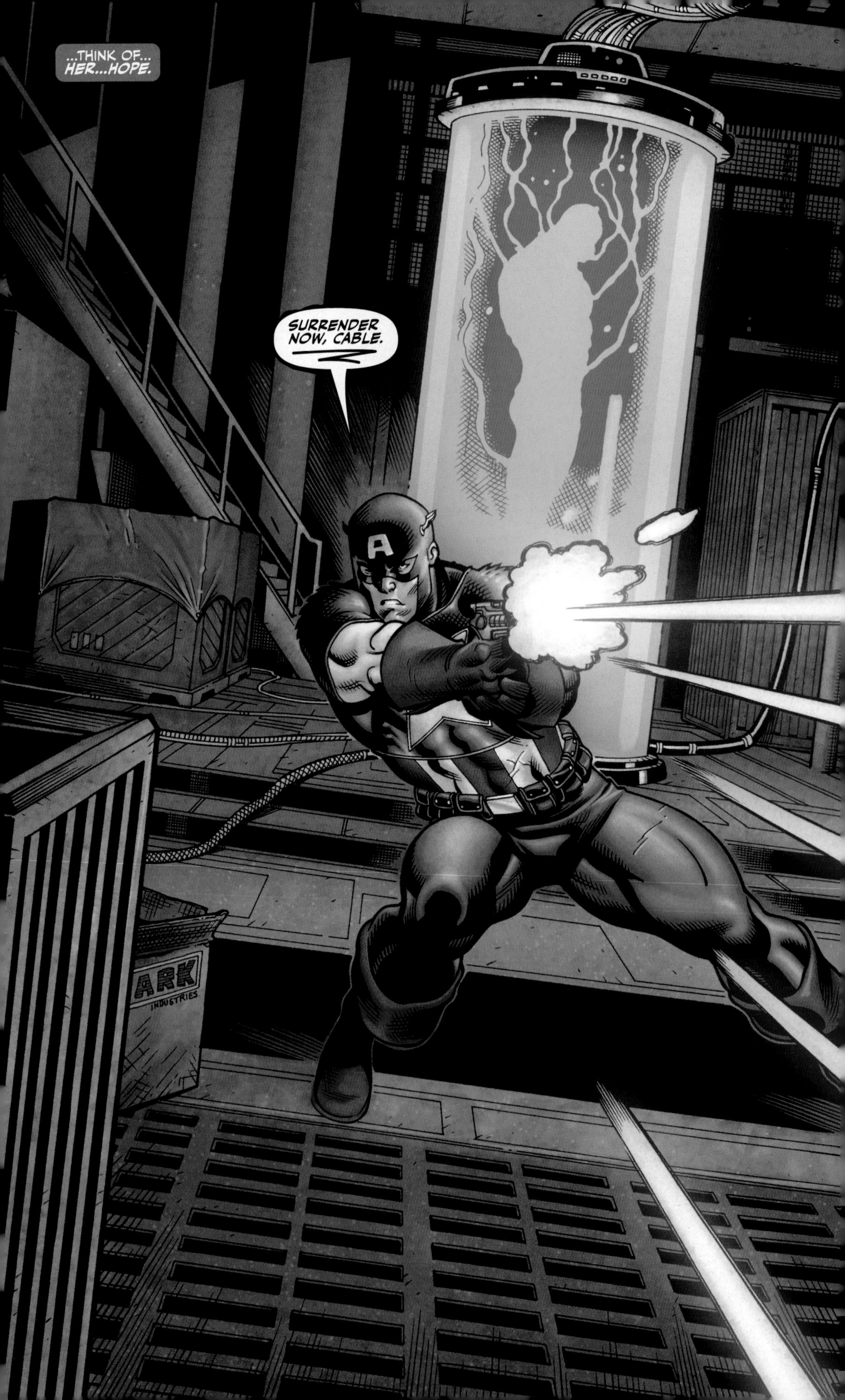
...THINK OF... HER...HOPE.
SURRENDER NOW, CABLE.
ARK INDUSTRIES

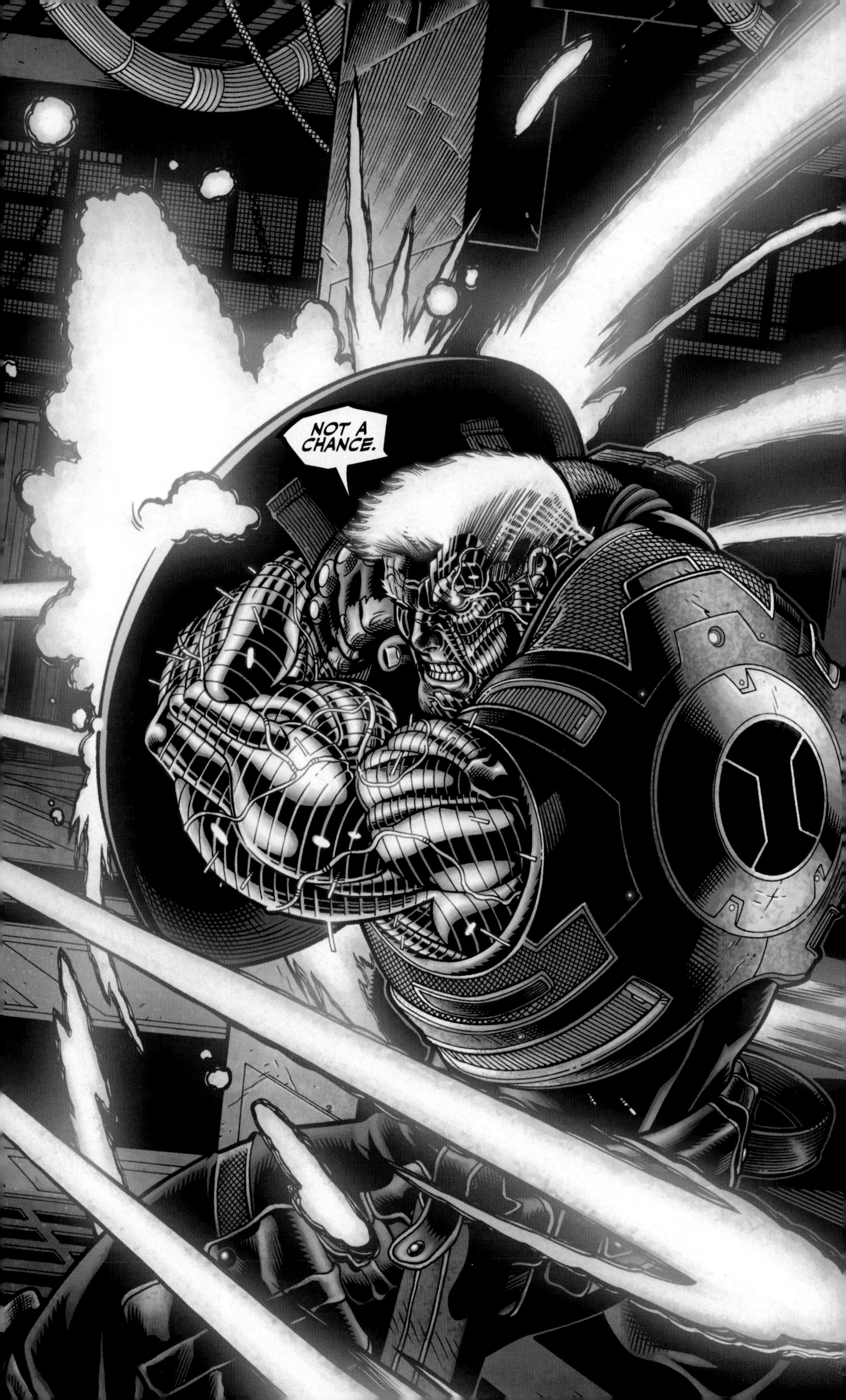
NOT A CHANCE.

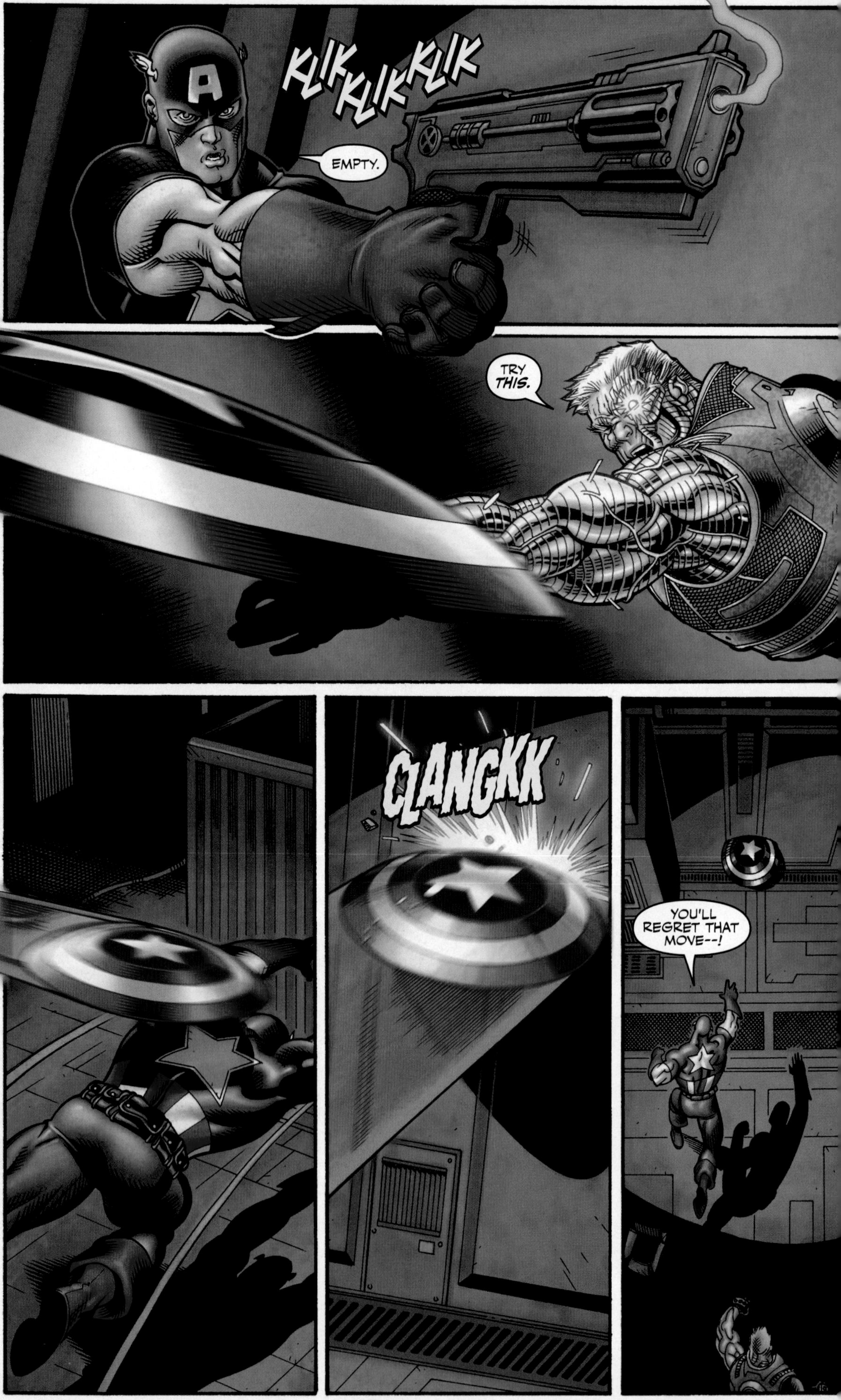
KLIK KLIK KLIK KLIK
EMPTY.
TRY THIS.
CLANGKK
YOU'LL REGRET THAT MOVE--!

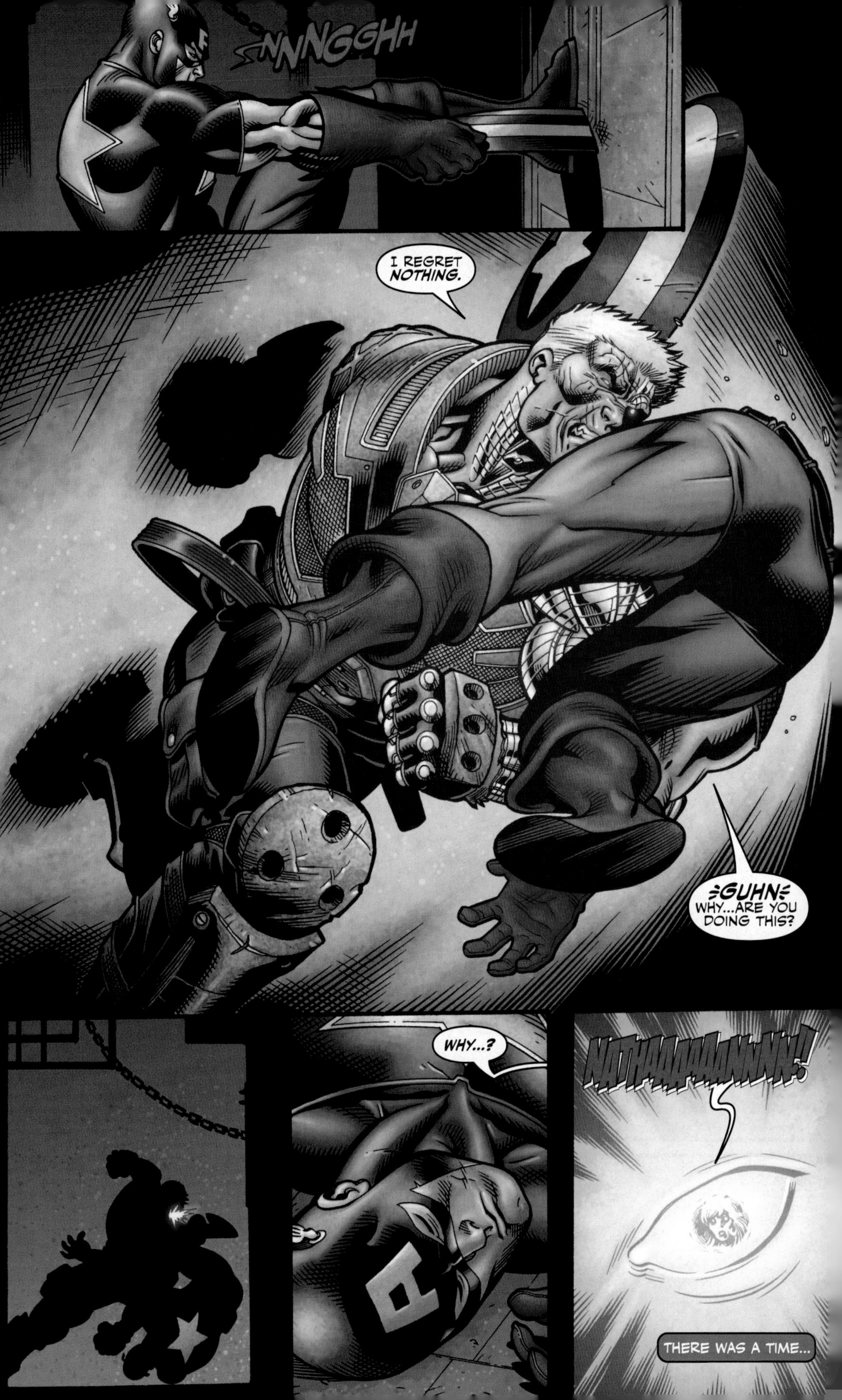
SNNNGGHH
I REGRET NOTHING.
GUHN WHY...ARE YOU DOING THIS?
WHY...?
NATHAAAAAANNNN!!
THERE WAS A TIME...

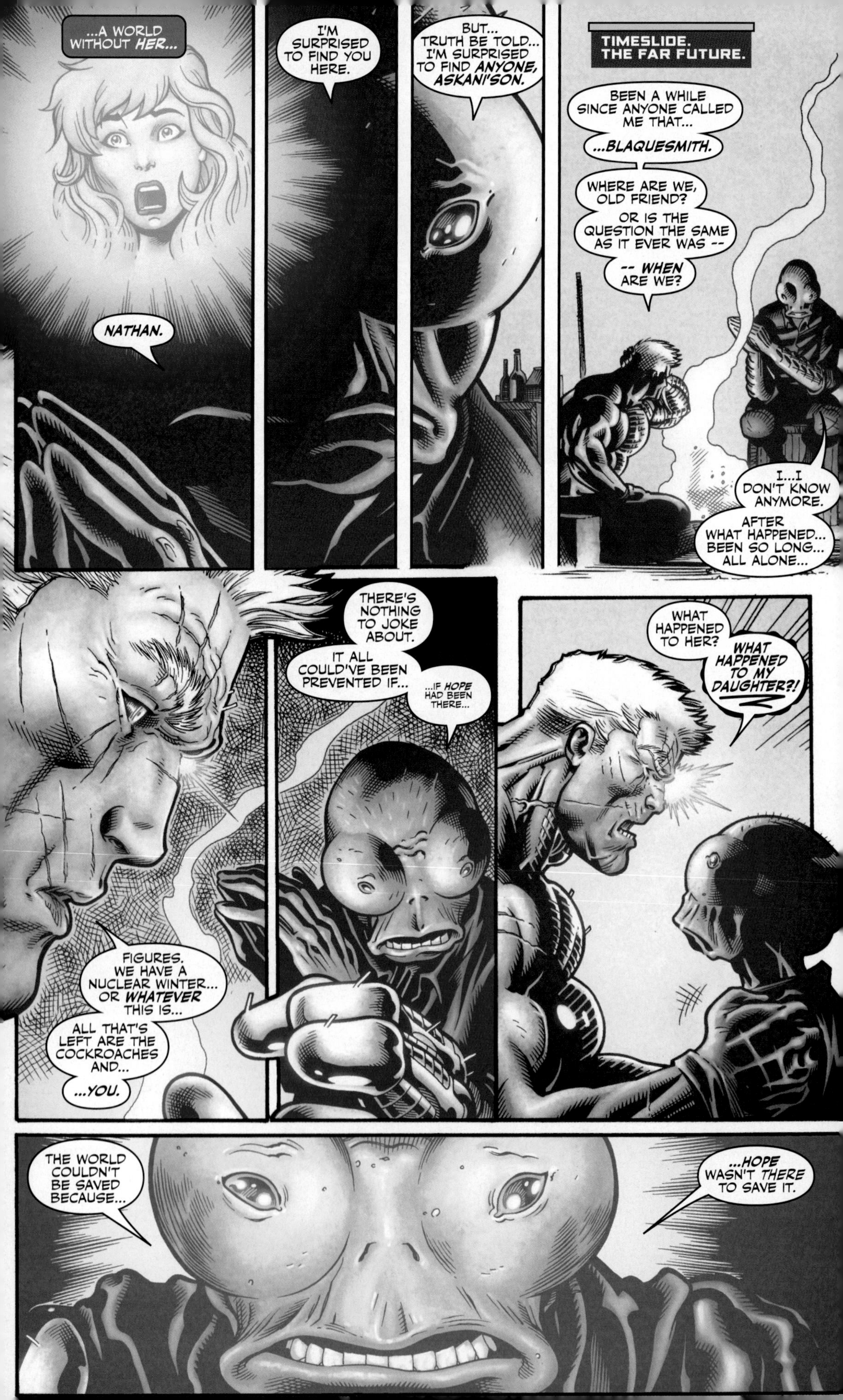
...A WORLD WITHOUT *HER*...
NATHAN.
I'M SURPRISED TO FIND YOU HERE.
BUT... TRUTH BE TOLD... I'M SURPRISED TO FIND *ANYONE, ASKANI'SON.*
TIMESLIDE. THE FAR FUTURE.
BEEN A WHILE SINCE ANYONE CALLED ME THAT...
...BLAQUESMITH.
WHERE ARE WE, OLD FRIEND?
OR IS THE QUESTION THE SAME AS IT EVER WAS --
-- *WHEN* ARE WE?
I...I DON'T KNOW ANYMORE.
AFTER WHAT HAPPENED... BEEN SO LONG... ALL ALONE...
FIGURES. WE HAVE A NUCLEAR WINTER... OR *WHATEVER* THIS IS...
ALL THAT'S LEFT ARE THE COCKROACHES AND...
...YOU.
THERE'S NOTHING TO JOKE ABOUT.
IT ALL COULD'VE BEEN PREVENTED IF...
...IF *HOPE* HAD BEEN THERE...
WHAT HAPPENED TO HER?
WHAT HAPPENED TO MY DAUGHTER?!
THE WORLD COULDN'T BE SAVED BECAUSE...
...HOPE WASN'T *THERE* TO SAVE IT.

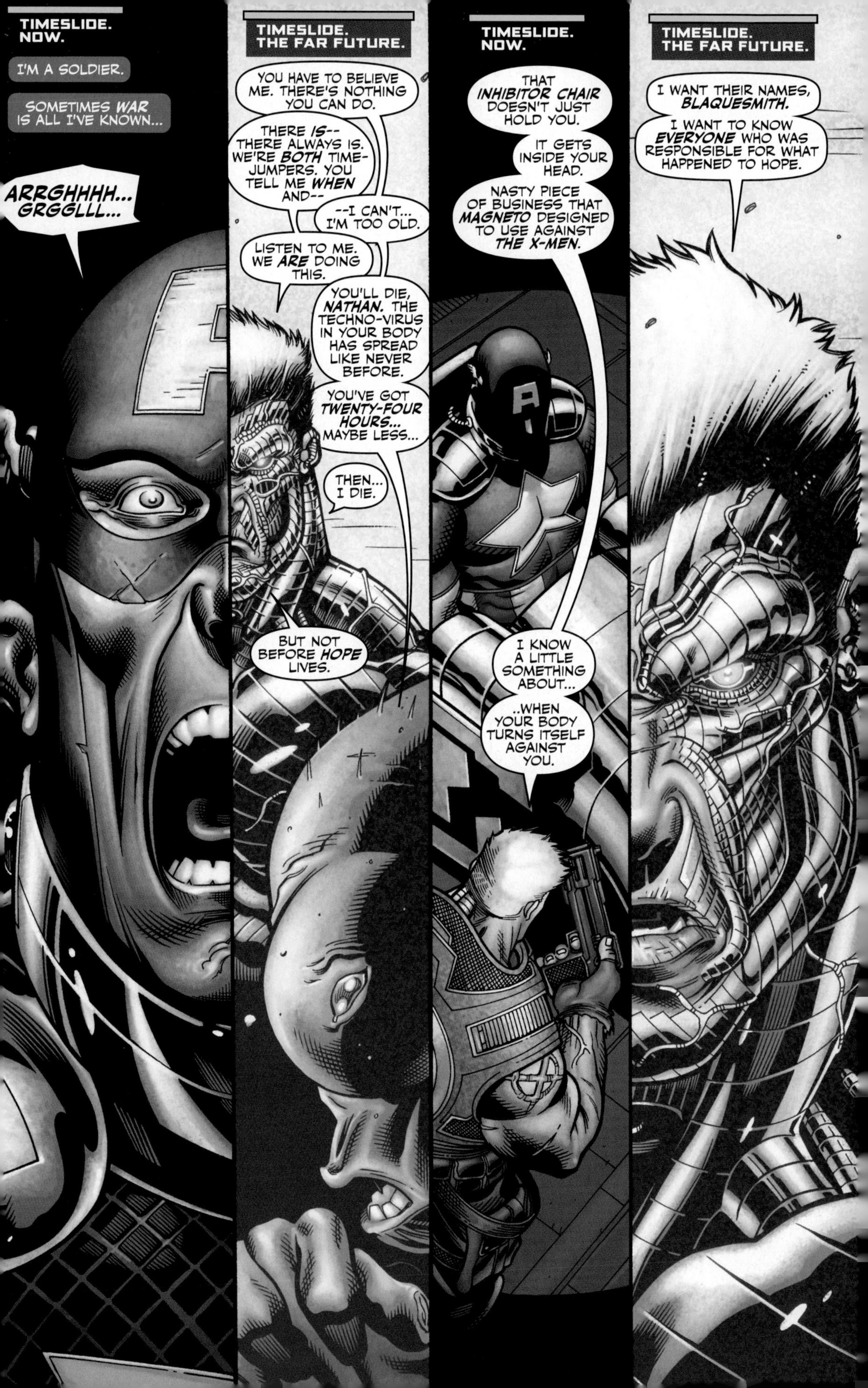
TIMESLIDE. NOW.
I'M A SOLDIER.
SOMETIMES WAR IS ALL I'VE KNOWN...
ARRGHHHH... GRGGLLL...
TIMESLIDE. THE FAR FUTURE.
YOU HAVE TO BELIEVE ME. THERE'S NOTHING YOU CAN DO.
THERE IS-- THERE ALWAYS IS. WE'RE BOTH TIME-JUMPERS. YOU TELL ME WHEN AND--
--I CAN'T... I'M TOO OLD.
LISTEN TO ME. WE ARE DOING THIS.
YOU'LL DIE, NATHAN. THE TECHNO-VIRUS IN YOUR BODY HAS SPREAD LIKE NEVER BEFORE.
YOU'VE GOT TWENTY-FOUR HOURS... MAYBE LESS...
THEN... I DIE.
BUT NOT BEFORE HOPE LIVES.
TIMESLIDE. NOW.
THAT INHIBITOR CHAIR DOESN'T JUST HOLD YOU.
IT GETS INSIDE YOUR HEAD.
NASTY PIECE OF BUSINESS THAT MAGNETO DESIGNED TO USE AGAINST THE X-MEN.
I KNOW A LITTLE SOMETHING ABOUT...
..WHEN YOUR BODY TURNS ITSELF AGAINST YOU.
TIMESLIDE. THE FAR FUTURE.
I WANT THEIR NAMES, BLAQUESMITH.
I WANT TO KNOW EVERYONE WHO WAS RESPONSIBLE FOR WHAT HAPPENED TO HOPE.

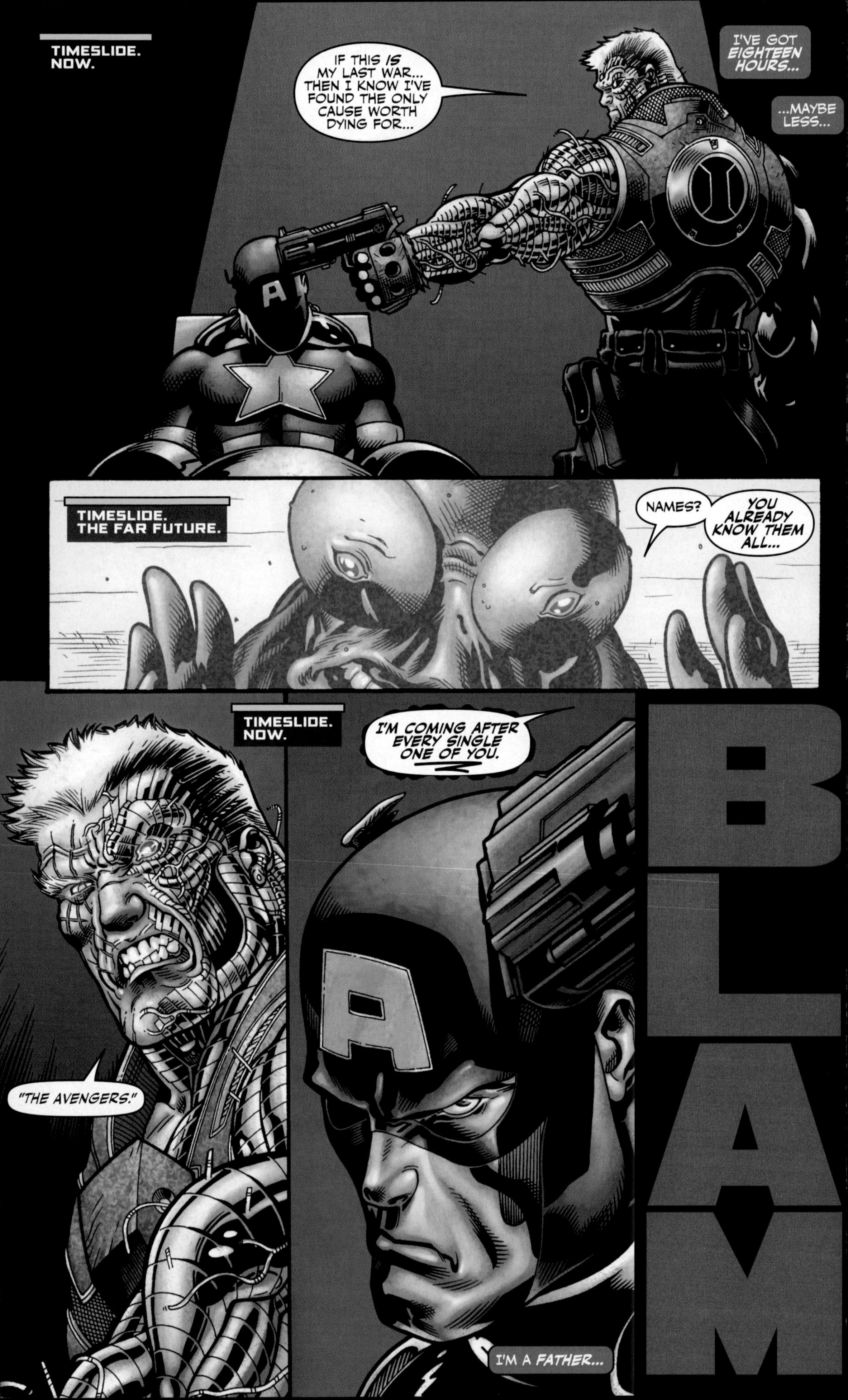
TIMESLIDE. NOW.
IF THIS IS MY LAST WAR... THEN I KNOW I'VE FOUND THE ONLY CAUSE WORTH DYING FOR...
I'VE GOT EIGHTEEN HOURS...
...MAYBE LESS...
TIMESLIDE. THE FAR FUTURE.
NAMES?
YOU ALREADY KNOW THEM ALL...
TIMESLIDE. NOW.
"THE AVENGERS."
I'M COMING AFTER EVERY SINGLE ONE OF YOU.
I'M A FATHER...
BLAM

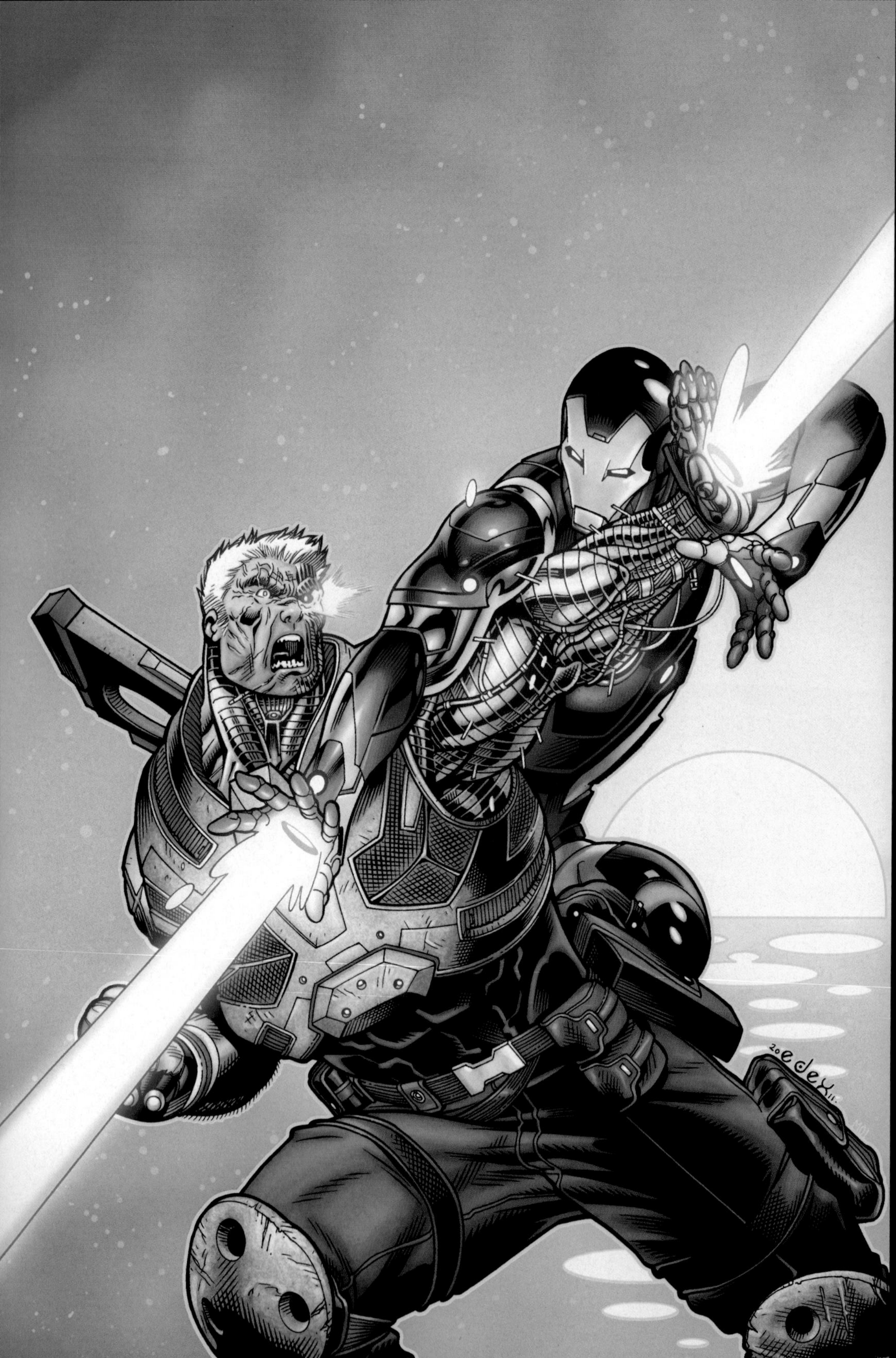

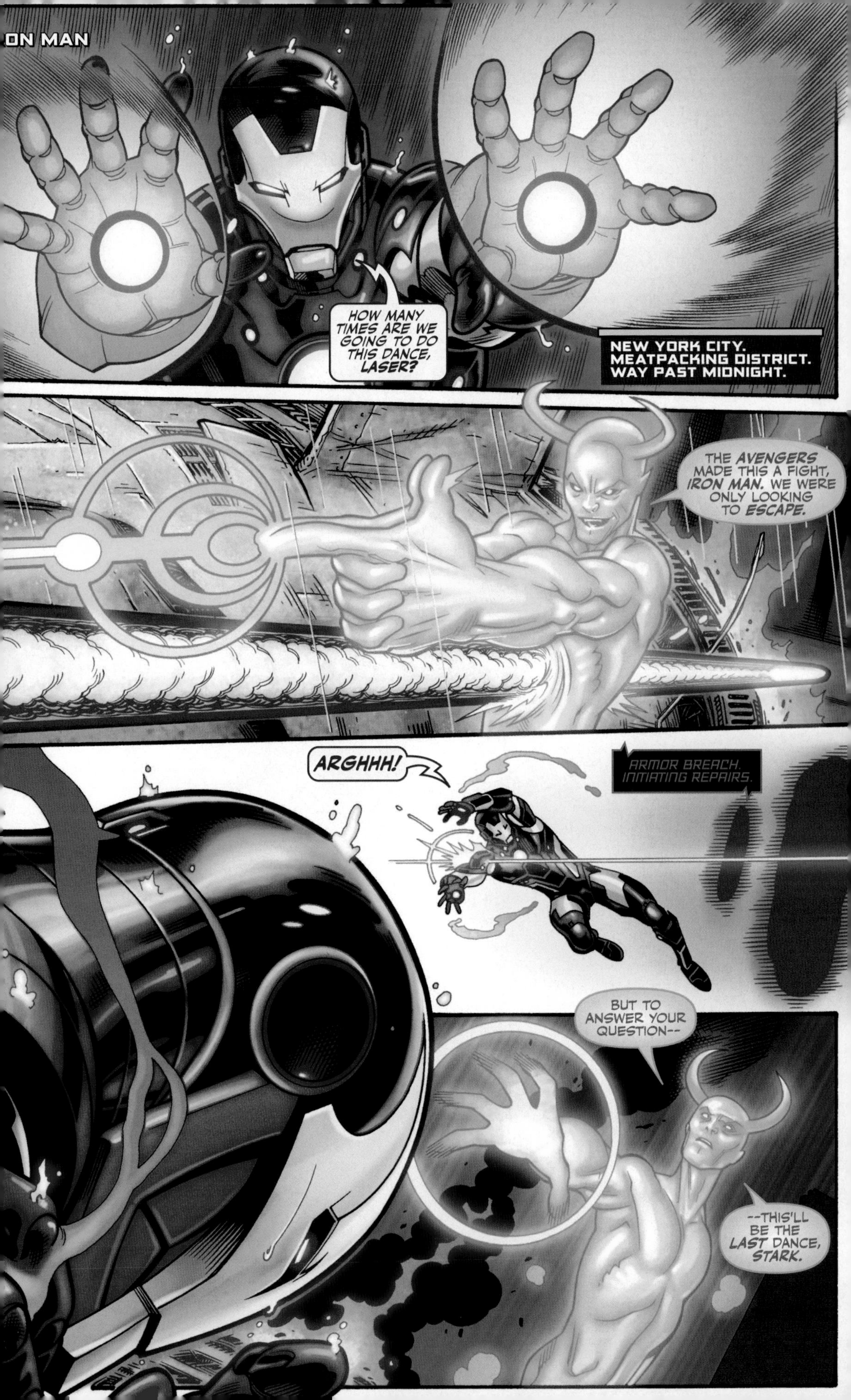
HOW MANY TIMES ARE WE GOING TO DO THIS DANCE, LASER?
NEW YORK CITY. MEATPACKING DISTRICT. WAY PAST MIDNIGHT.
THE AVENGERS MADE THIS A FIGHT, IRON MAN. WE WERE ONLY LOOKING TO ESCAPE.
ARGHHH!
ARMOR BREACH. INITIATING REPAIRS.
BUT TO ANSWER YOUR QUESTION--
--THIS'LL BE THE LAST DANCE, STARK.

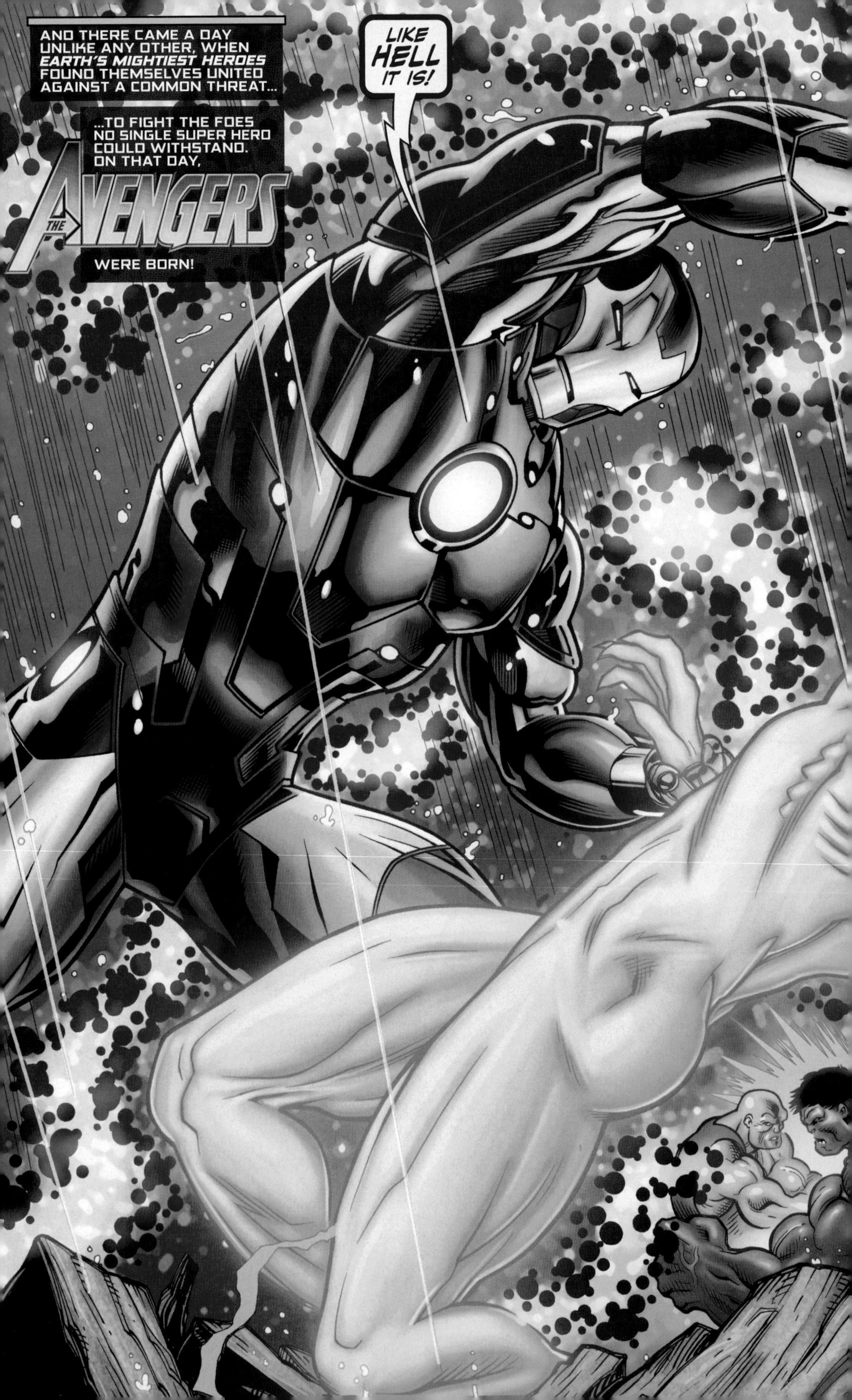

AND THERE CAME A DAY UNLIKE ANY OTHER, WHEN *EARTH'S MIGHTIEST HEROES* FOUND THEMSELVES UNITED AGAINST A COMMON THREAT...
LIKE HELL IT IS!
...TO FIGHT THE FOES NO SINGLE SUPER HERO COULD WITHSTAND. ON THAT DAY,
THE AVENGERS
WERE BORN!

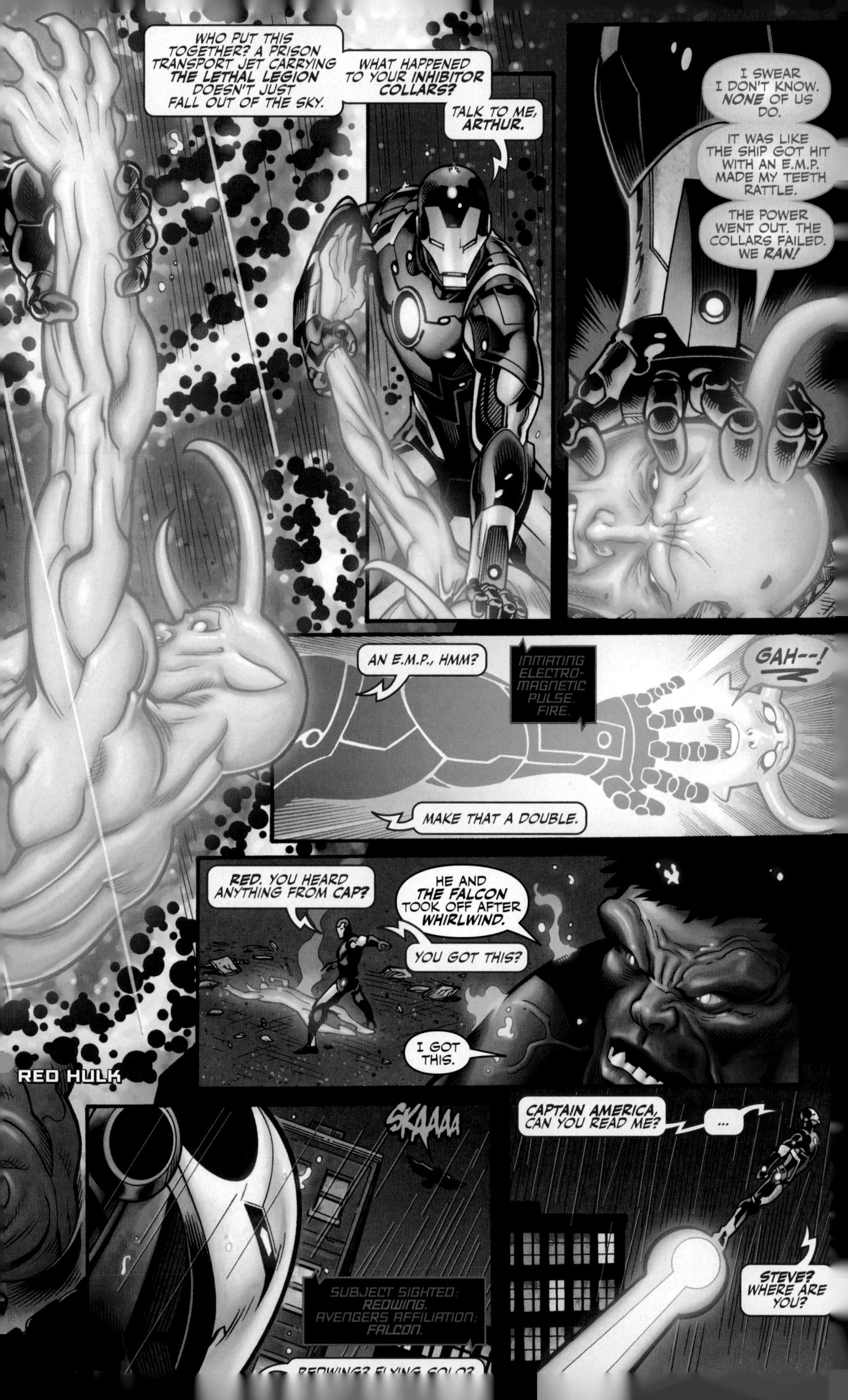
WHO PUT THIS TOGETHER? A PRISON TRANSPORT JET CARRYING THE LETHAL LEGION DOESN'T JUST FALL OUT OF THE SKY.
WHAT HAPPENED TO YOUR INHIBITOR COLLARS?
TALK TO ME, ARTHUR.
I SWEAR I DON'T KNOW. NONE OF US DO.
IT WAS LIKE THE SHIP GOT HIT WITH AN E.M.P. MADE MY TEETH RATTLE.
THE POWER WENT OUT. THE COLLARS FAILED. WE RAN!
AN E.M.P., HMM?
INITIATING ELECTRO-MAGNETIC PULSE. FIRE.
GAH--!
MAKE THAT A DOUBLE.
RED. YOU HEARD ANYTHING FROM CAP?
HE AND THE FALCON TOOK OFF AFTER WHIRLWIND.
YOU GOT THIS?
I GOT THIS.
RED HULK
SKAAAA
SUBJECT SIGHTED: REDWING. AVENGERS AFFILIATION: FALCON.
CAPTAIN AMERICA, CAN YOU READ ME?
...
STEVE? WHERE ARE YOU?

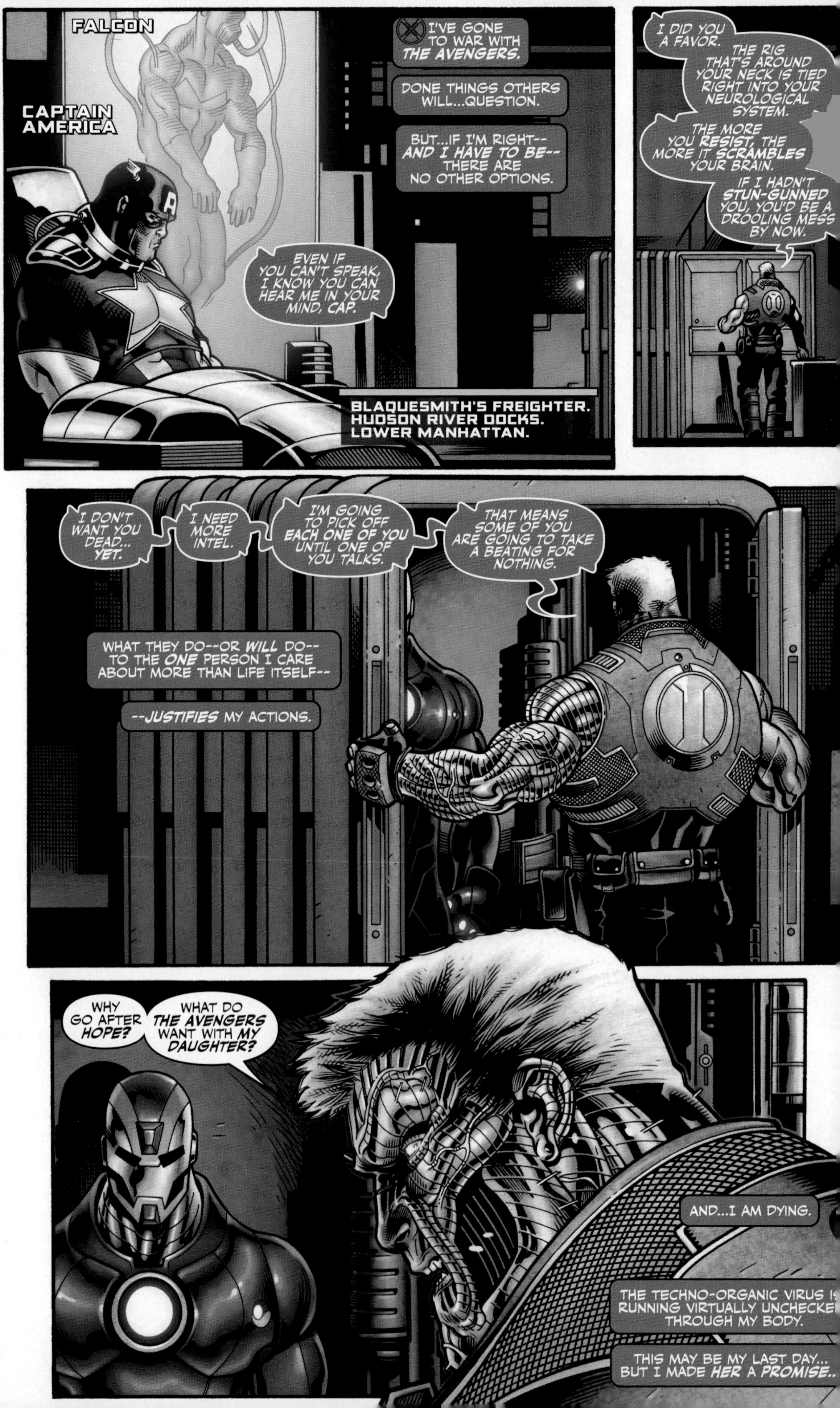
FALCON
CAPTAIN AMERICA
I'VE GONE TO WAR WITH THE AVENGERS.
DONE THINGS OTHERS WILL...QUESTION.
BUT...IF I'M RIGHT-- AND I HAVE TO BE-- THERE ARE NO OTHER OPTIONS.
EVEN IF YOU CAN'T SPEAK, I KNOW YOU CAN HEAR ME IN YOUR MIND, CAP.
BLAQUESMITH'S FREIGHTER. HUDSON RIVER DOCKS. LOWER MANHATTAN.
I DID YOU A FAVOR.
THE RIG THAT'S AROUND YOUR NECK IS TIED RIGHT INTO YOUR NEUROLOGICAL SYSTEM.
THE MORE YOU RESIST, THE MORE IT SCRAMBLES YOUR BRAIN.
IF I HADN'T STUN-GUNNED YOU, YOU'D BE A DROOLING MESS BY NOW.
I DON'T WANT YOU DEAD... YET.
I NEED MORE INTEL.
I'M GOING TO PICK OFF EACH ONE OF YOU UNTIL ONE OF YOU TALKS.
THAT MEANS SOME OF YOU ARE GOING TO TAKE A BEATING FOR NOTHING.
WHAT THEY DO--OR WILL DO-- TO THE ONE PERSON I CARE ABOUT MORE THAN LIFE ITSELF--
--JUSTIFIES MY ACTIONS.
WHY GO AFTER HOPE?
WHAT DO THE AVENGERS WANT WITH MY DAUGHTER?
AND...I AM DYING.
THE TECHNO-ORGANIC VIRUS IS RUNNING VIRTUALLY UNCHECKED THROUGH MY BODY.
THIS MAY BE MY LAST DAY... BUT I MADE HER A PROMISE..

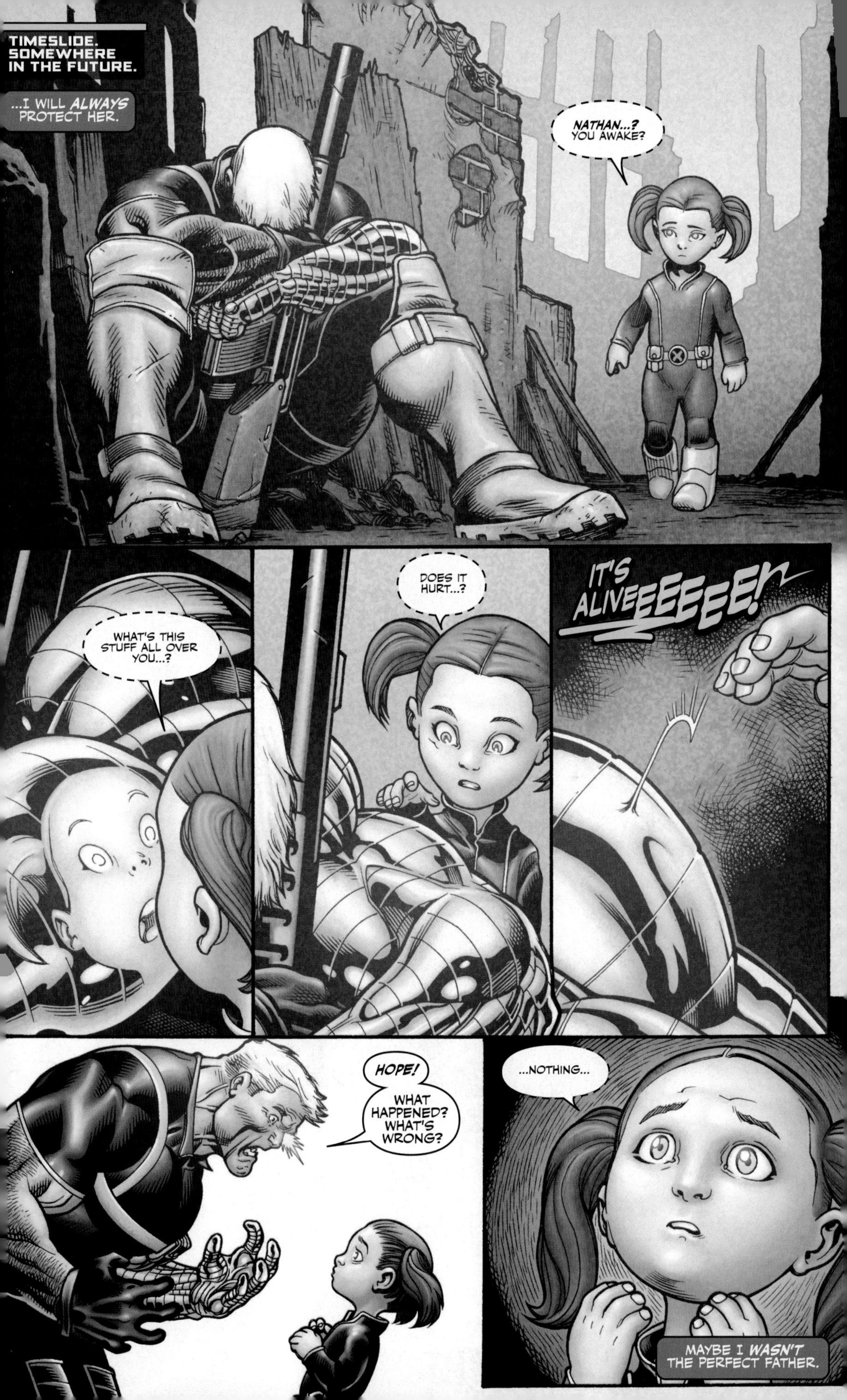
TIMESLIDE. SOMEWHERE IN THE FUTURE.
...I WILL ALWAYS PROTECT HER.
NATHAN...? YOU AWAKE?
WHAT'S THIS STUFF ALL OVER YOU...?
DOES IT HURT...?
IT'S ALIVEEEEEEE!
HOPE! WHAT HAPPENED? WHAT'S WRONG?
...NOTHING...
MAYBE I WASN'T THE PERFECT FATHER.

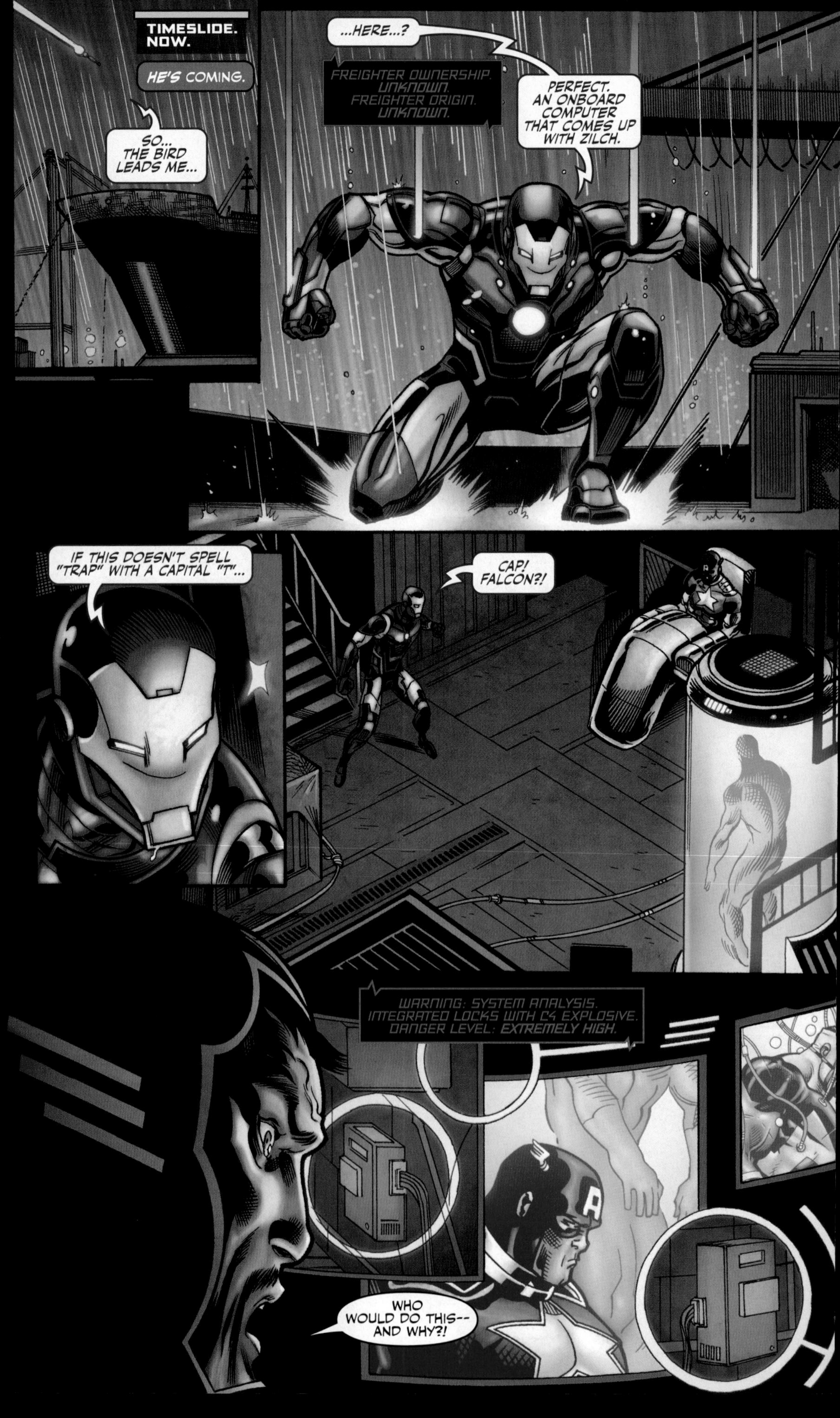
TIMESLIDE. NOW.
HE'S COMING.
SO... THE BIRD LEADS ME...
...HERE...?
FREIGHTER OWNERSHIP. UNKNOWN. FREIGHTER ORIGIN. UNKNOWN.
PERFECT. AN ONBOARD COMPUTER THAT COMES UP WITH ZILCH.
IF THIS DOESN'T SPELL "TRAP" WITH A CAPITAL "T"...
CAP! FALCON?!
WARNING: SYSTEM ANALYSIS. INTEGRATED LOCKS WITH C4 EXPLOSIVE. DANGER LEVEL: EXTREMELY HIGH.
WHO WOULD DO THIS-- AND WHY?!

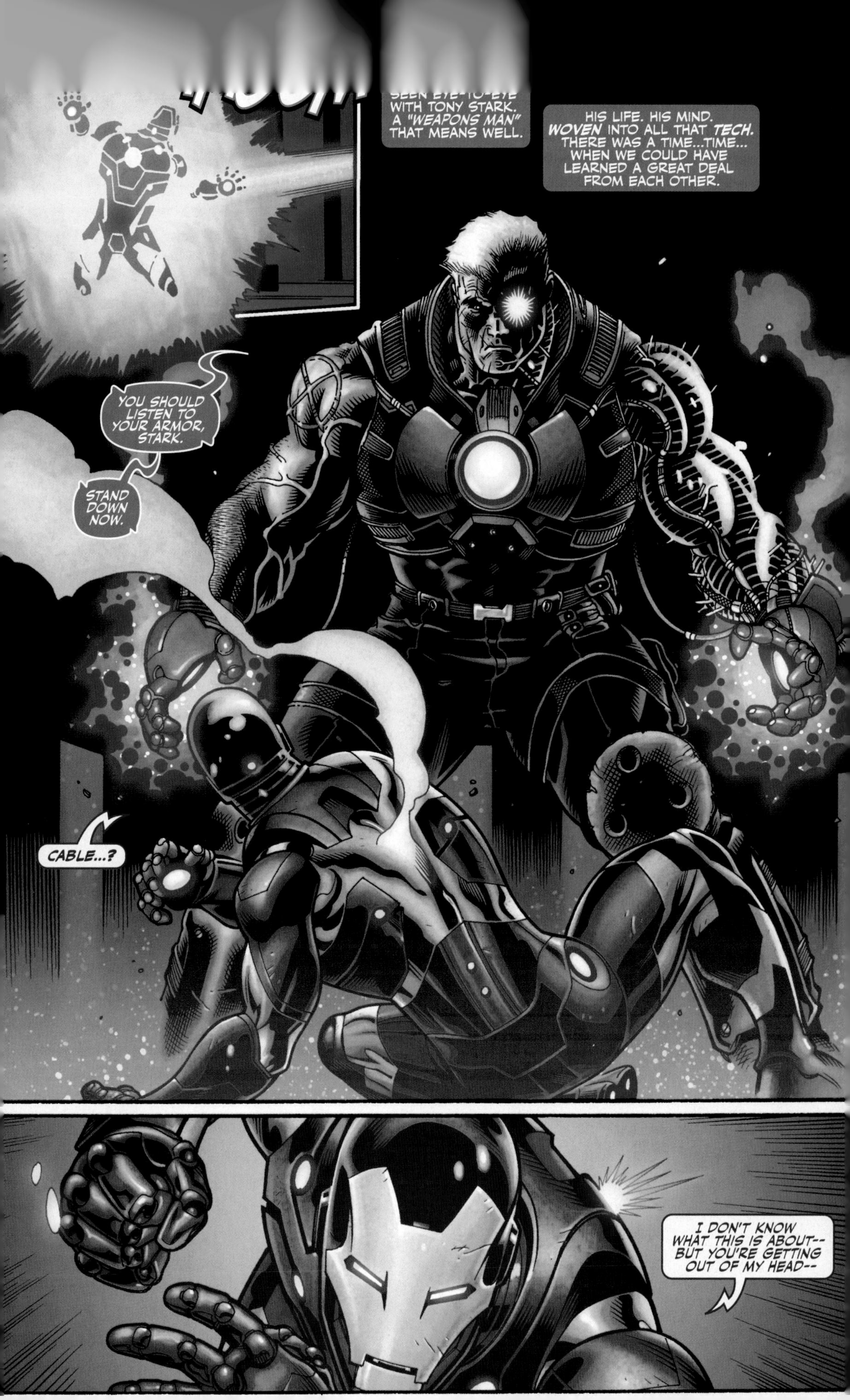
WITH TONY STARK. A "WEAPONS MAN" THAT MEANS WELL.
HIS LIFE. HIS MIND. WOVEN INTO ALL THAT TECH. THERE WAS A TIME...TIME... WHEN WE COULD HAVE LEARNED A GREAT DEAL FROM EACH OTHER.
YOU SHOULD LISTEN TO YOUR ARMOR, STARK.
STAND DOWN NOW.
CABLE...?
I DON'T KNOW WHAT THIS IS ABOUT-- BUT YOU'RE GETTING OUT OF MY HEAD--

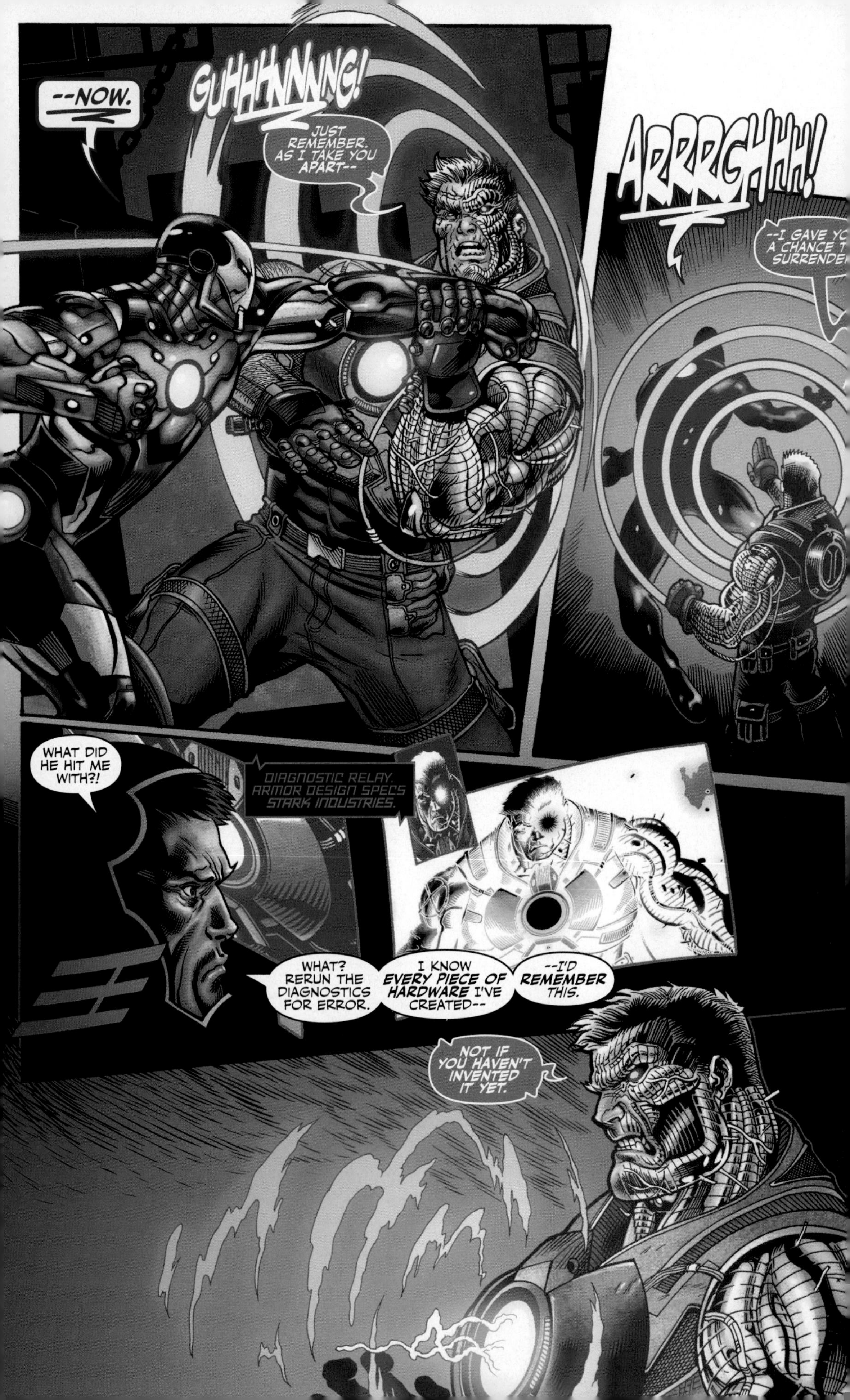
--NOW.
GUHHHNNNNG!
JUST REMEMBER. AS I TAKE YOU APART--
ARRRGHHH!
--I GAVE YO A CHANCE T SURRENDE
WHAT DID HE HIT ME WITH?!
DIAGNOSTIC RELAY. ARMOR DESIGN SPECS STARK INDUSTRIES.
WHAT? RERUN THE DIAGNOSTICS FOR ERROR.
I KNOW EVERY PIECE OF HARDWARE I'VE CREATED--
--I'D REMEMBER THIS.
NOT IF YOU HAVEN'T INVENTED IT YET.

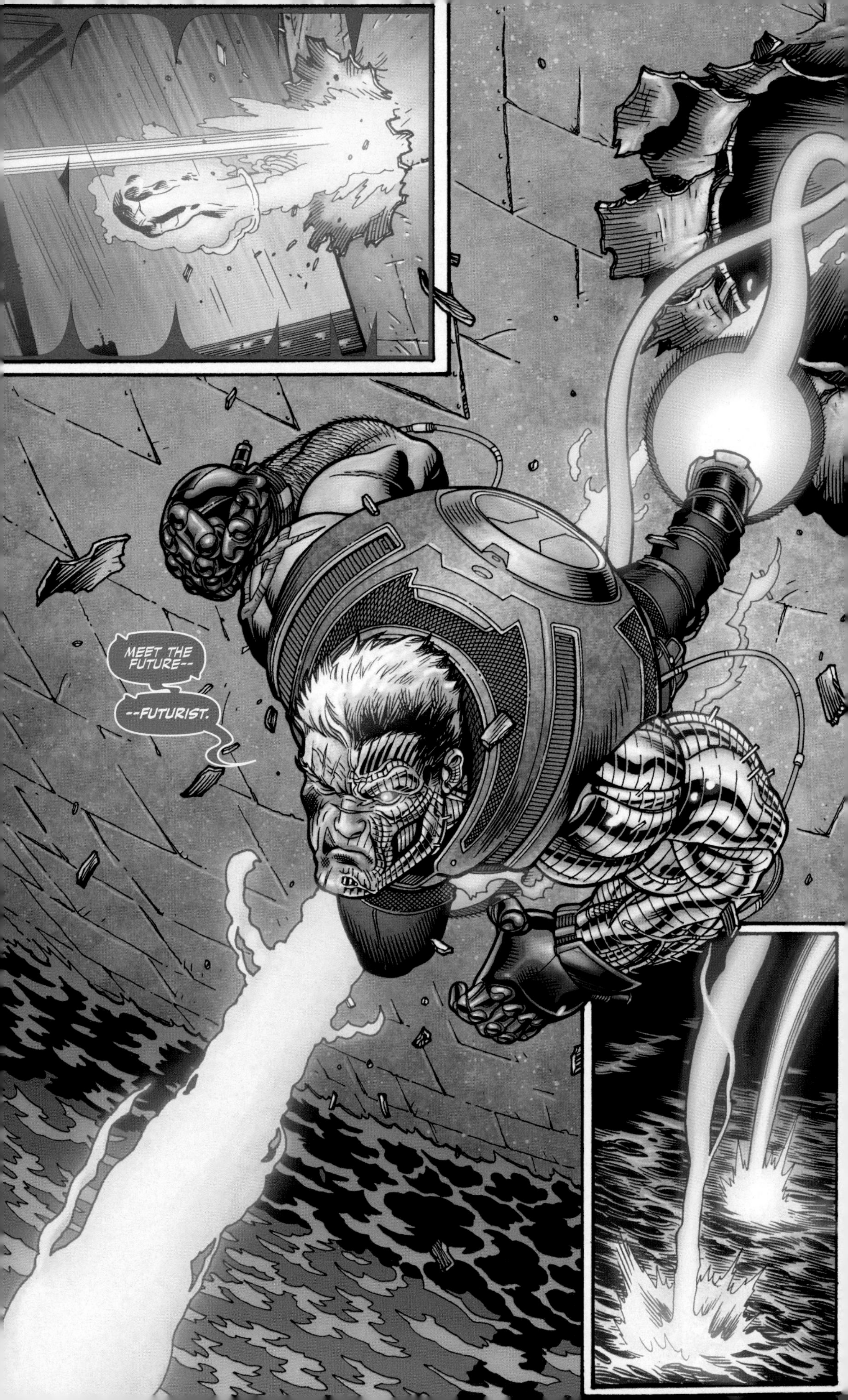
MEET THE FUTURE--
--FUTURIST.

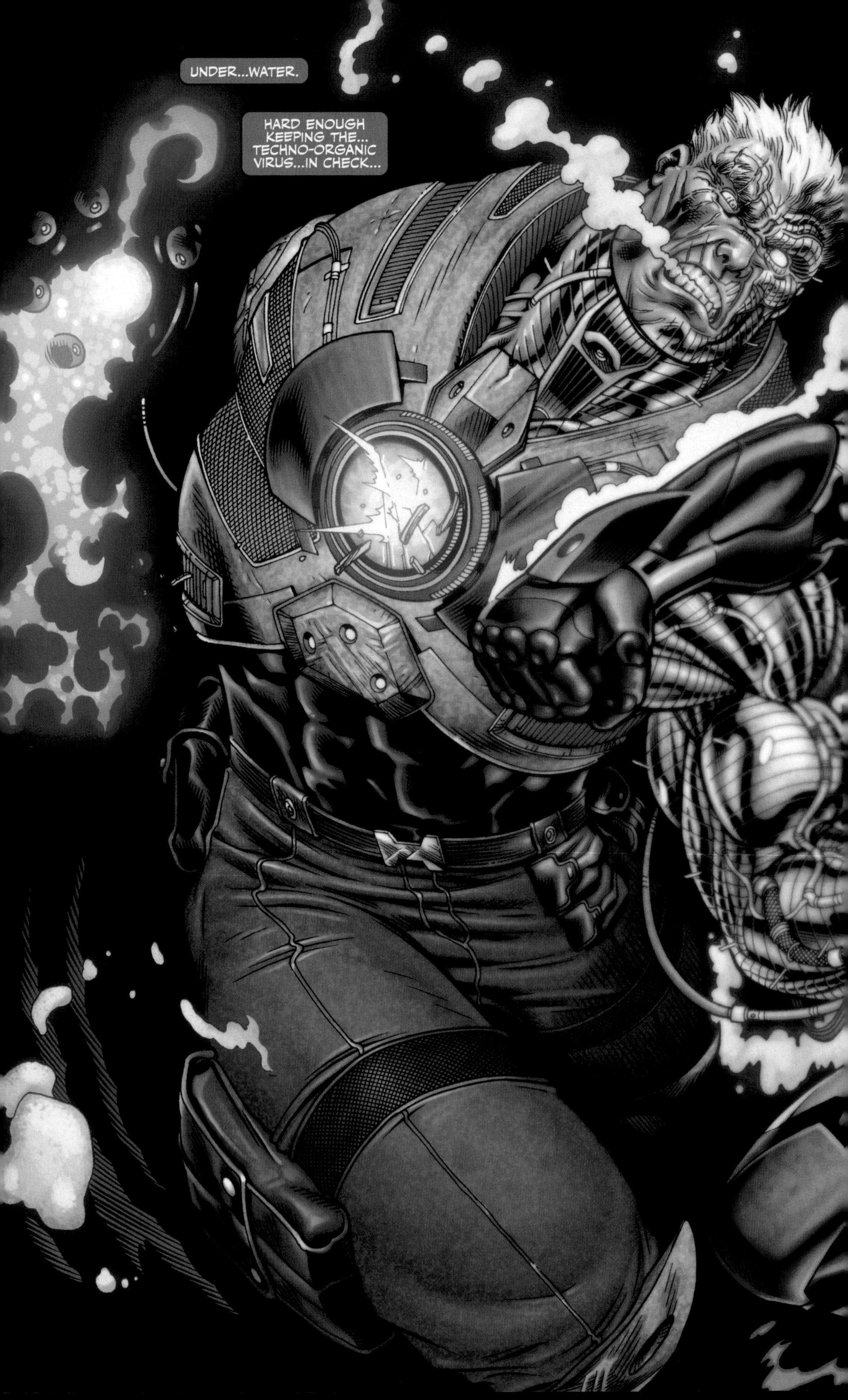
UNDER...WATER.
HARD ENOUGH KEEPING THE... TECHNO-ORGANIC VIRUS...IN CHECK...

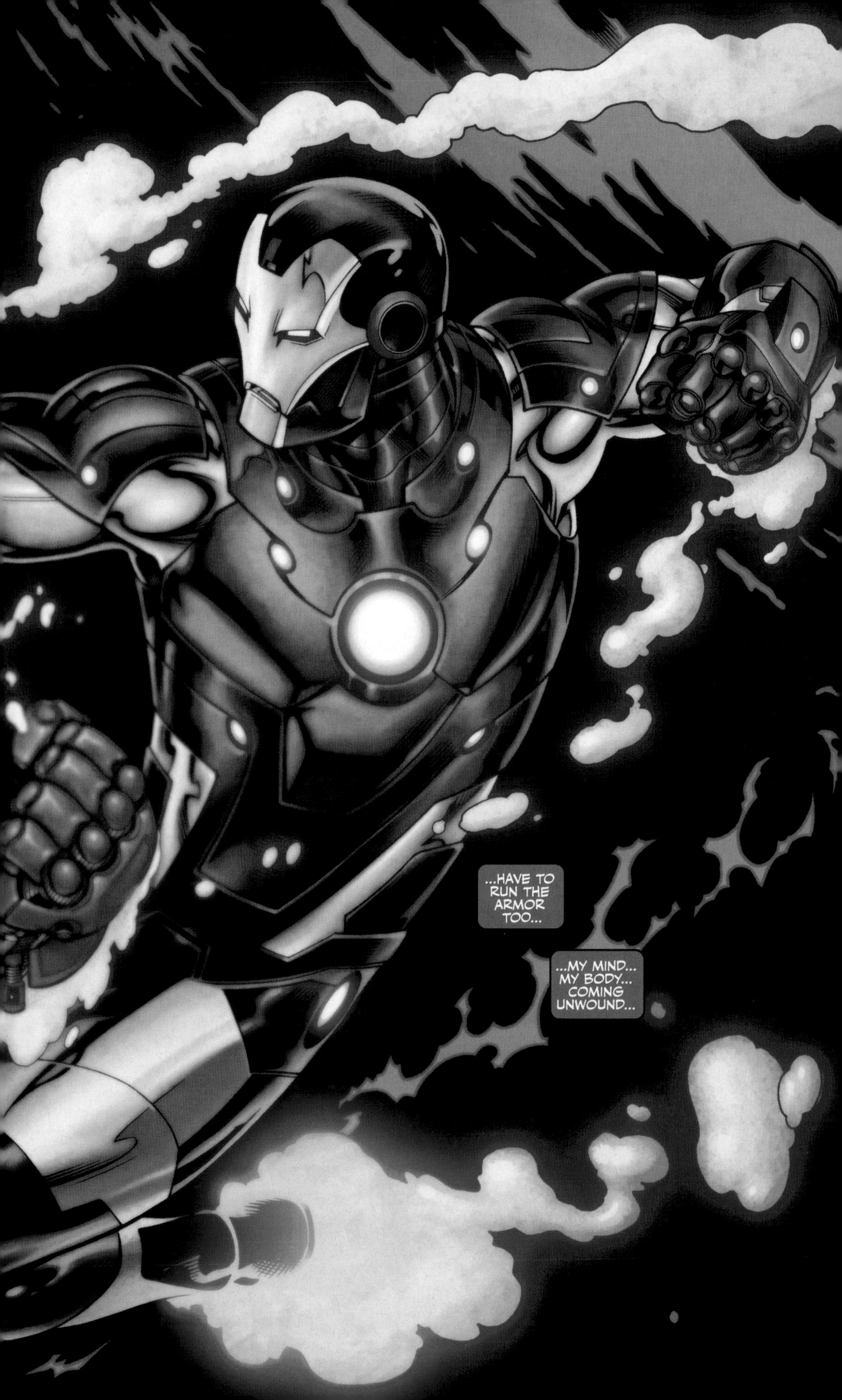
...HAVE TO RUN THE ARMOR TOO...
...MY MIND... MY BODY... COMING UNWOUND...

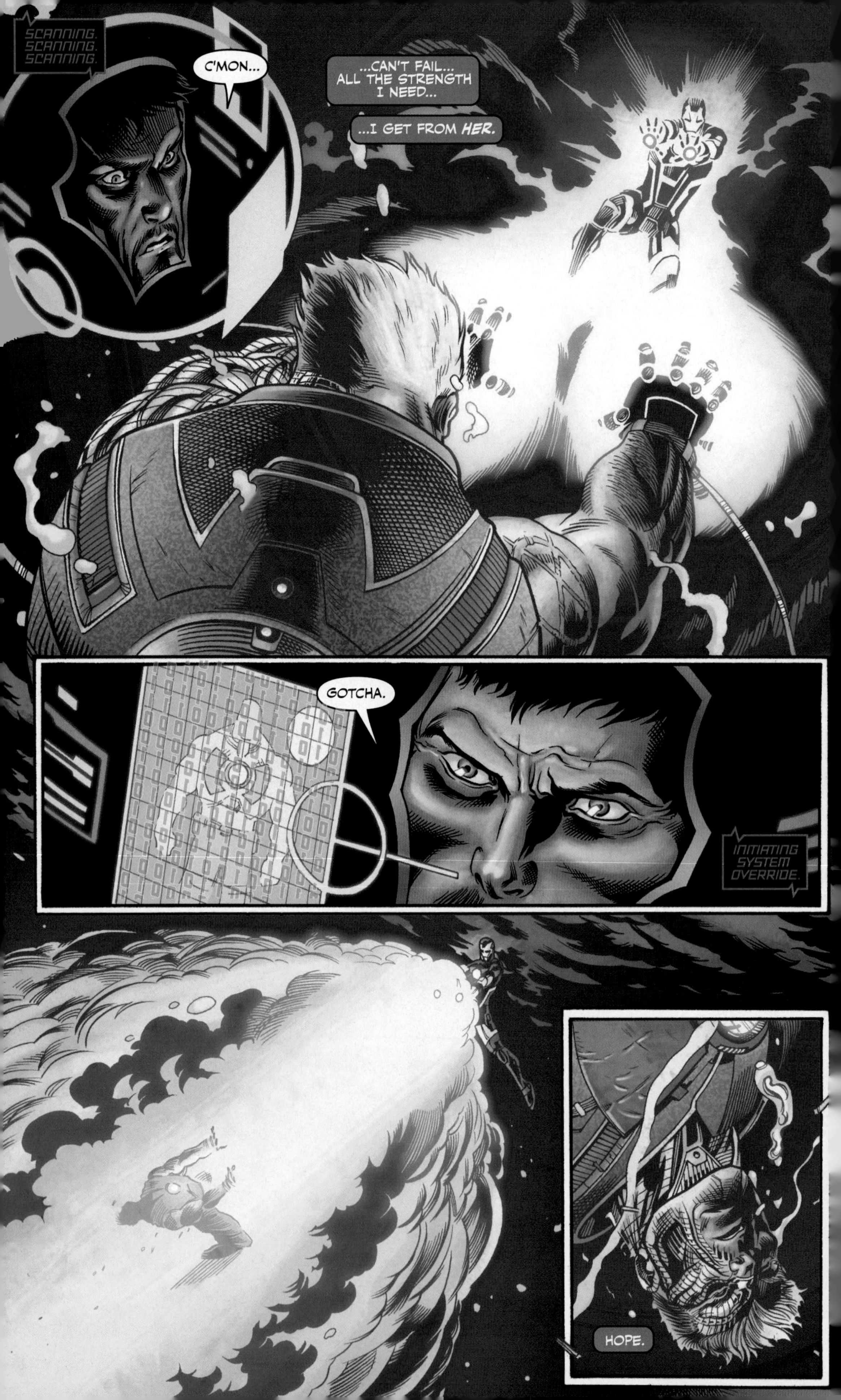

SCANNING. SCANNING. SCANNING.
C'MON...
...CAN'T FAIL... ALL THE STRENGTH I NEED...
...I GET FROM HER.
GOTCHA.
INITIATING SYSTEM OVERRIDE.
HOPE.

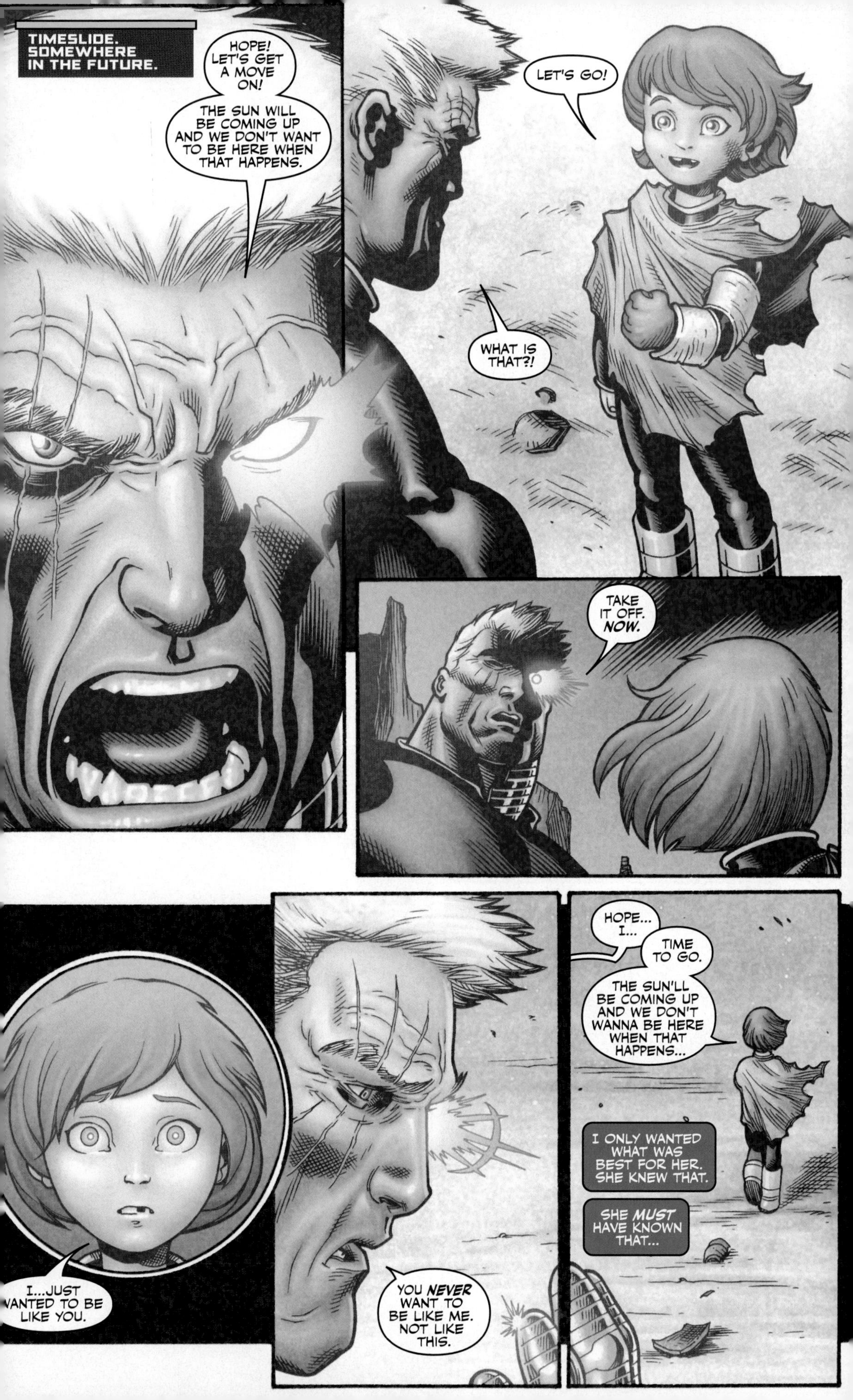
TIMESLIDE. SOMEWHERE IN THE FUTURE.
HOPE! LET'S GET A MOVE ON!
THE SUN WILL BE COMING UP AND WE DON'T WANT TO BE HERE WHEN THAT HAPPENS.
LET'S GO!
WHAT IS THAT?!
TAKE IT OFF. NOW.
I...JUST WANTED TO BE LIKE YOU.
YOU NEVER WANT TO BE LIKE ME. NOT LIKE THIS.
HOPE... I...
TIME TO GO.
THE SUN'LL BE COMING UP AND WE DON'T WANNA BE HERE WHEN THAT HAPPENS...
I ONLY WANTED WHAT WAS BEST FOR HER. SHE KNEW THAT.
SHE MUST HAVE KNOWN THAT...

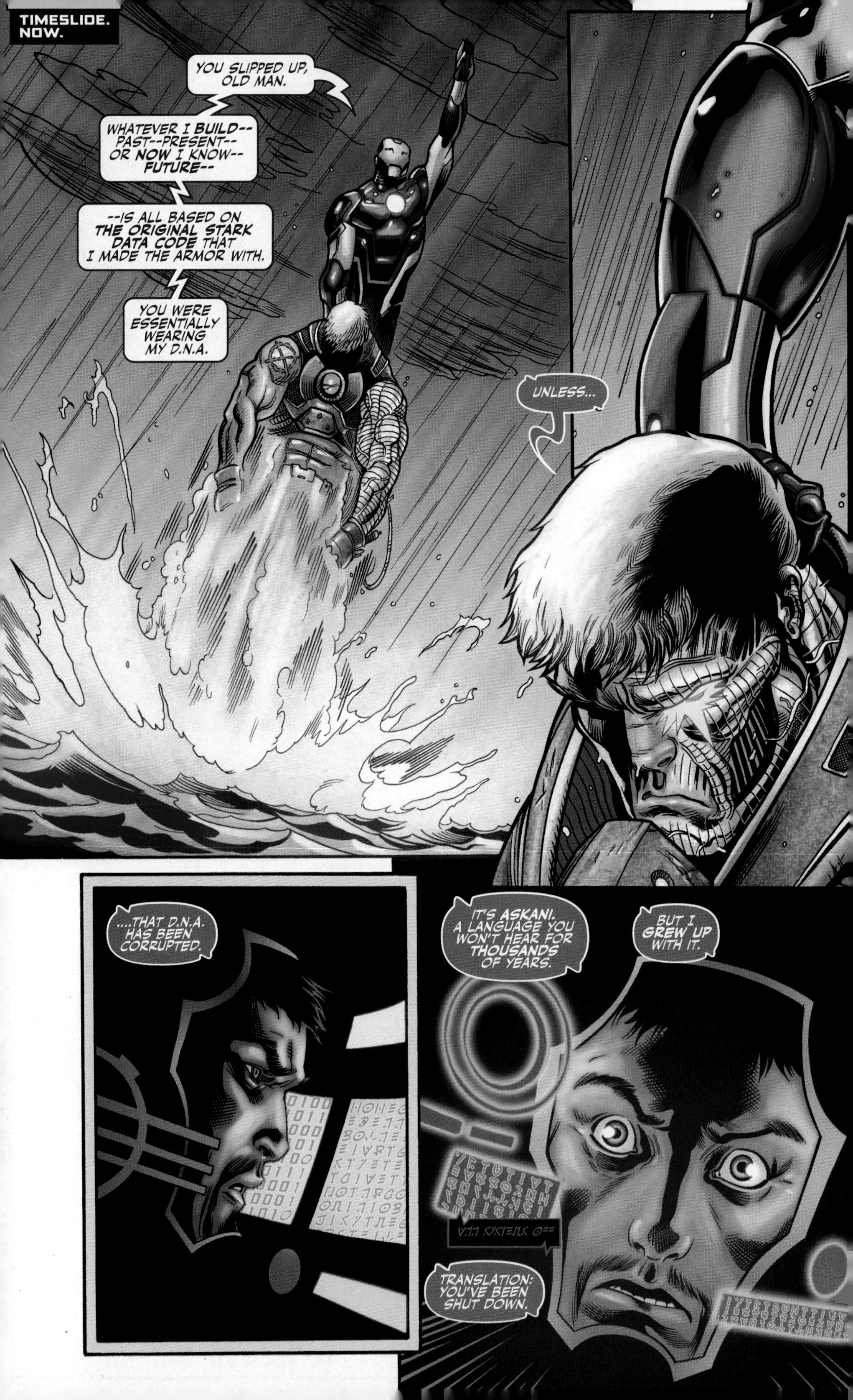
TIMESLIDE. NOW.
YOU SLIPPED UP, OLD MAN.
WHATEVER I BUILD-- PAST--PRESENT-- OR NOW I KNOW-- FUTURE--
--IS ALL BASED ON THE ORIGINAL STARK DATA CODE THAT I MADE THE ARMOR WITH.
YOU WERE ESSENTIALLY WEARING MY D.N.A.
UNLESS...
....THAT D.N.A. HAS BEEN CORRUPTED.
IT'S ASKANI. A LANGUAGE YOU WON'T HEAR FOR THOUSANDS OF YEARS.
BUT I GREW UP WITH IT.
TRANSLATION: YOU'VE BEEN SHUT DOWN.

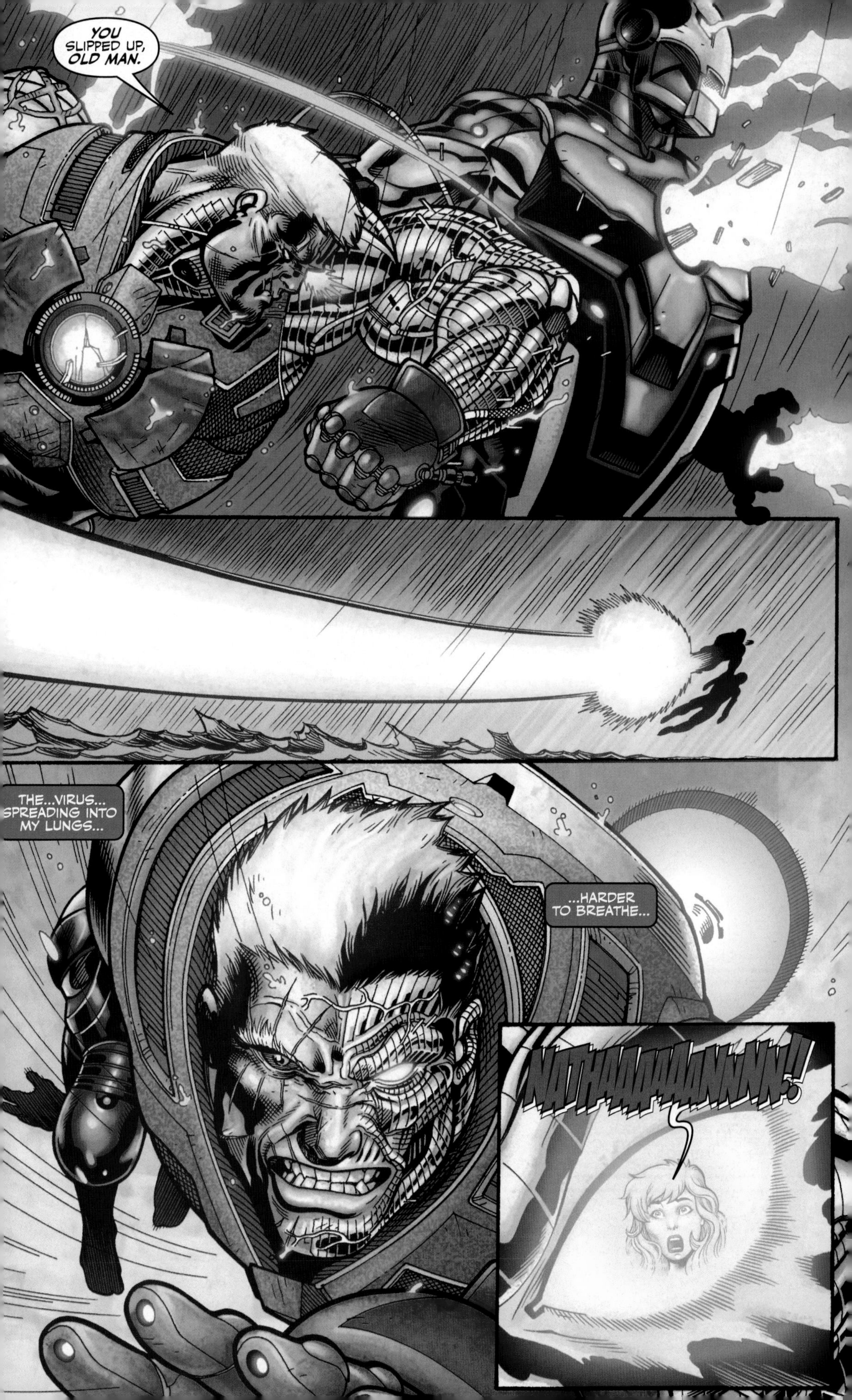
YOU SLIPPED UP, OLD MAN.
THE...VIRUS... SPREADING INTO MY LUNGS...
...HARDER TO BREATHE...
NATHAAAAAANNNN!!

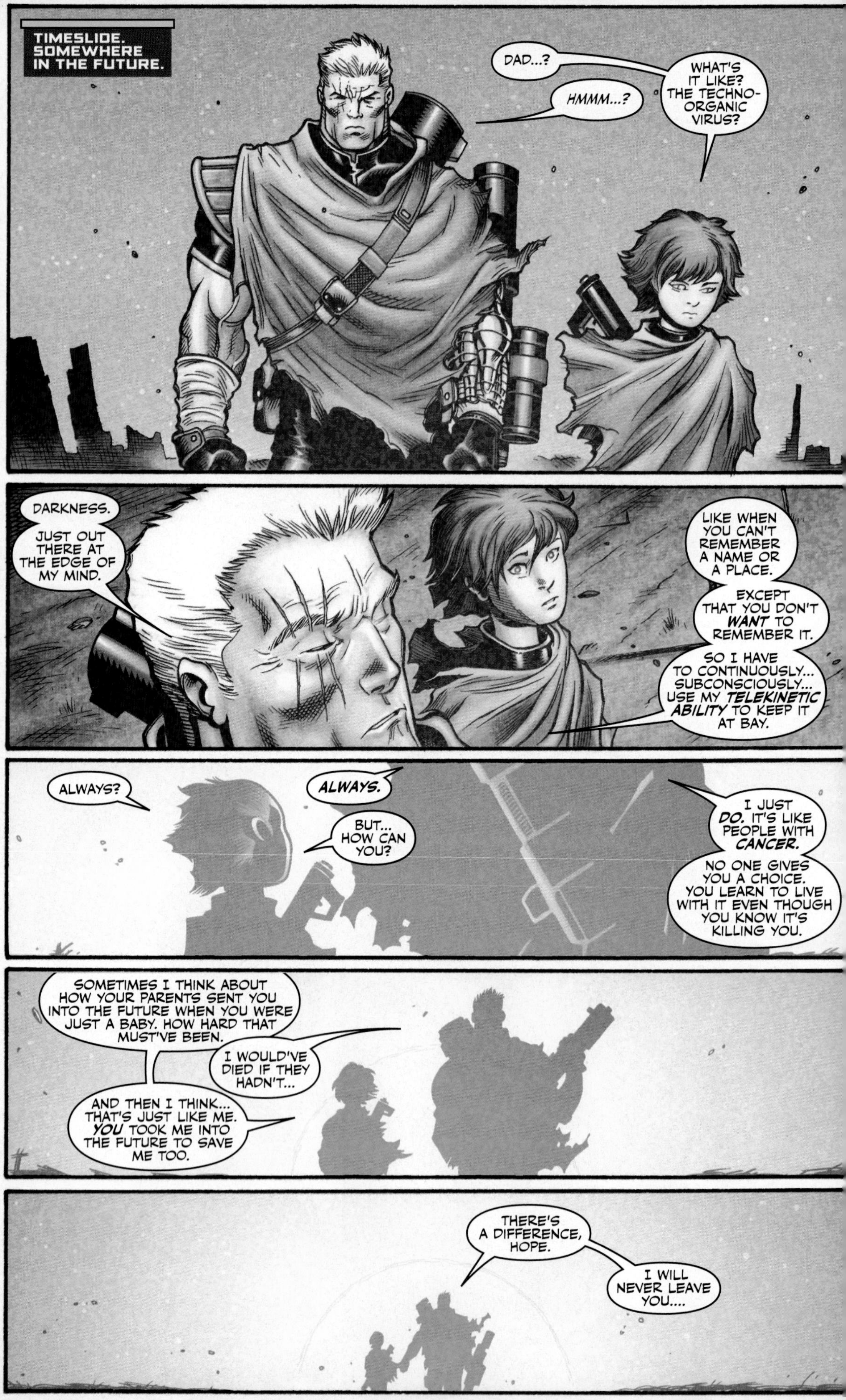
TIMESLIDE. SOMEWHERE IN THE FUTURE.
DAD...?
HMMM...?
WHAT'S IT LIKE? THE TECHNO-ORGANIC VIRUS?
DARKNESS.
JUST OUT THERE AT THE EDGE OF MY MIND.
LIKE WHEN YOU CAN'T REMEMBER A NAME OR A PLACE.
EXCEPT THAT YOU DON'T WANT TO REMEMBER IT.
SO I HAVE TO CONTINUOUSLY... SUBCONSCIOUSLY... USE MY TELEKINETIC ABILITY TO KEEP IT AT BAY.
ALWAYS?
ALWAYS.
BUT... HOW CAN YOU?
I JUST DO. IT'S LIKE PEOPLE WITH CANCER.
NO ONE GIVES YOU A CHOICE. YOU LEARN TO LIVE WITH IT EVEN THOUGH YOU KNOW IT'S KILLING YOU.
SOMETIMES I THINK ABOUT HOW YOUR PARENTS SENT YOU INTO THE FUTURE WHEN YOU WERE JUST A BABY. HOW HARD THAT MUST'VE BEEN.
I WOULD'VE DIED IF THEY HADN'T...
AND THEN I THINK... THAT'S JUST LIKE ME. YOU TOOK ME INTO THE FUTURE TO SAVE ME TOO.
THERE'S A DIFFERENCE, HOPE.
I WILL NEVER LEAVE YOU....

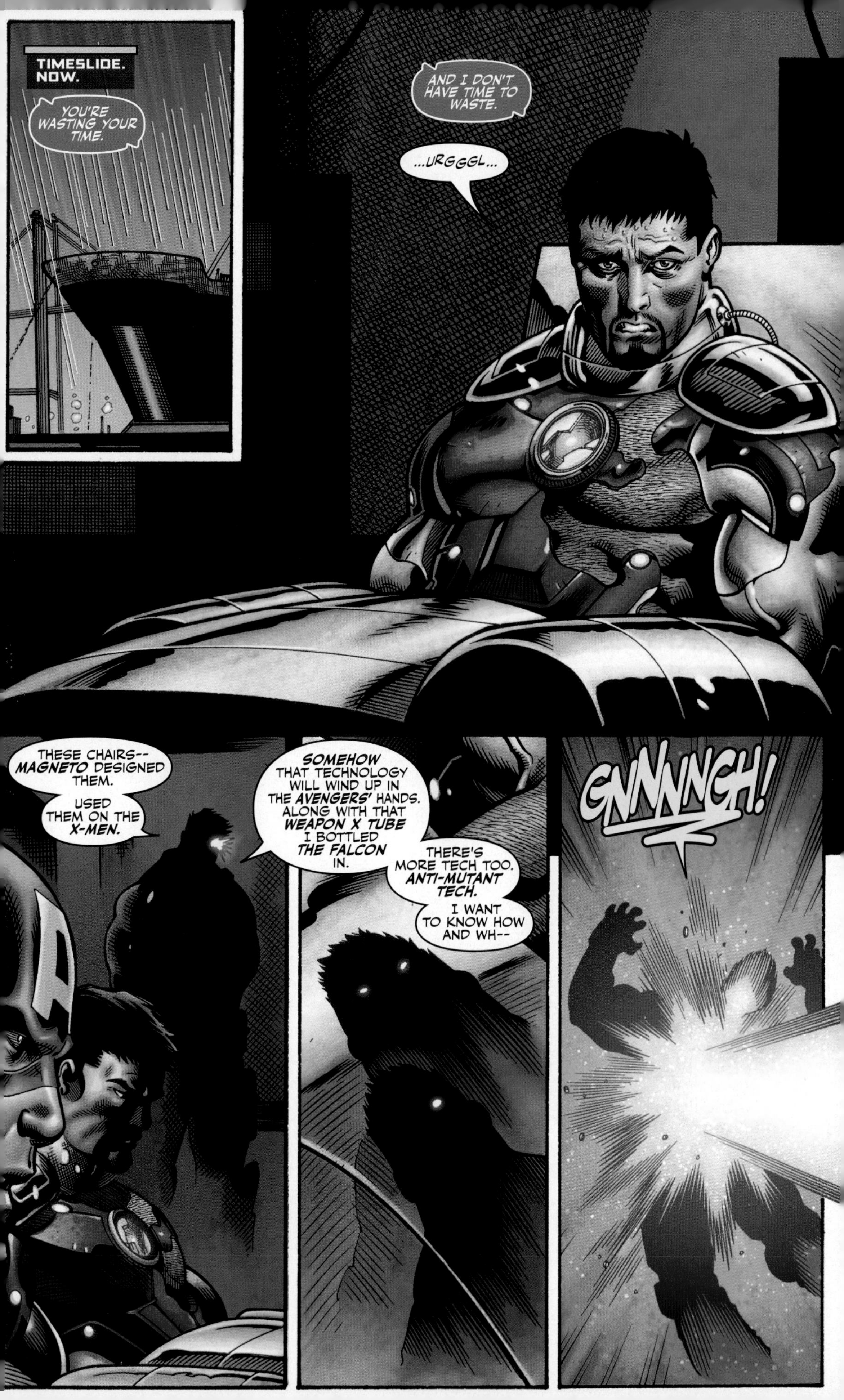
TIMESLIDE. NOW.
YOU'RE WASTING YOUR TIME.
AND I DON'T HAVE TIME TO WASTE.
...URGGGL...
THESE CHAIRS-- MAGNETO DESIGNED THEM.
USED THEM ON THE X-MEN.
SOMEHOW THAT TECHNOLOGY WILL WIND UP IN THE AVENGERS' HANDS. ALONG WITH THAT WEAPON X TUBE I BOTTLED THE FALCON IN.
THERE'S MORE TECH TOO. ANTI-MUTANT TECH.
I WANT TO KNOW HOW AND WH--
GNNNNGH!

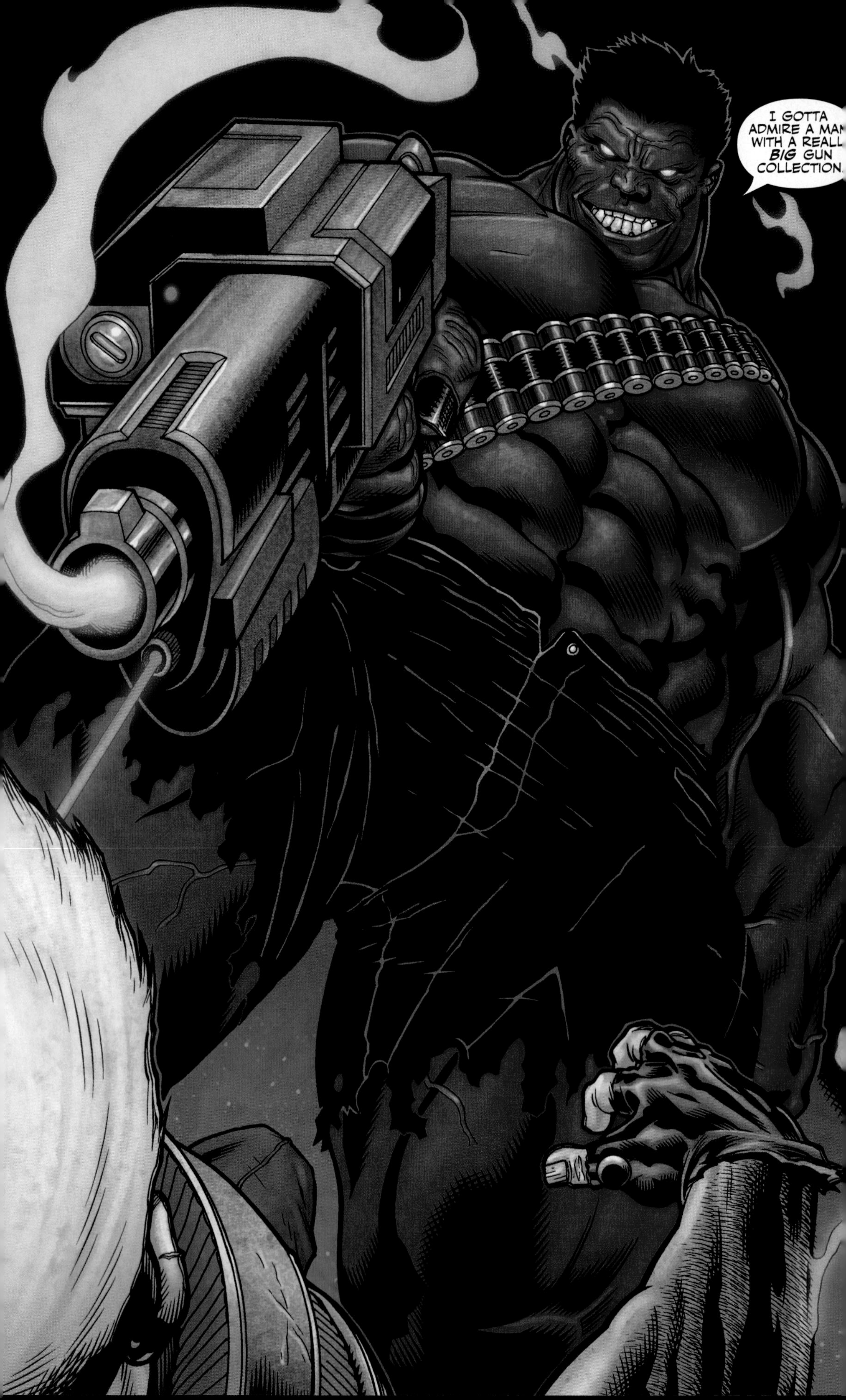
I GOTTA ADMIRE A MAN WITH A REALL BIG GUN COLLECTION.

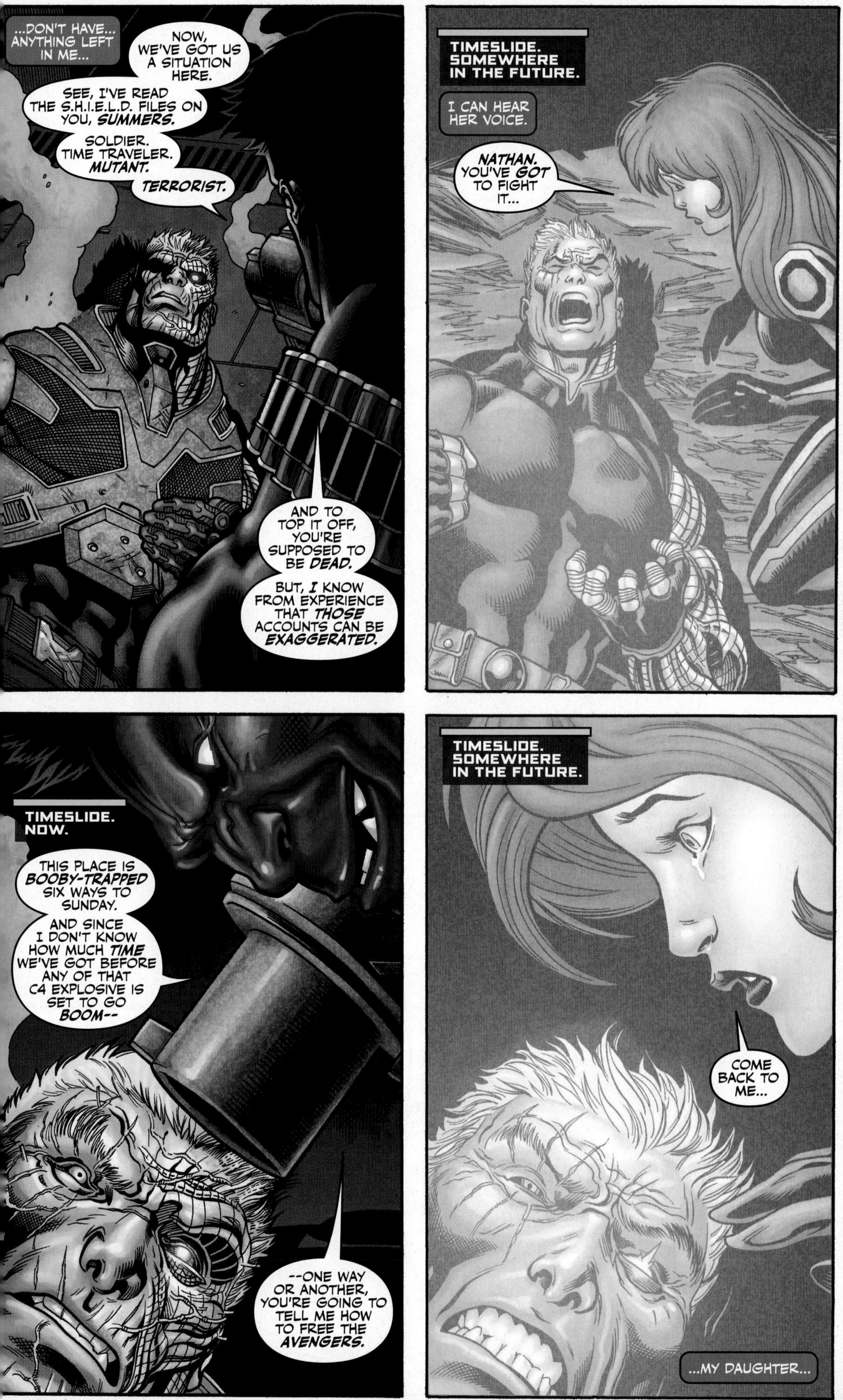
...DON'T HAVE... ANYTHING LEFT IN ME...
NOW, WE'VE GOT US A SITUATION HERE.
SEE, I'VE READ THE S.H.I.E.L.D. FILES ON YOU, SUMMERS.
SOLDIER. TIME TRAVELER. MUTANT.
TERRORIST.
AND TO TOP IT OFF, YOU'RE SUPPOSED TO BE DEAD.
BUT, I KNOW FROM EXPERIENCE THAT THOSE ACCOUNTS CAN BE EXAGGERATED.
TIMESLIDE. SOMEWHERE IN THE FUTURE.
I CAN HEAR HER VOICE.
NATHAN. YOU'VE GOT TO FIGHT IT...
TIMESLIDE. NOW.
THIS PLACE IS BOOBY-TRAPPED SIX WAYS TO SUNDAY.
AND SINCE I DON'T KNOW HOW MUCH TIME WE'VE GOT BEFORE ANY OF THAT C4 EXPLOSIVE IS SET TO GO BOOM--
--ONE WAY OR ANOTHER, YOU'RE GOING TO TELL ME HOW TO FREE THE AVENGERS.
TIMESLIDE. SOMEWHERE IN THE FUTURE.
COME BACK TO ME...
...MY DAUGHTER...

TIMESLIDE. NOW.

...TALBOT...

WHO...?

...FOUGHT YOU BEFORE... AND *EVERY* TIME... YOU LOSE.

TIMESLIDE. SOMEWHERE IN THE FUTURE.

YOU MADE ME A PROMISE...

TIMESLIDE. NOW.

WELL...I'VE GOT GOOD NEWS AND BAD NEWS.

THE GOOD NEWS IS YOU'RE STILL ALIVE.

THE BAD NEWS IS-- I'M *NOT* TALBOT. AND WE'VE *NEVER* MET BEFORE.

SO, YOU'RE DEALING WITH *A HULK OF A DIFFERENT COLOR*...

TIMESLIDE. SOMEWHERE IN THE FUTURE.

...YOU SAID...

...YOU WOULD NEVER LEAVE ME...

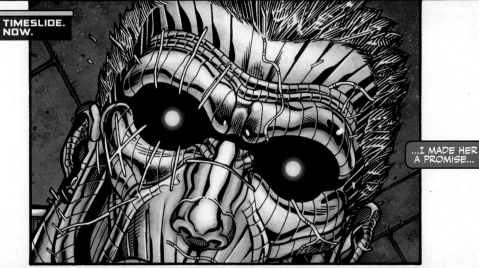

TIMESLIDE. NOW.

...I MADE HER A PROMISE...

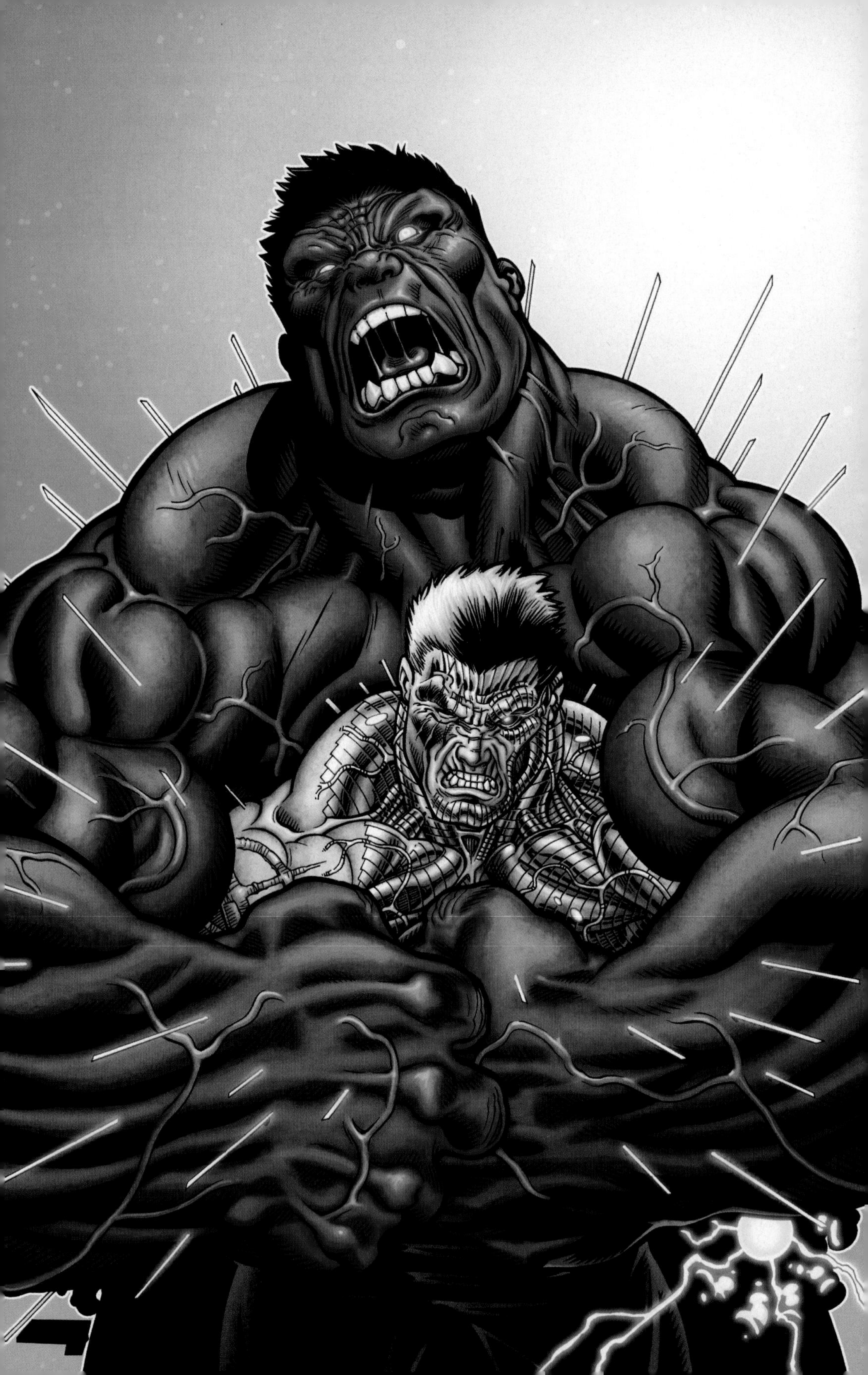

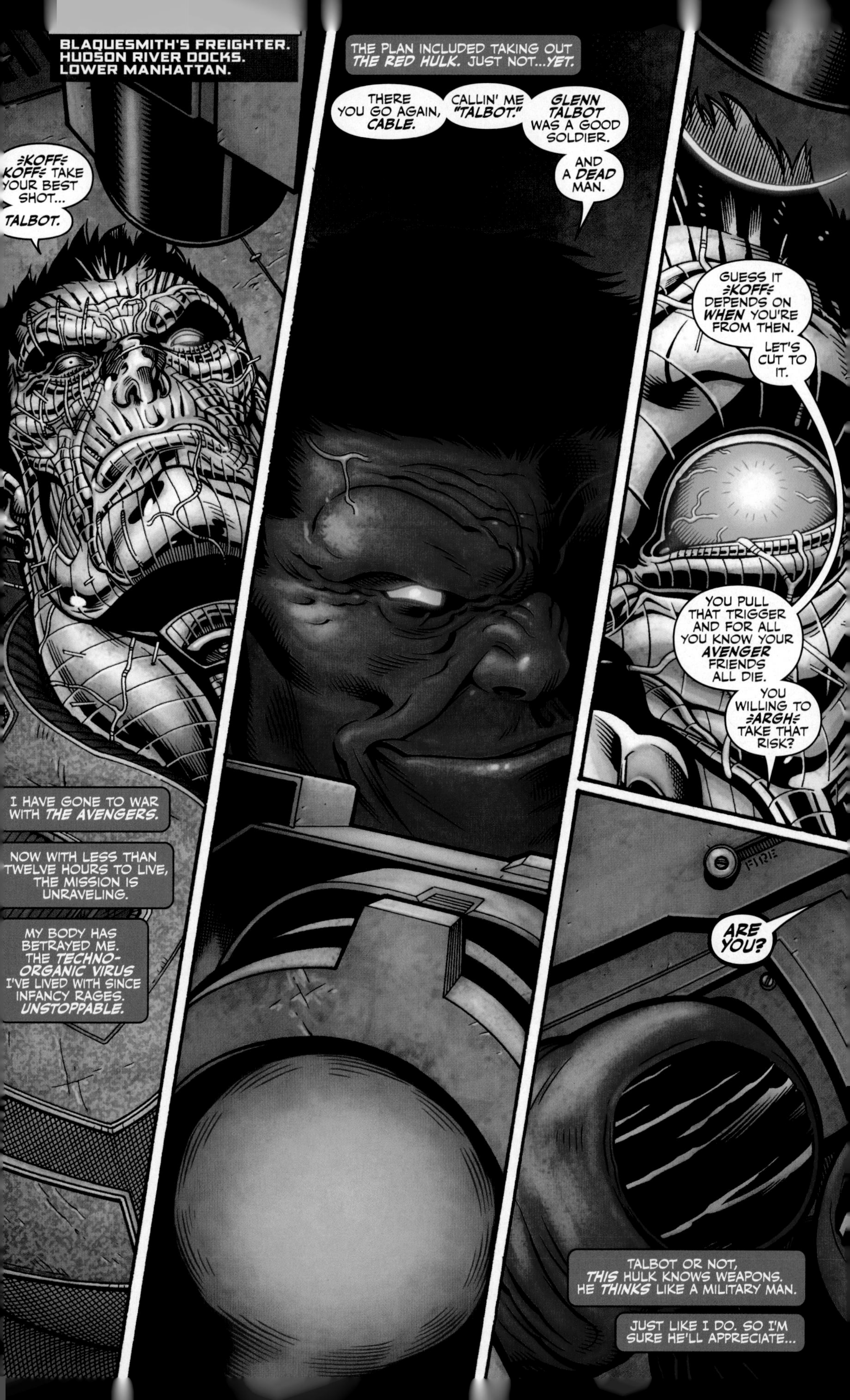
BLAQUESMITH'S FREIGHTER. HUDSON RIVER DOCKS. LOWER MANHATTAN.
=KOFF= KOFF= TAKE YOUR BEST SHOT... TALBOT.
I HAVE GONE TO WAR WITH THE AVENGERS.
NOW WITH LESS THAN TWELVE HOURS TO LIVE, THE MISSION IS UNRAVELING.
MY BODY HAS BETRAYED ME. THE TECHNO-ORGANIC VIRUS I'VE LIVED WITH SINCE INFANCY RAGES. UNSTOPPABLE.
THE PLAN INCLUDED TAKING OUT THE RED HULK. JUST NOT...YET.
THERE YOU GO AGAIN, CABLE.
CALLIN' ME "TALBOT."
GLENN TALBOT WAS A GOOD SOLDIER.
AND A DEAD MAN.
GUESS IT =KOFF= DEPENDS ON WHEN YOU'RE FROM THEN.
LET'S CUT TO IT.
YOU PULL THAT TRIGGER AND FOR ALL YOU KNOW YOUR AVENGER FRIENDS ALL DIE.
YOU WILLING TO =ARGH= TAKE THAT RISK?
FIRE
ARE YOU?
TALBOT OR NOT, THIS HULK KNOWS WEAPONS. HE THINKS LIKE A MILITARY MAN.
JUST LIKE I DO. SO I'M SURE HE'LL APPRECIATE...

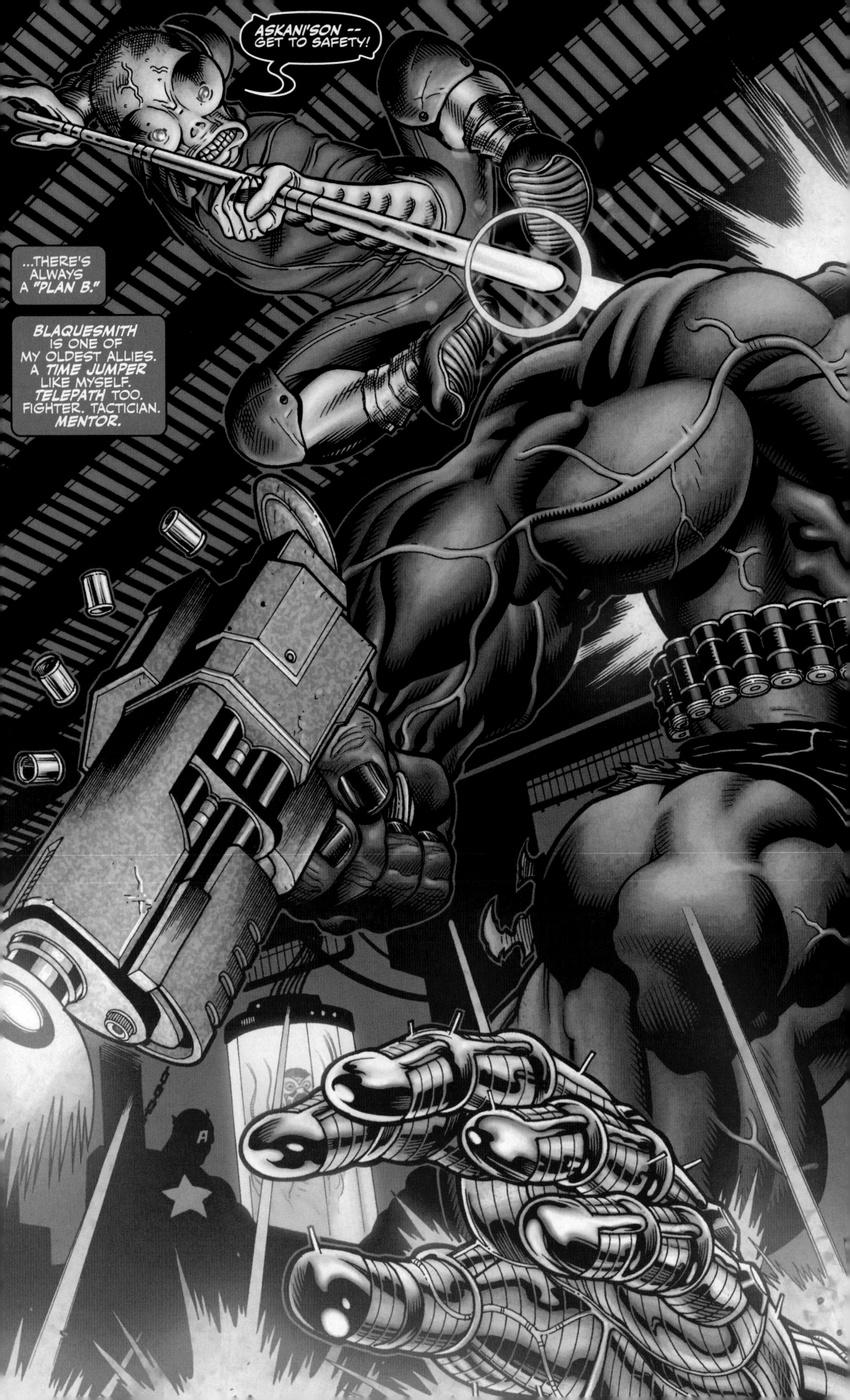
ASKANI'SON -- GET TO SAFETY!
...THERE'S ALWAYS A "PLAN B."
BLAQUESMITH IS ONE OF MY OLDEST ALLIES. A TIME JUMPER LIKE MYSELF. TELEPATH TOO. FIGHTER. TACTICIAN. MENTOR.

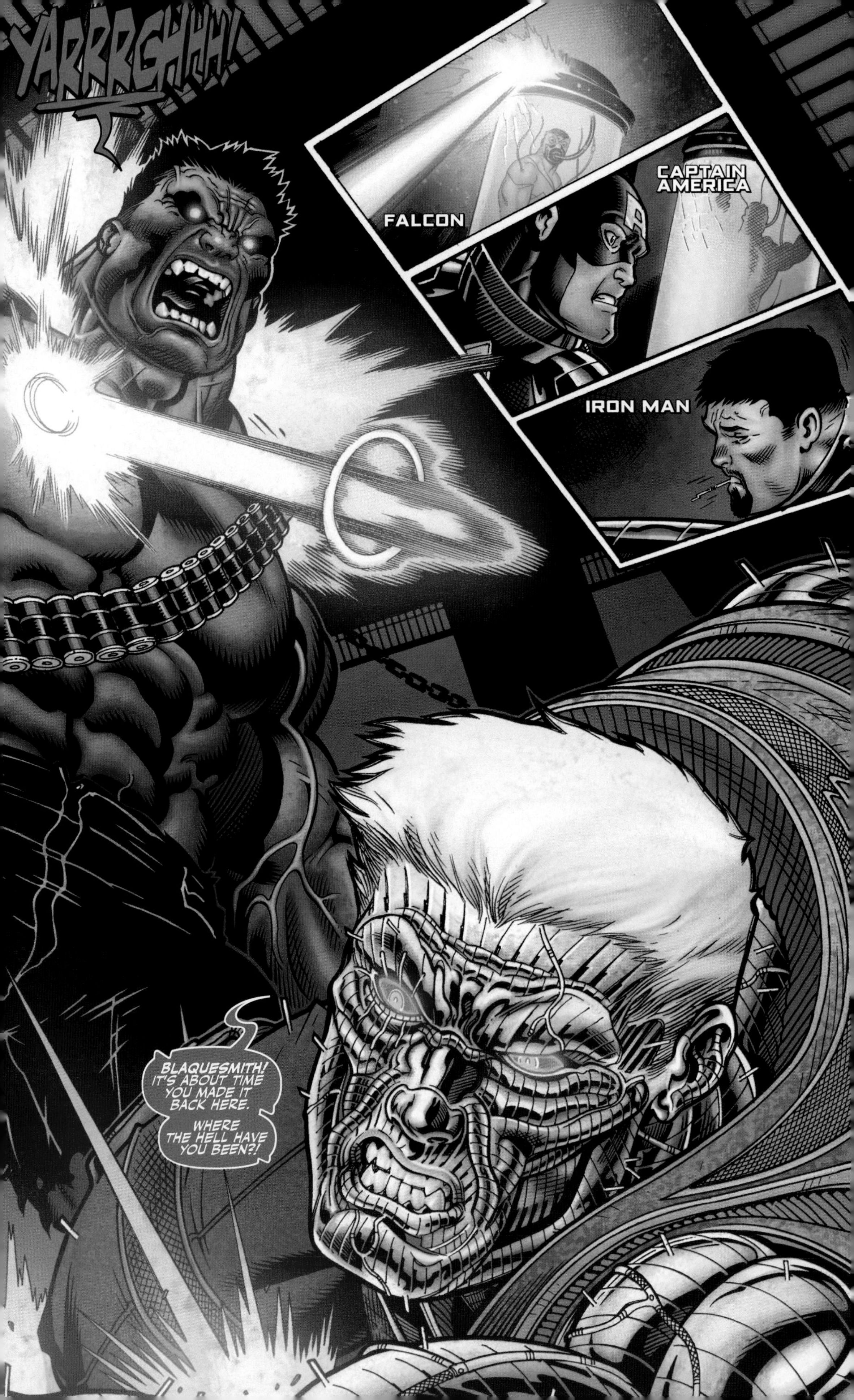
YARRRGHHH!
FALCON
CAPTAIN AMERICA
IRON MAN
BLAQUESMITH! IT'S ABOUT TIME YOU MADE IT BACK HERE.
WHERE THE HELL HAVE YOU BEEN?!

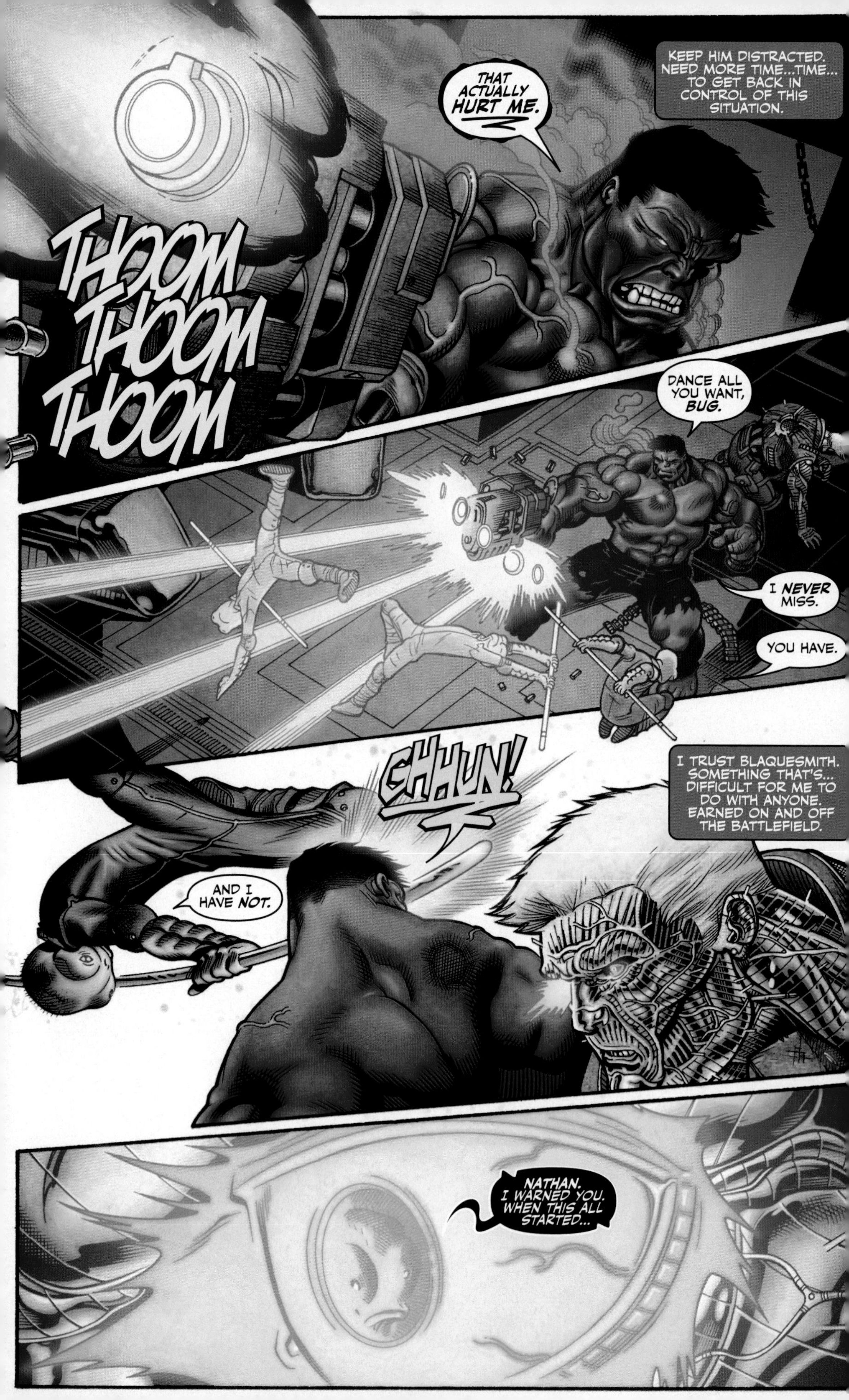
THAT ACTUALLY HURT ME.
KEEP HIM DISTRACTED. NEED MORE TIME...TIME... TO GET BACK IN CONTROL OF THIS SITUATION.
THOOM THOOM THOOM
DANCE ALL YOU WANT, BUG.
I NEVER MISS.
YOU HAVE.
CHHUN!
I TRUST BLAQUESMITH. SOMETHING THAT'S... DIFFICULT FOR ME TO DO WITH ANYONE. EARNED ON AND OFF THE BATTLEFIELD.
AND I HAVE NOT.
NATHAN. I WARNED YOU. WHEN THIS ALL STARTED...

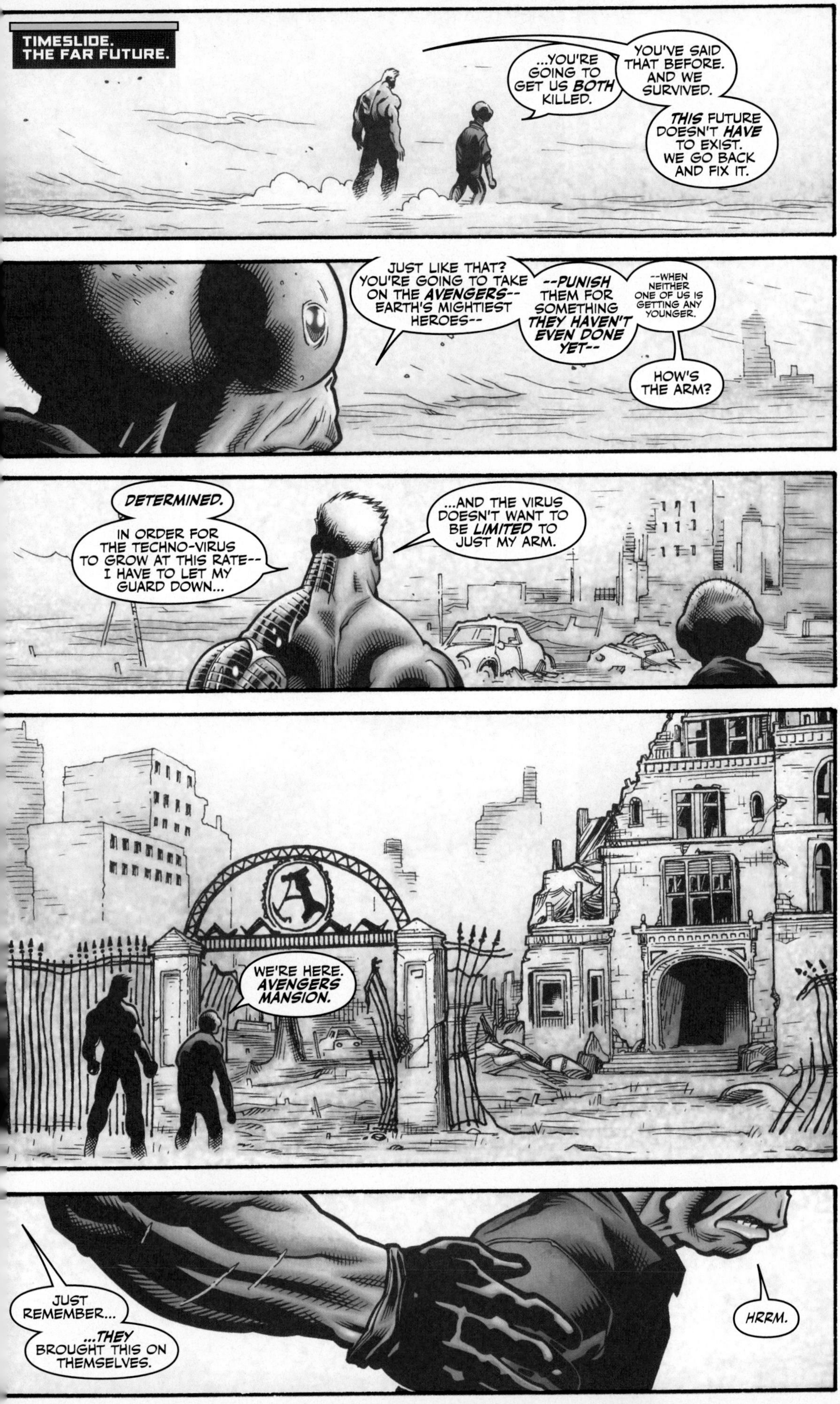
TIMESLIDE. THE FAR FUTURE.
...YOU'RE GOING TO GET US BOTH KILLED.
YOU'VE SAID THAT BEFORE. AND WE SURVIVED.
THIS FUTURE DOESN'T HAVE TO EXIST. WE GO BACK AND FIX IT.
JUST LIKE THAT? YOU'RE GOING TO TAKE ON THE AVENGERS-- EARTH'S MIGHTIEST HEROES--
--PUNISH THEM FOR SOMETHING THEY HAVEN'T EVEN DONE YET--
--WHEN NEITHER ONE OF US IS GETTING ANY YOUNGER.
HOW'S THE ARM?
DETERMINED.
IN ORDER FOR THE TECHNO-VIRUS TO GROW AT THIS RATE-- I HAVE TO LET MY GUARD DOWN...
...AND THE VIRUS DOESN'T WANT TO BE LIMITED TO JUST MY ARM.
WE'RE HERE. AVENGERS MANSION.
JUST REMEMBER...
...THEY BROUGHT THIS ON THEMSELVES.
HRRM.

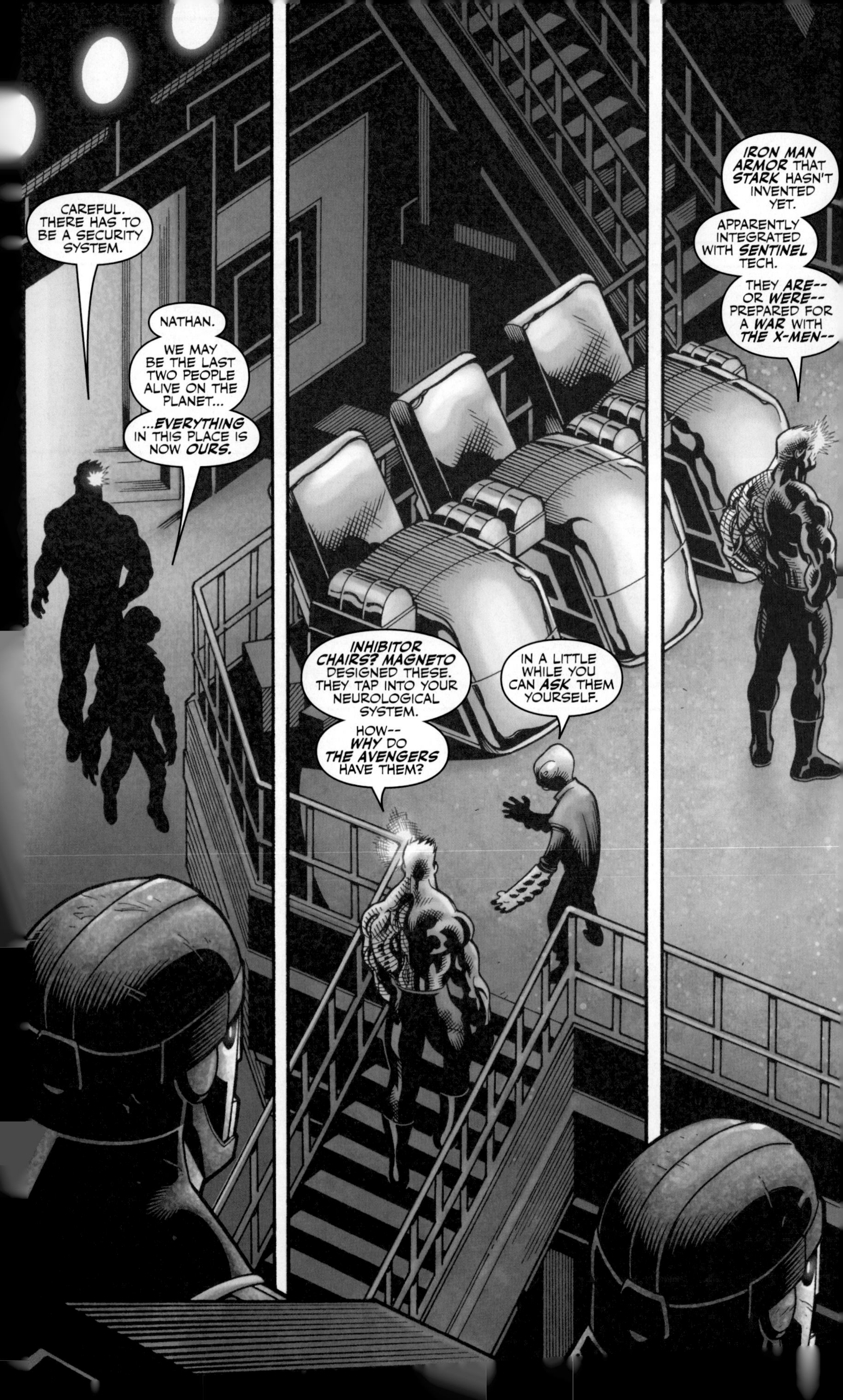
CAREFUL. THERE HAS TO BE A SECURITY SYSTEM.
NATHAN.
WE MAY BE THE LAST TWO PEOPLE ALIVE ON THE PLANET...
...EVERYTHING IN THIS PLACE IS NOW OURS.
INHIBITOR CHAIRS? MAGNETO DESIGNED THESE. THEY TAP INTO YOUR NEUROLOGICAL SYSTEM.
HOW-- WHY DO THE AVENGERS HAVE THEM?
IN A LITTLE WHILE YOU CAN ASK THEM YOURSELF.
IRON MAN ARMOR THAT STARK HASN'T INVENTED YET.
APPARENTLY INTEGRATED WITH SENTINEL TECH.
THEY ARE-- OR WERE-- PREPARED FOR A WAR WITH THE X-MEN--

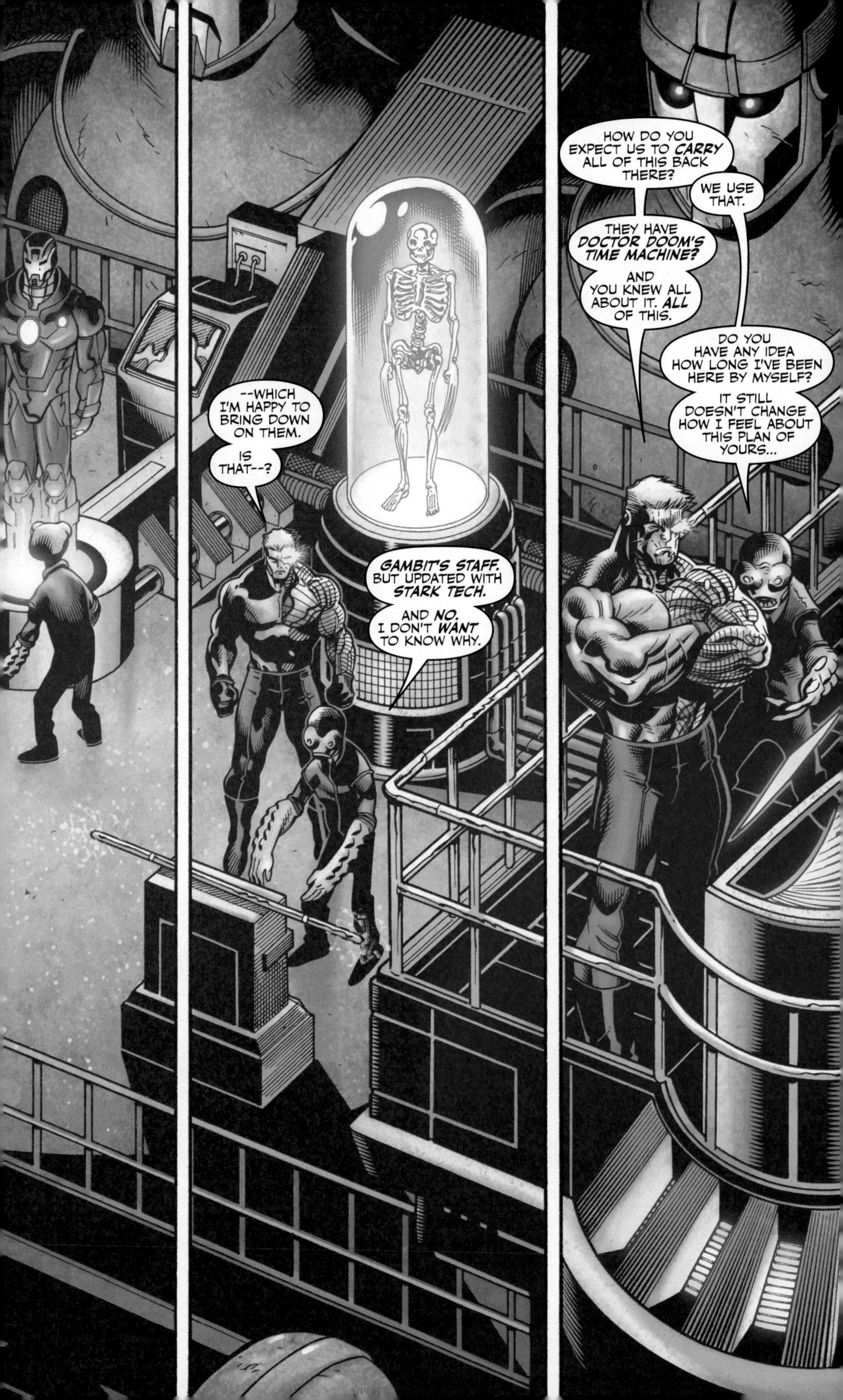
--WHICH I'M HAPPY TO BRING DOWN ON THEM.
IS THAT--?
GAMBIT'S STAFF. BUT UPDATED WITH STARK TECH.
AND NO. I DON'T WANT TO KNOW WHY.
HOW DO YOU EXPECT US TO CARRY ALL OF THIS BACK THERE?
WE USE THAT.
THEY HAVE DOCTOR DOOM'S TIME MACHINE?
AND YOU KNEW ALL ABOUT IT. ALL OF THIS.
DO YOU HAVE ANY IDEA HOW LONG I'VE BEEN HERE BY MYSELF?
IT STILL DOESN'T CHANGE HOW I FEEL ABOUT THIS PLAN OF YOURS...

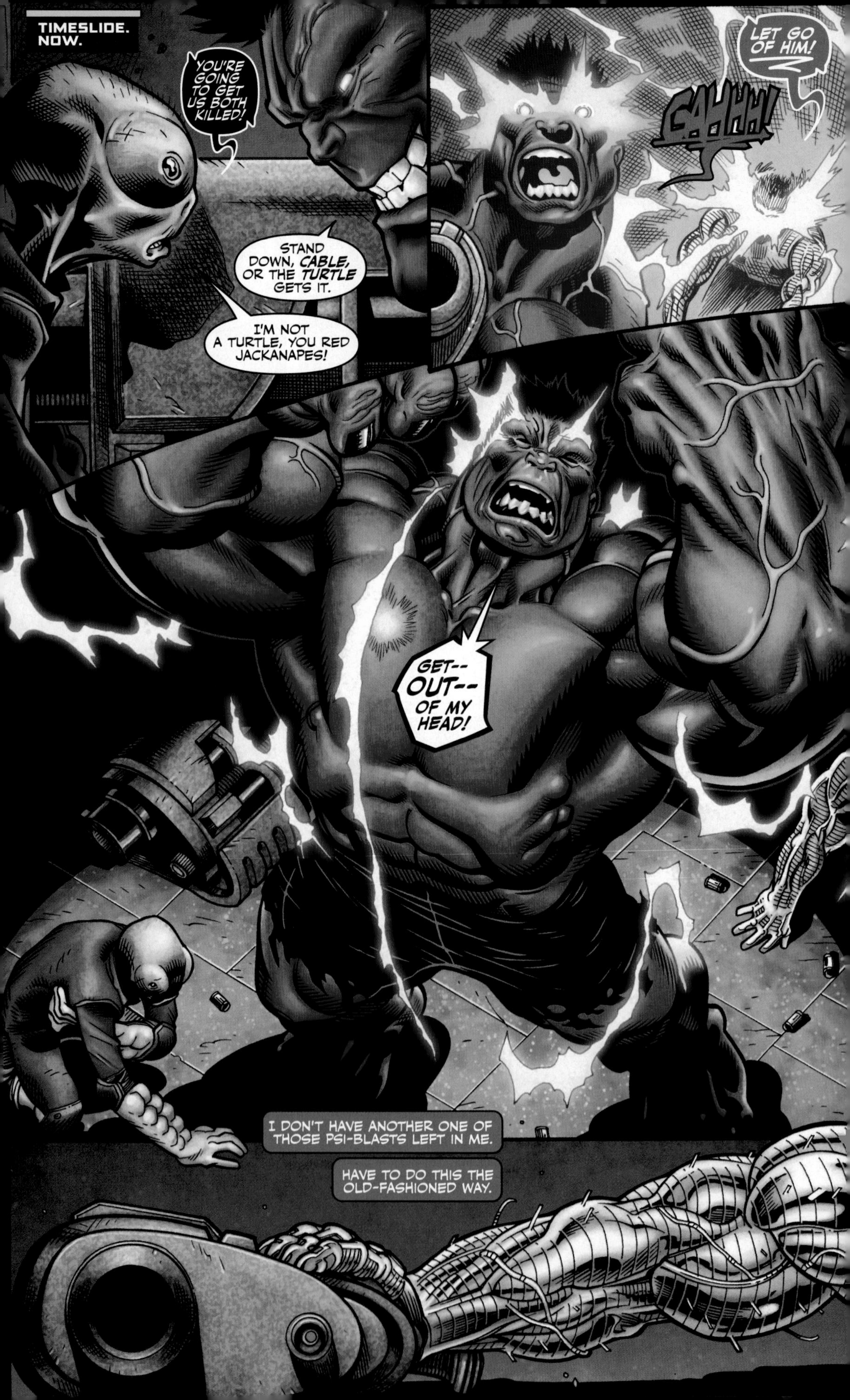
TIMESLIDE.
NOW.
YOU'RE GOING TO GET US BOTH KILLED!
STAND DOWN, CABLE, OR THE TURTLE GETS IT.
I'M NOT A TURTLE, YOU RED JACKANAPES!
LET GO OF HIM!
GAHHH!
GET-- OUT-- OF MY HEAD!
I DON'T HAVE ANOTHER ONE OF THOSE PSI-BLASTS LEFT IN ME.
HAVE TO DO THIS THE OLD-FASHIONED WAY.

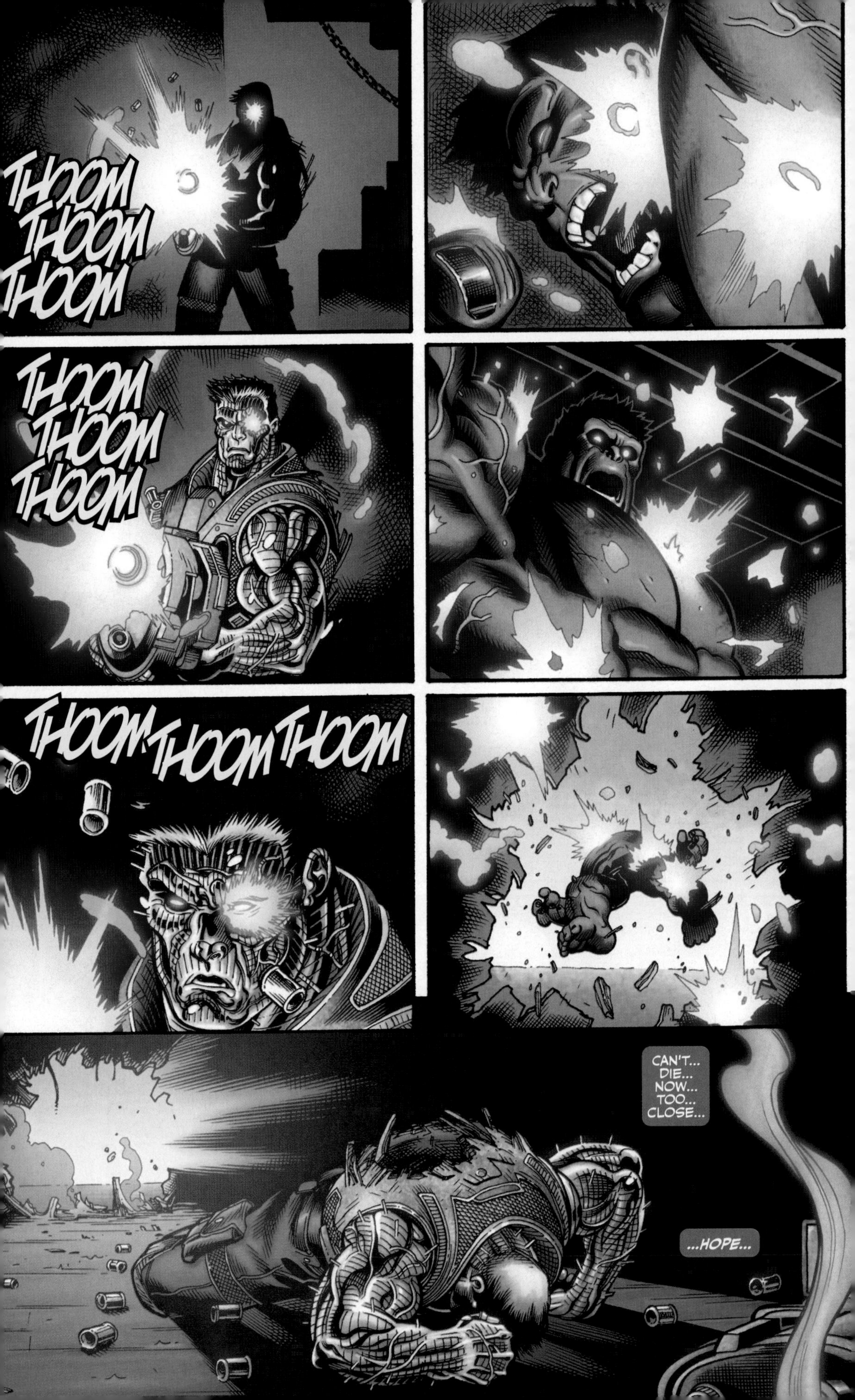
THOOM THOOM THOOM
THOOM THOOM THOOM
THOOM THOOM THOOM
CAN'T... DIE... NOW... TOO... CLOSE...
...HOPE...

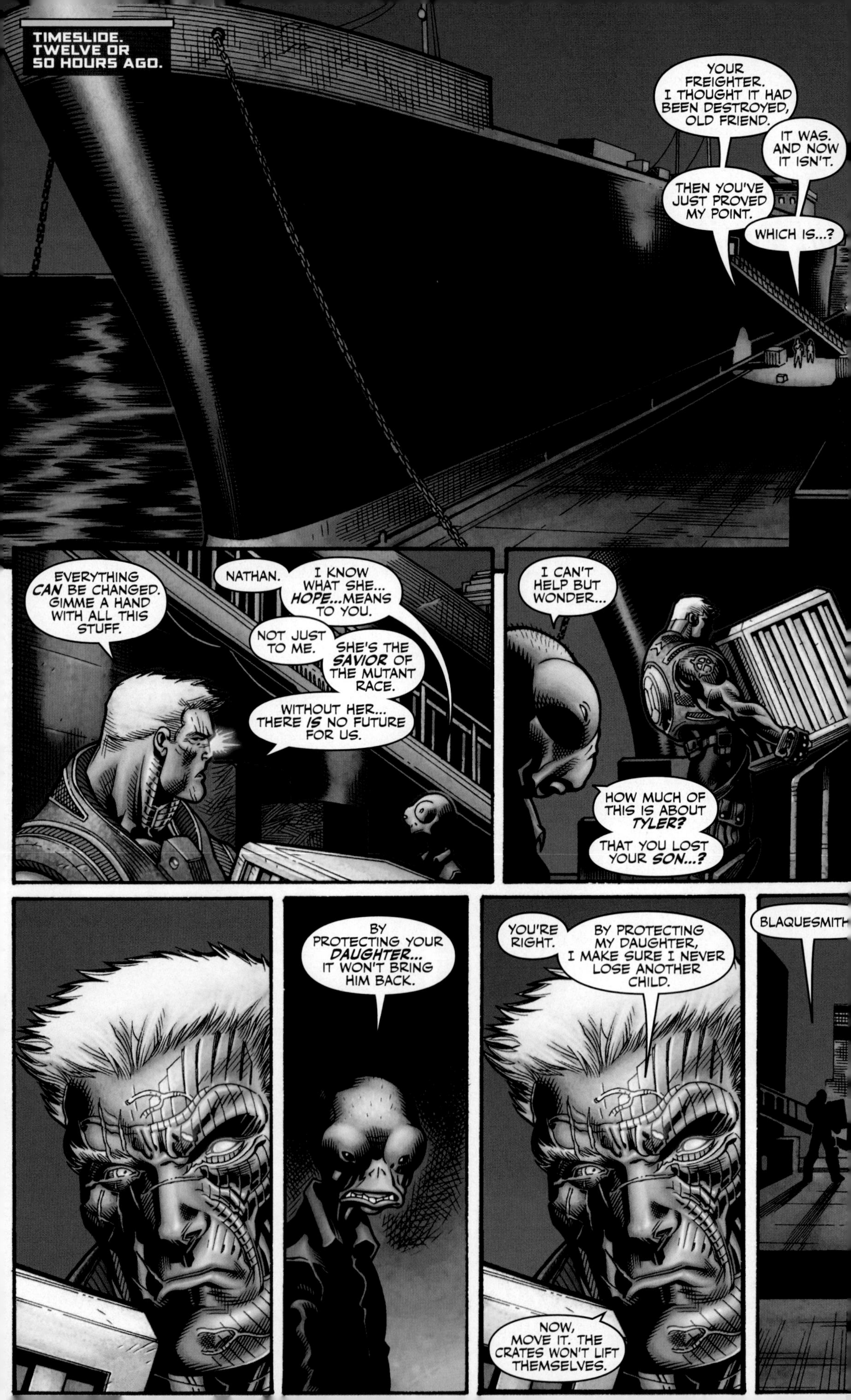
TIMESLIDE. TWELVE OR SO HOURS AGO.
YOUR FREIGHTER. I THOUGHT IT HAD BEEN DESTROYED, OLD FRIEND.
IT WAS. AND NOW IT ISN'T.
THEN YOU'VE JUST PROVED MY POINT.
WHICH IS...?
EVERYTHING CAN BE CHANGED. GIMME A HAND WITH ALL THIS STUFF.
NATHAN.
I KNOW WHAT SHE... HOPE...MEANS TO YOU.
NOT JUST TO ME.
SHE'S THE SAVIOR OF THE MUTANT RACE.
WITHOUT HER... THERE IS NO FUTURE FOR US.
I CAN'T HELP BUT WONDER...
HOW MUCH OF THIS IS ABOUT TYLER?
THAT YOU LOST YOUR SON...?
BY PROTECTING YOUR DAUGHTER... IT WON'T BRING HIM BACK.
YOU'RE RIGHT.
BY PROTECTING MY DAUGHTER, I MAKE SURE I NEVER LOSE ANOTHER CHILD.
NOW, MOVE IT. THE CRATES WON'T LIFT THEMSELVES.
BLAQUESMITH

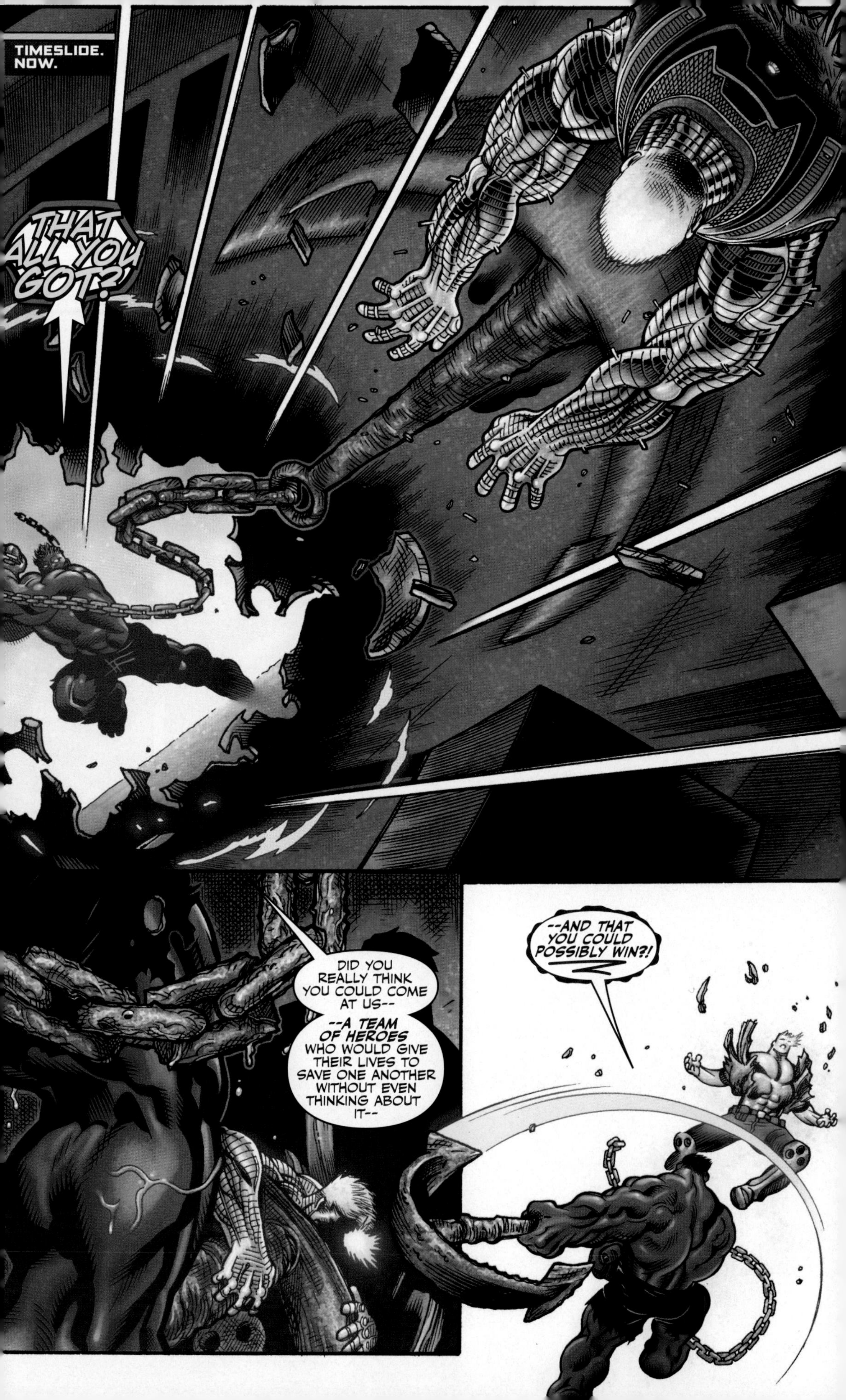
TIMESLIDE. NOW.
THAT ALL YOU GOT?!
DID YOU REALLY THINK YOU COULD COME AT US--
--A TEAM OF HEROES WHO WOULD GIVE THEIR LIVES TO SAVE ONE ANOTHER WITHOUT EVEN THINKING ABOUT IT--
--AND THAT YOU COULD POSSIBLY WIN?!

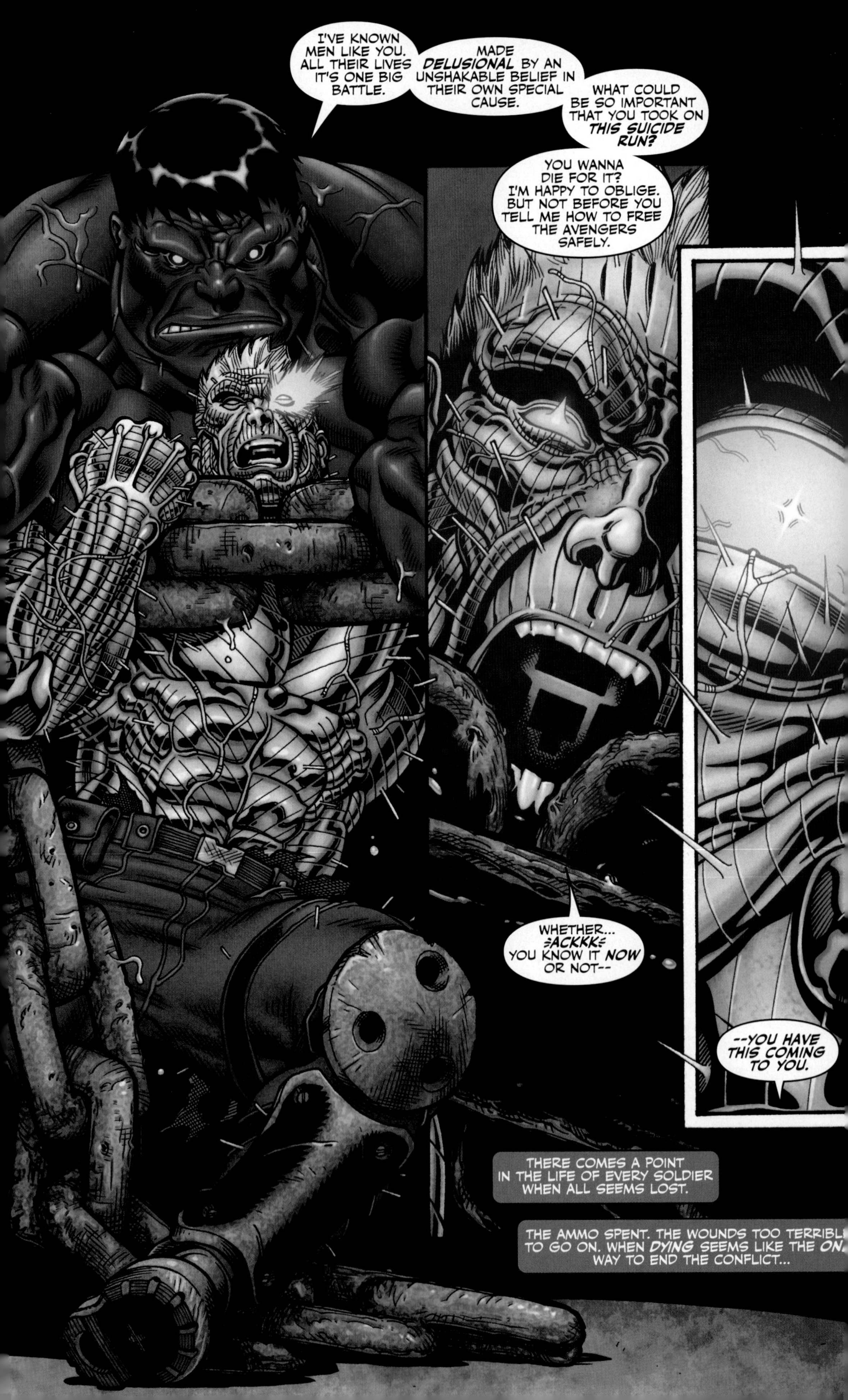
I'VE KNOWN MEN LIKE YOU. ALL THEIR LIVES IT'S ONE BIG BATTLE.
MADE DELUSIONAL BY AN UNSHAKABLE BELIEF IN THEIR OWN SPECIAL CAUSE.
WHAT COULD BE SO IMPORTANT THAT YOU TOOK ON THIS SUICIDE RUN?
YOU WANNA DIE FOR IT? I'M HAPPY TO OBLIGE. BUT NOT BEFORE YOU TELL ME HOW TO FREE THE AVENGERS SAFELY.
WHETHER... ACKKK YOU KNOW IT NOW OR NOT--
--YOU HAVE THIS COMING TO YOU.
THERE COMES A POINT IN THE LIFE OF EVERY SOLDIER WHEN ALL SEEMS LOST.
THE AMMO SPENT. THE WOUNDS TOO TERRIBL TO GO ON. WHEN DYING SEEMS LIKE THE ON WAY TO END THE CONFLICT...

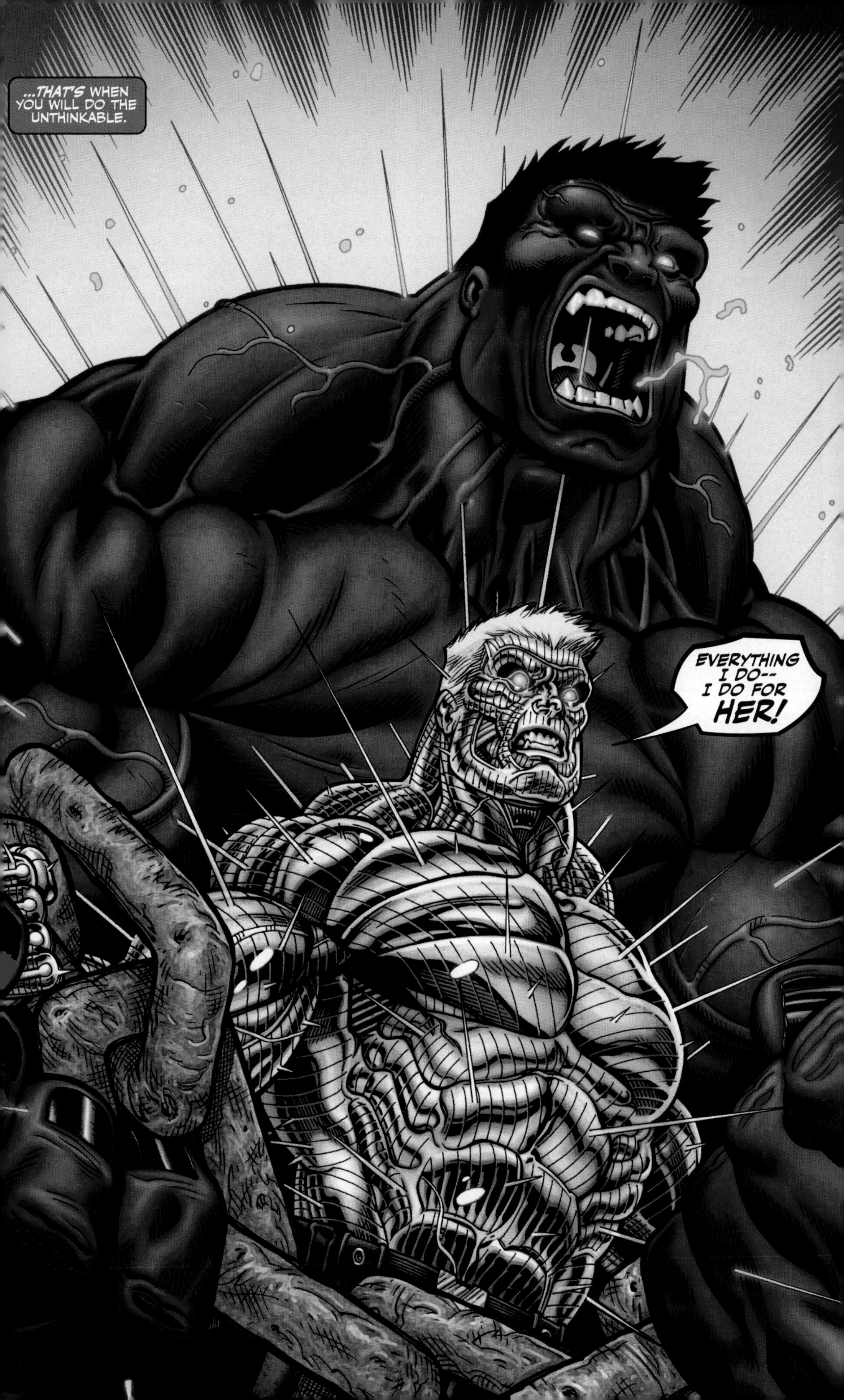
...THAT'S WHEN YOU WILL DO THE UNTHINKABLE.
EVERYTHING I DO-- I DO FOR HER!

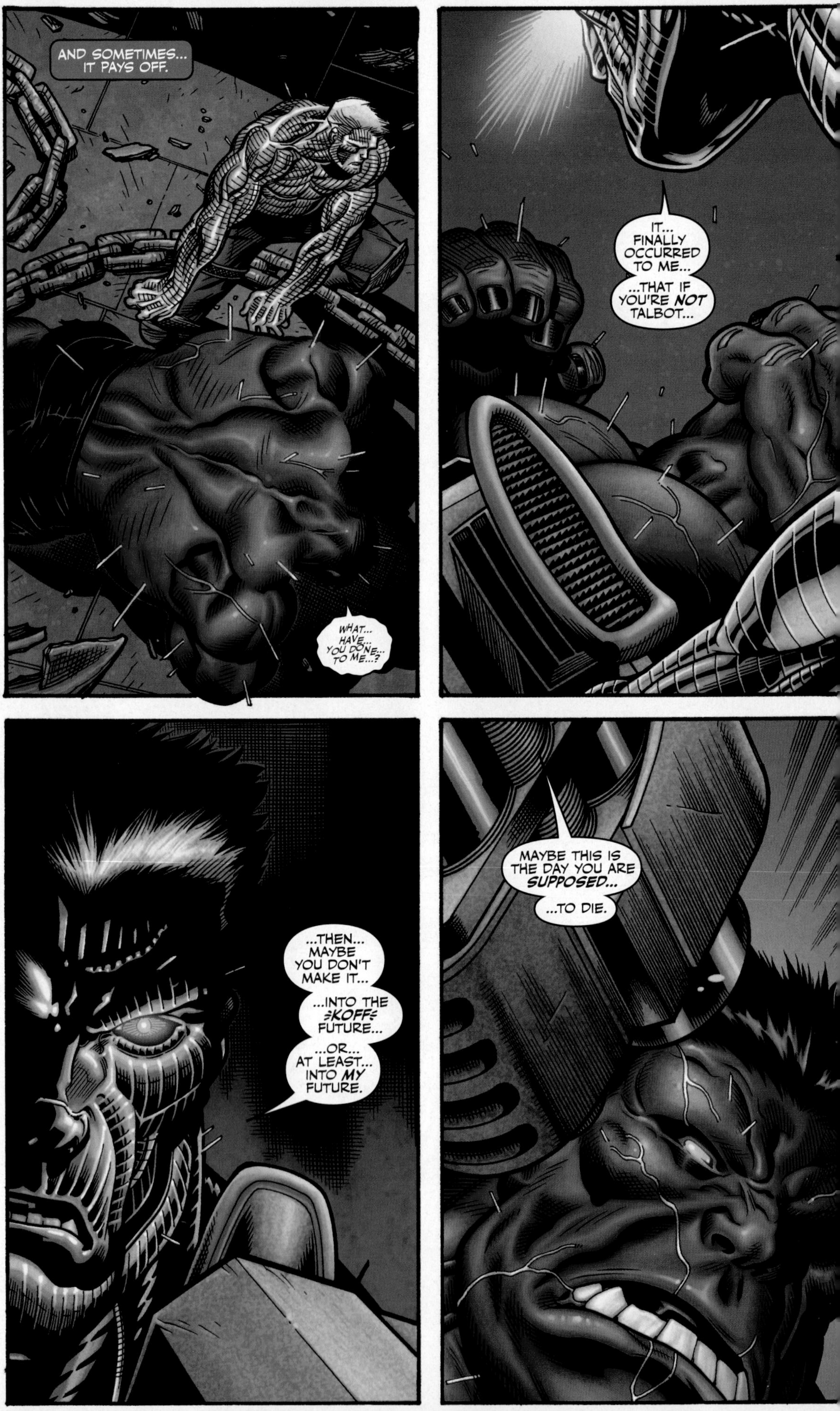
AND SOMETIMES... IT PAYS OFF.
WHAT... HAVE... YOU DONE... TO ME...?
IT... FINALLY OCCURRED TO ME...
...THAT IF YOU'RE NOT TALBOT...
...THEN... MAYBE YOU DON'T MAKE IT...
...INTO THE KOFF FUTURE...
...OR... AT LEAST... INTO MY FUTURE.
MAYBE THIS IS THE DAY YOU ARE SUPPOSED...
...TO DIE.

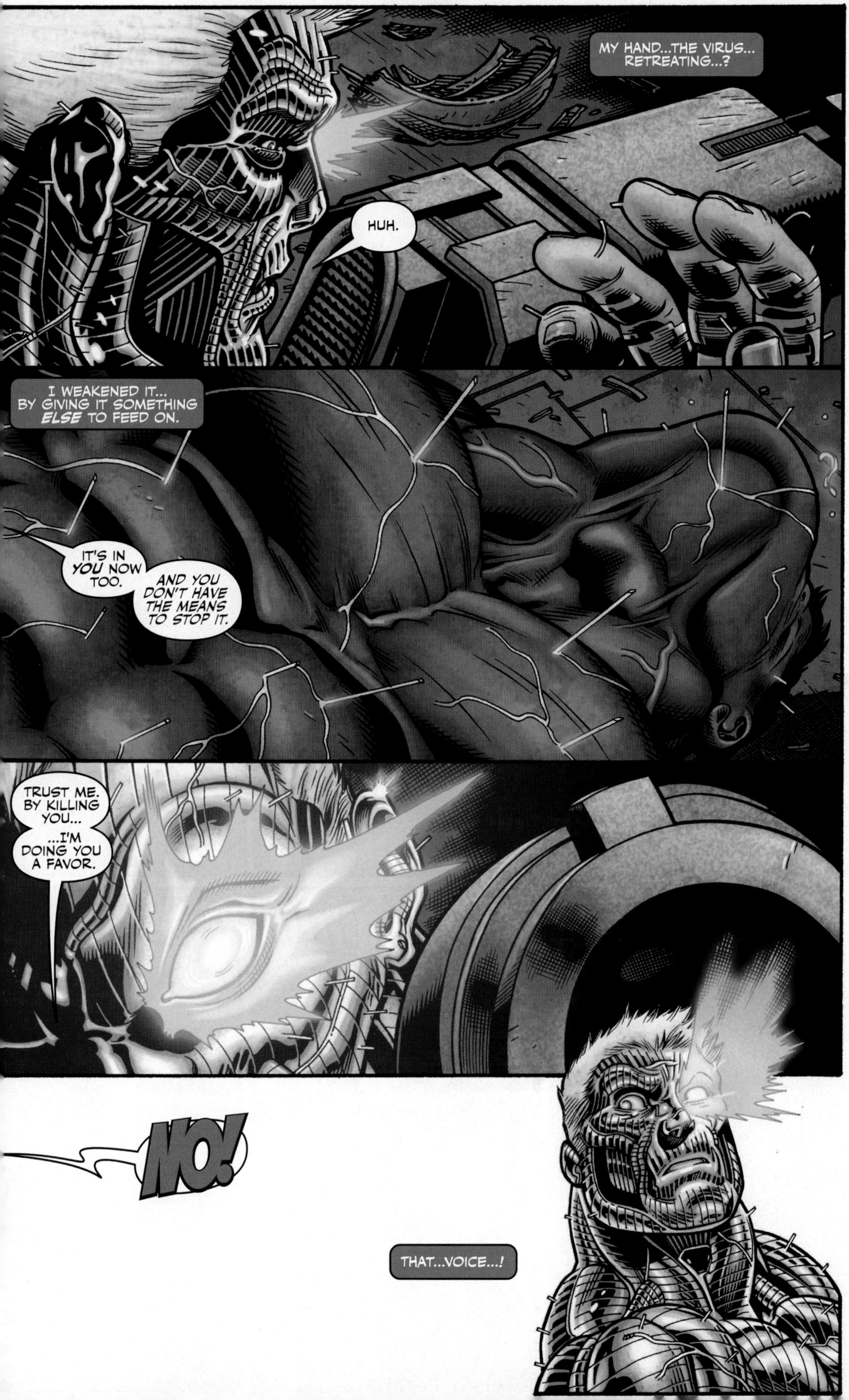
MY HAND...THE VIRUS... RETREATING...?
HUH.
I WEAKENED IT... BY GIVING IT SOMETHING ELSE TO FEED ON.
IT'S IN YOU NOW TOO.
AND YOU DON'T HAVE THE MEANS TO STOP IT.
TRUST ME. BY KILLING YOU...
...I'M DOING YOU A FAVOR.
NO!
THAT...VOICE...!

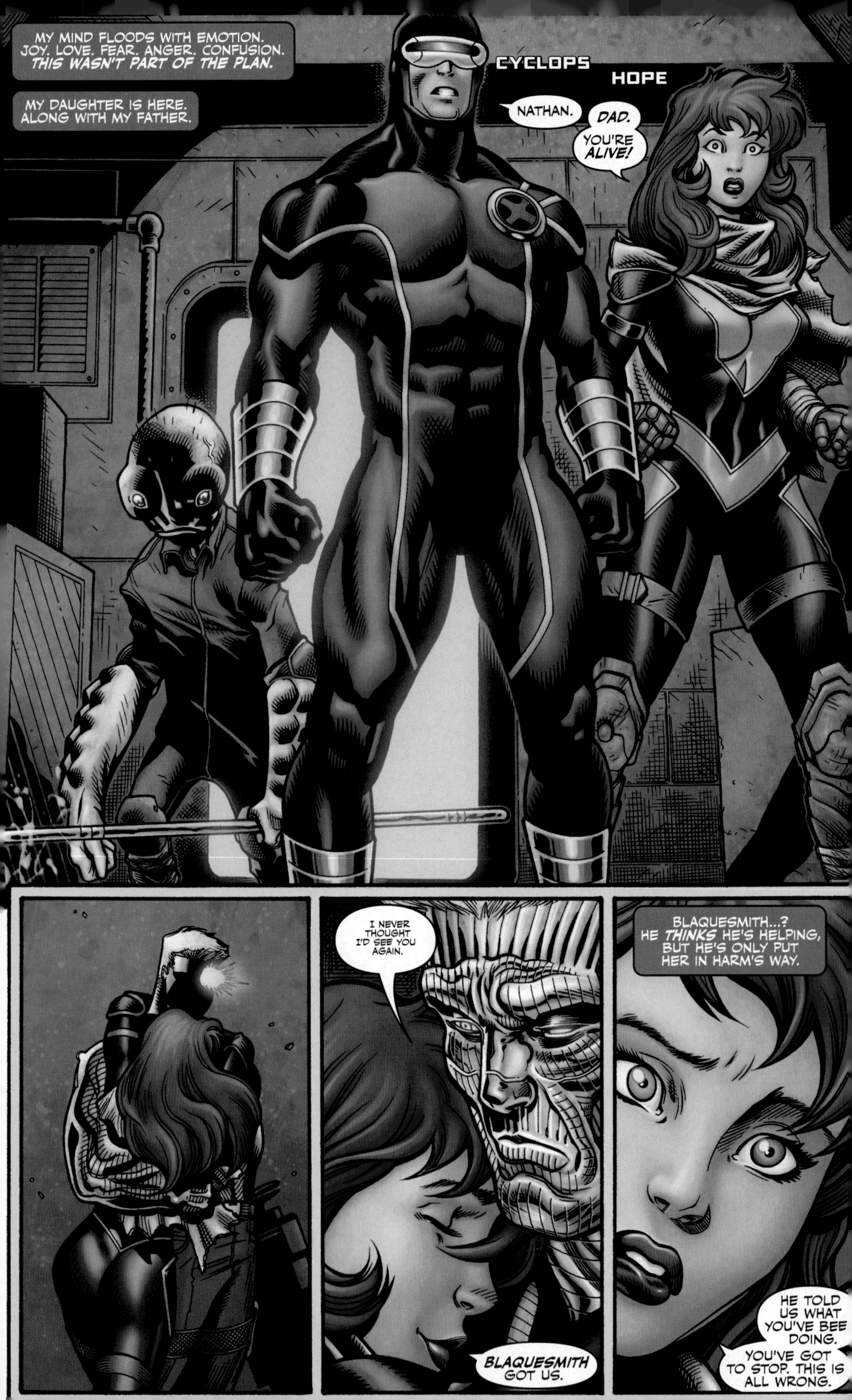

MY MIND FLOODS WITH EMOTION. JOY. LOVE. FEAR. ANGER. CONFUSION. *THIS WASN'T PART OF THE PLAN.*
MY DAUGHTER IS HERE. ALONG WITH MY FATHER.
CYCLOPS
HOPE
NATHAN.
DAD. YOU'RE *ALIVE!*
I NEVER THOUGHT I'D SEE YOU AGAIN.
BLAQUESMITH GOT US.
BLAQUESMITH...? HE *THINKS* HE'S HELPING, BUT HE'S ONLY PUT HER IN HARM'S WAY.
HE TOLD US WHAT YOU'VE BEE DOING. YOU'VE GOT TO STOP. THIS IS ALL WRONG.

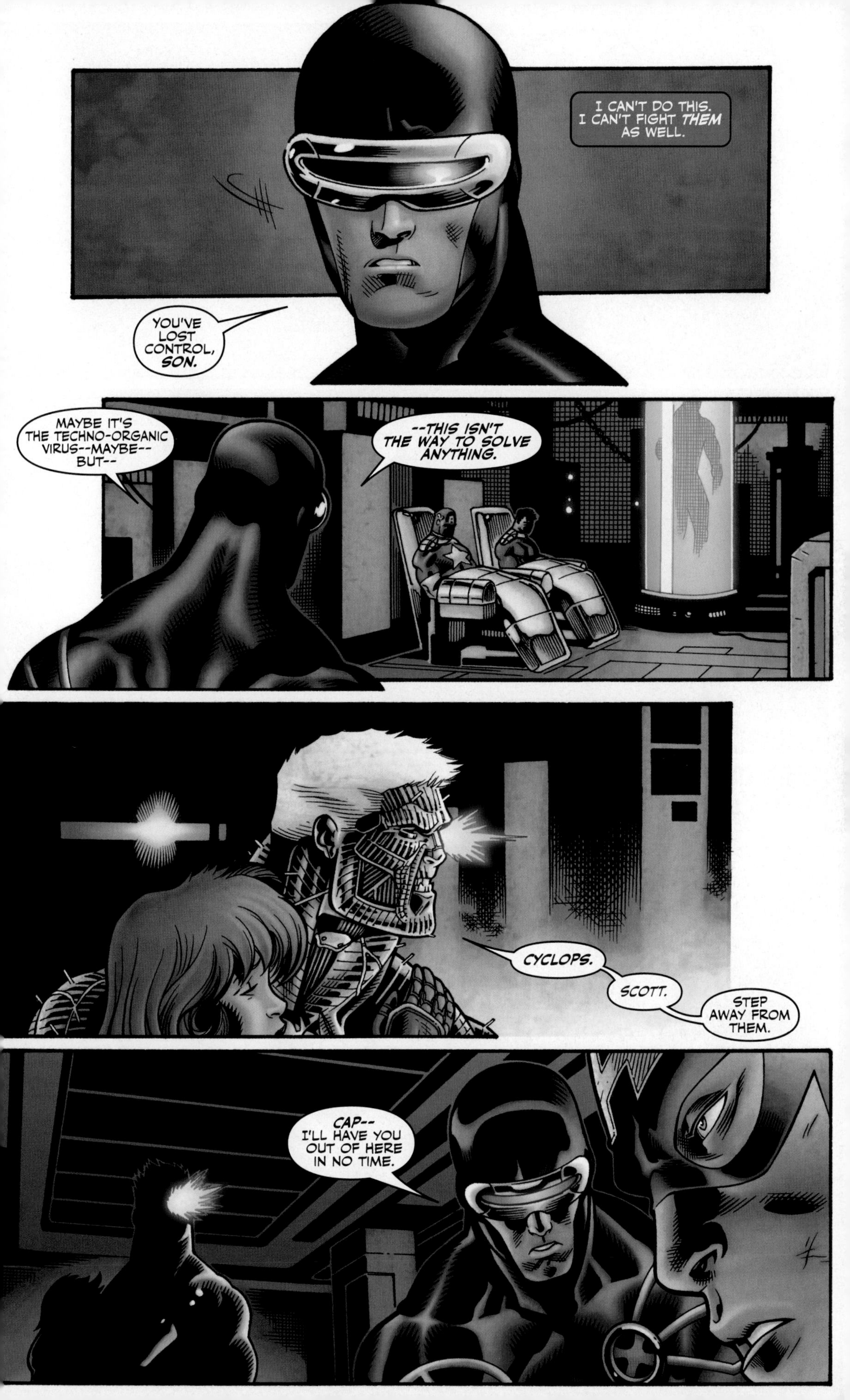
I CAN'T DO THIS. I CAN'T FIGHT THEM AS WELL.
YOU'VE LOST CONTROL, SON.
MAYBE IT'S THE TECHNO-ORGANIC VIRUS--MAYBE-- BUT--
--THIS ISN'T THE WAY TO SOLVE ANYTHING.
CYCLOPS.
SCOTT.
STEP AWAY FROM THEM.
CAP-- I'LL HAVE YOU OUT OF HERE IN NO TIME.

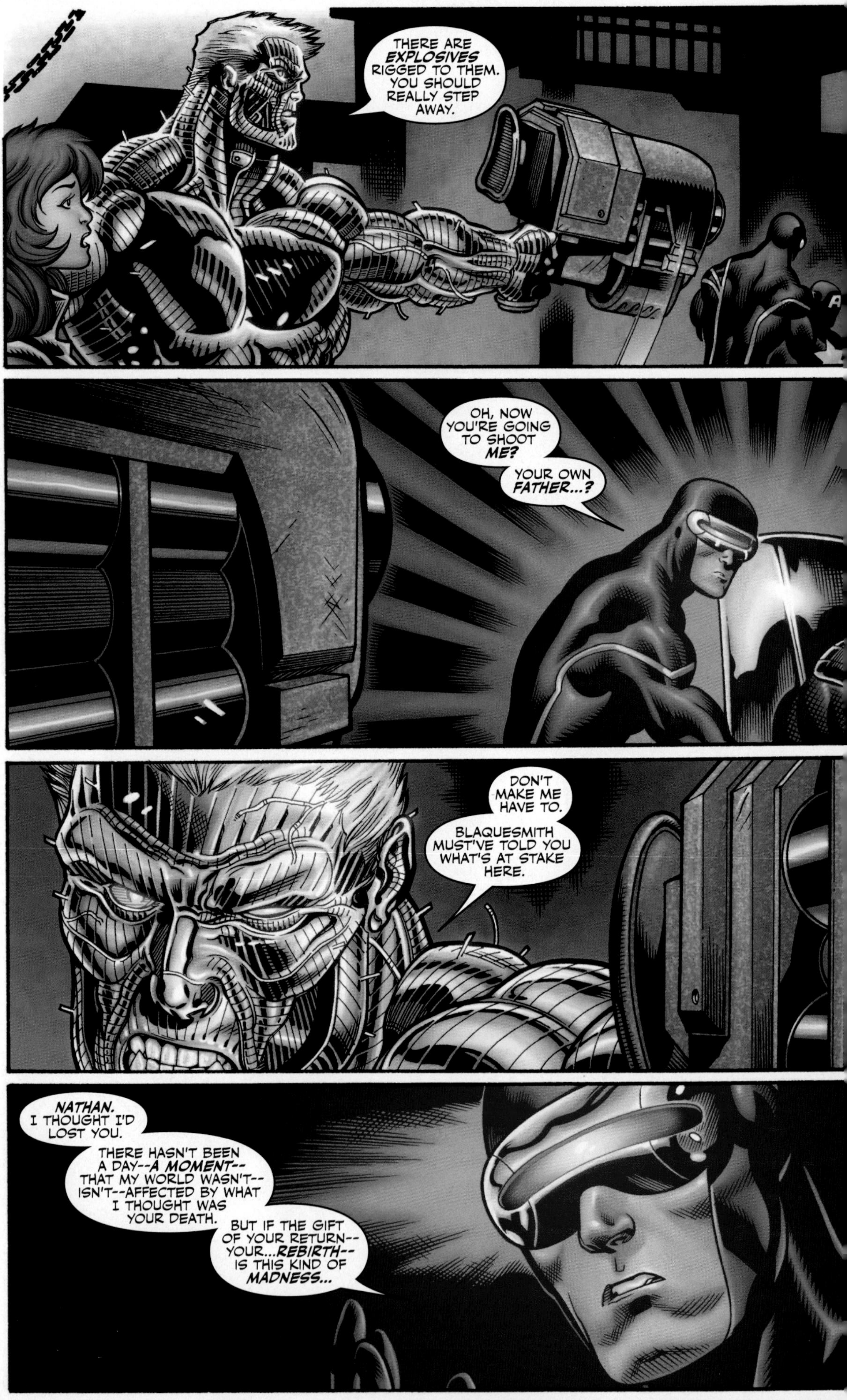
THERE ARE EXPLOSIVES RIGGED TO THEM. YOU SHOULD REALLY STEP AWAY.
OH, NOW YOU'RE GOING TO SHOOT ME?
YOUR OWN FATHER...?
DON'T MAKE ME HAVE TO.
BLAQUESMITH MUST'VE TOLD YOU WHAT'S AT STAKE HERE.
NATHAN. I THOUGHT I'D LOST YOU.
THERE HASN'T BEEN A DAY--A MOMENT--THAT MY WORLD WASN'T--ISN'T--AFFECTED BY WHAT I THOUGHT WAS YOUR DEATH.
BUT IF THE GIFT OF YOUR RETURN--YOUR...REBIRTH--IS THIS KIND OF MADNESS...

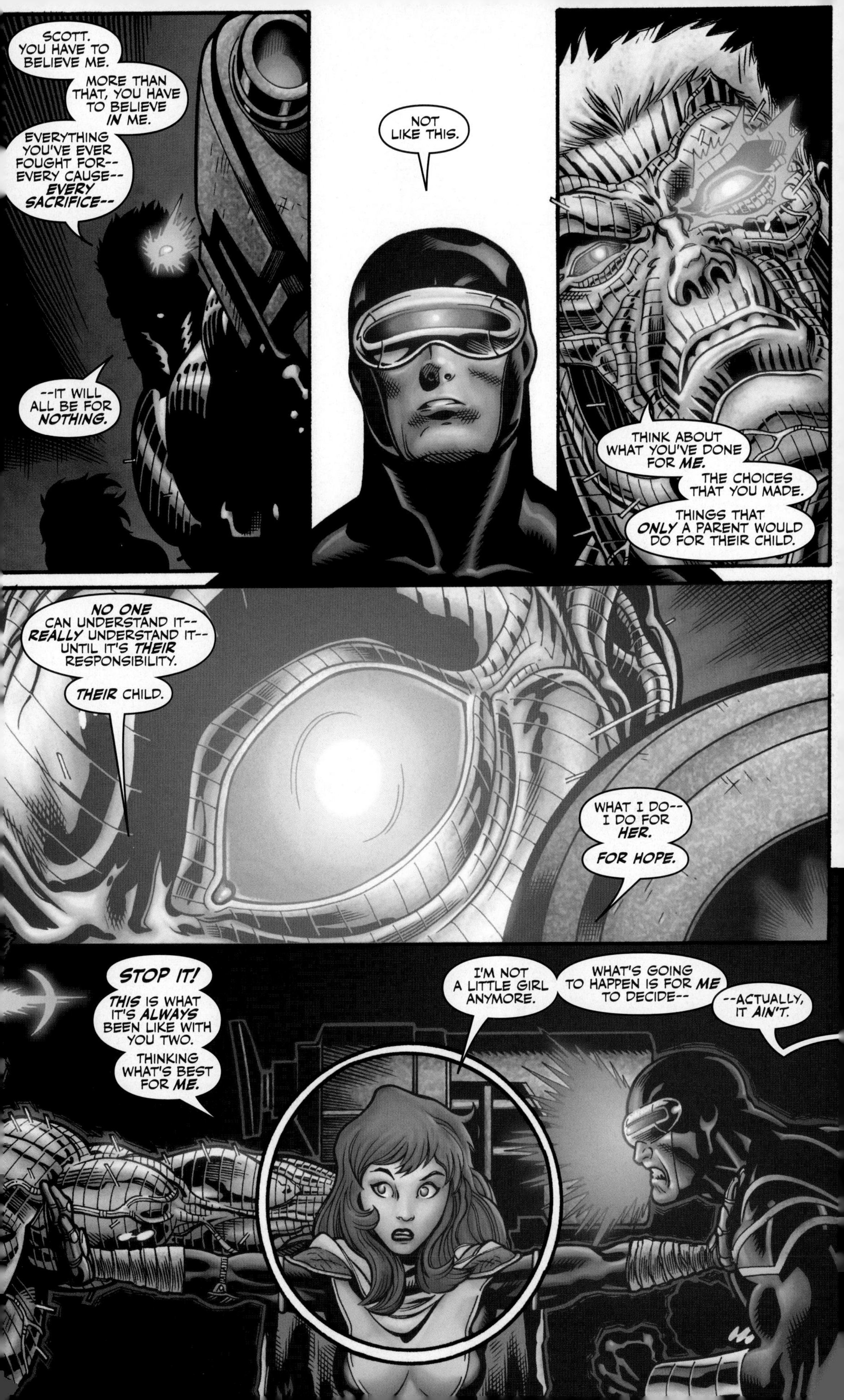
SCOTT. YOU HAVE TO BELIEVE ME.
MORE THAN THAT, YOU HAVE TO BELIEVE *IN* ME.
EVERYTHING YOU'VE EVER FOUGHT FOR-- EVERY CAUSE-- *EVERY SACRIFICE--*
--IT WILL ALL BE FOR *NOTHING.*
NOT LIKE THIS.
THINK ABOUT WHAT YOU'VE DONE FOR *ME.*
THE CHOICES THAT YOU MADE.
THINGS THAT *ONLY* A PARENT WOULD DO FOR THEIR CHILD.
NO ONE CAN UNDERSTAND IT-- *REALLY* UNDERSTAND IT-- UNTIL IT'S *THEIR* RESPONSIBILITY.
THEIR CHILD.
WHAT I DO-- I DO FOR *HER.*
FOR HOPE.
STOP IT!
THIS IS WHAT IT'S *ALWAYS* BEEN LIKE WITH YOU TWO.
THINKING WHAT'S BEST FOR *ME.*
I'M NOT A LITTLE GIRL ANYMORE.
WHAT'S GOING TO HAPPEN IS FOR *ME* TO DECIDE--
--ACTUALLY, IT *AIN'T.*

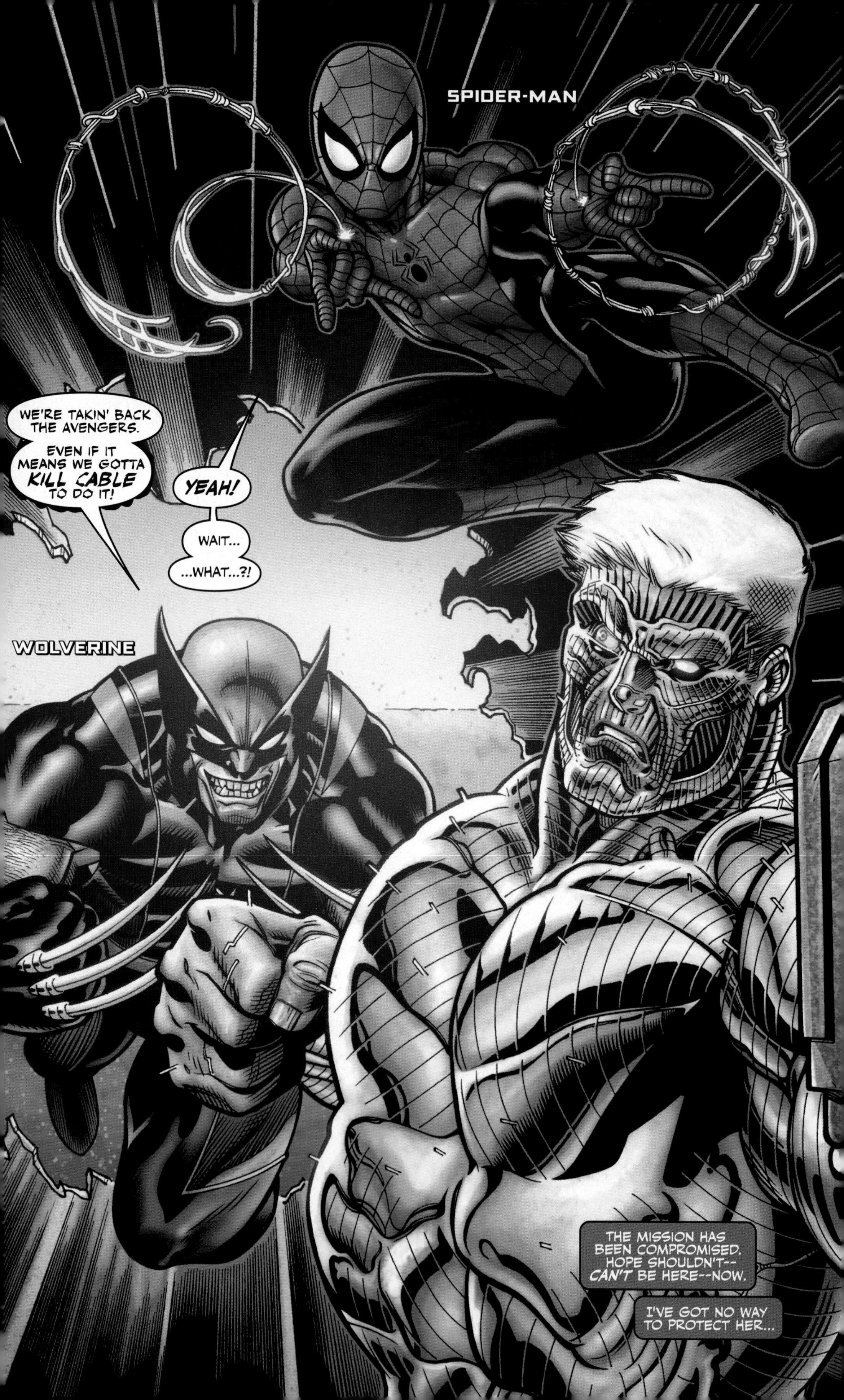
SPIDER-MAN
WE'RE TAKIN' BACK THE AVENGERS.
EVEN IF IT MEANS WE GOTTA KILL CABLE TO DO IT!
YEAH!
WAIT...
...WHAT...?!
WOLVERINE
THE MISSION HAS BEEN COMPROMISED. HOPE SHOULDN'T-- CAN'T BE HERE--NOW.
I'VE GOT NO WAY TO PROTECT HER...

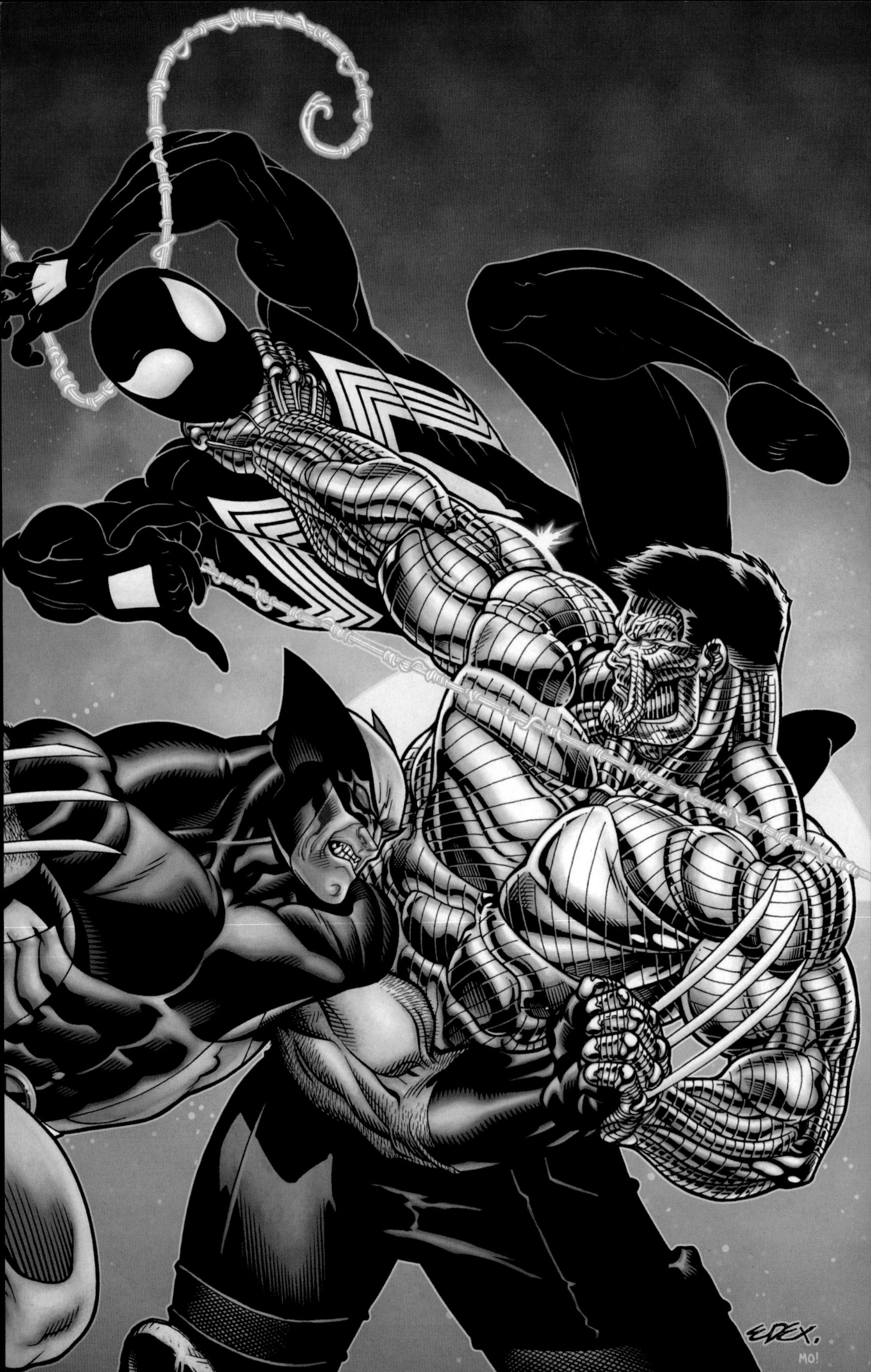

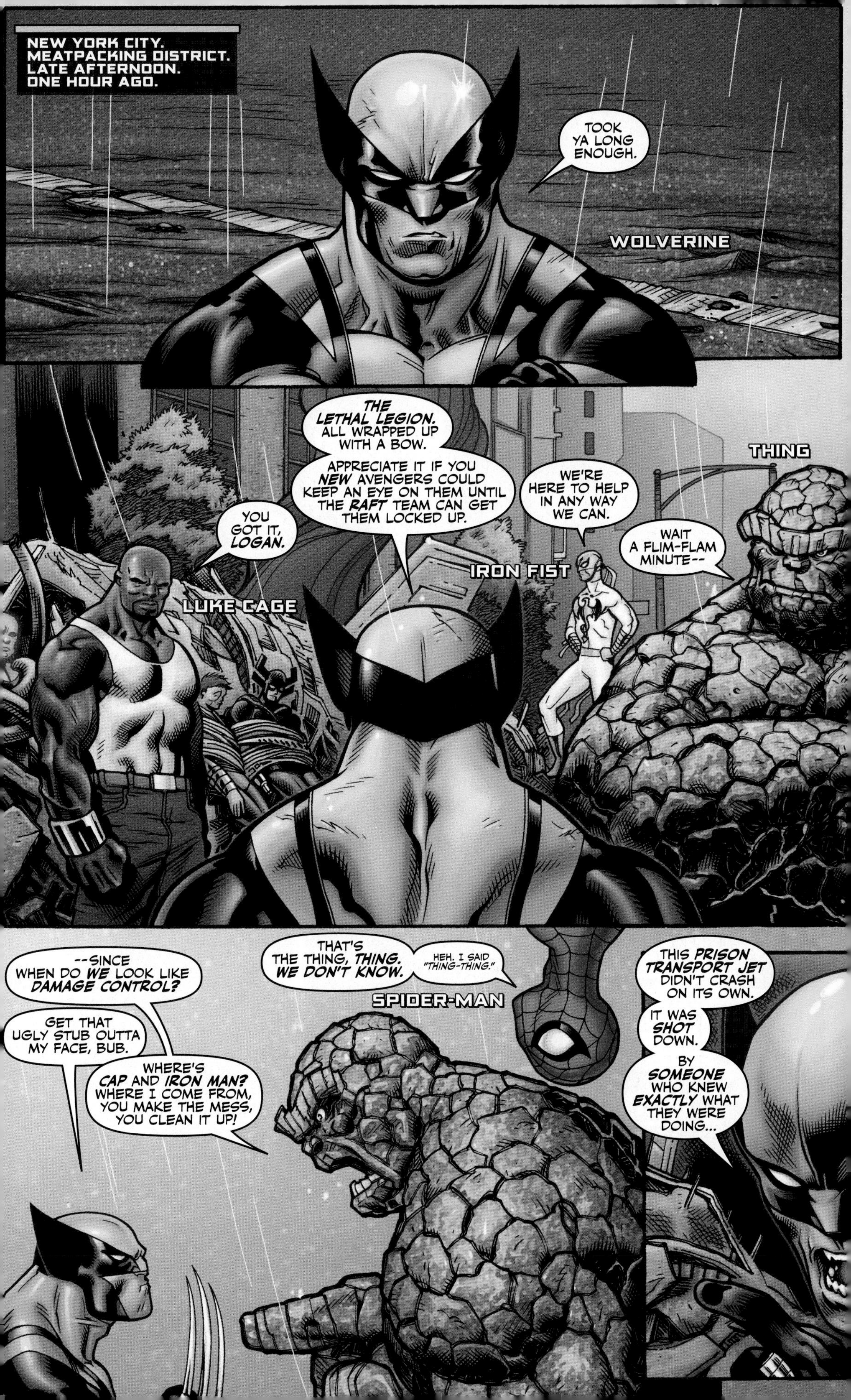
NEW YORK CITY. MEATPACKING DISTRICT. LATE AFTERNOON. ONE HOUR AGO.
TOOK YA LONG ENOUGH.
WOLVERINE
THE LETHAL LEGION. ALL WRAPPED UP WITH A BOW.
APPRECIATE IT IF YOU NEW AVENGERS COULD KEEP AN EYE ON THEM UNTIL THE RAFT TEAM CAN GET THEM LOCKED UP.
YOU GOT IT, LOGAN.
LUKE CAGE
WE'RE HERE TO HELP IN ANY WAY WE CAN.
IRON FIST
THING
WAIT A FLIM-FLAM MINUTE--
--SINCE WHEN DO WE LOOK LIKE DAMAGE CONTROL?
GET THAT UGLY STUB OUTTA MY FACE, BUB.
WHERE'S CAP AND IRON MAN? WHERE I COME FROM, YOU MAKE THE MESS, YOU CLEAN IT UP!
THAT'S THE THING, THING. WE DON'T KNOW.
HEH. I SAID "THING-THING."
SPIDER-MAN
THIS PRISON TRANSPORT JET DIDN'T CRASH ON ITS OWN.
IT WAS SHOT DOWN.
BY SOMEONE WHO KNEW EXACTLY WHAT THEY WERE DOING...

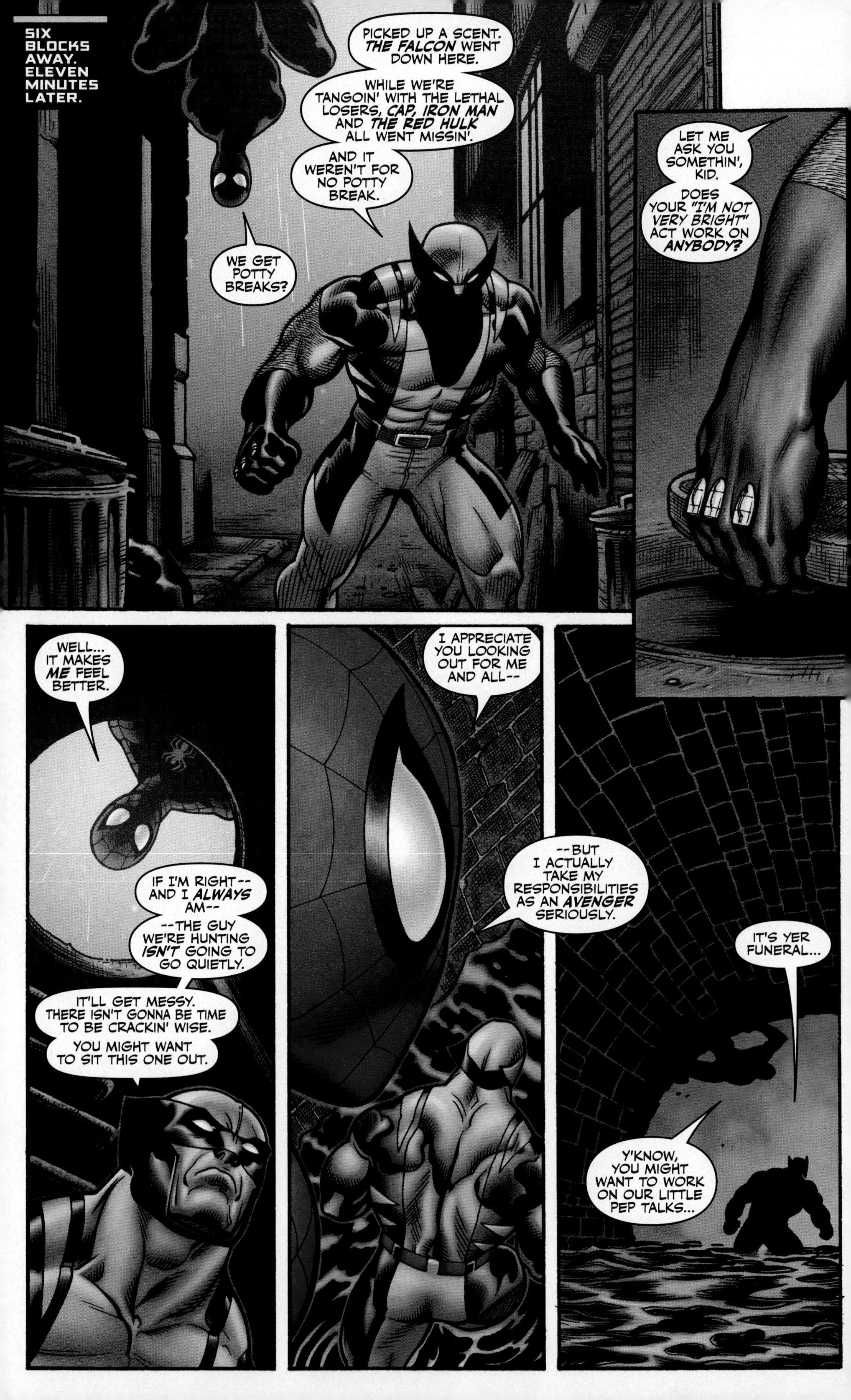
SIX BLOCKS AWAY. ELEVEN MINUTES LATER.
PICKED UP A SCENT. *THE FALCON* WENT DOWN HERE.
WHILE WE'RE TANGOIN' WITH THE LETHAL LOSERS, *CAP, IRON MAN* AND *THE RED HULK* ALL WENT MISSIN'.
AND IT WEREN'T FOR NO POTTY BREAK.
WE GET POTTY BREAKS?
LET ME ASK YOU SOMETHIN', KID.
DOES YOUR *"I'M NOT VERY BRIGHT"* ACT WORK ON *ANYBODY?*
WELL... IT MAKES *ME* FEEL BETTER.
IF I'M RIGHT-- AND I *ALWAYS* AM--
--THE GUY WE'RE HUNTING *ISN'T* GOING TO GO QUIETLY.
IT'LL GET MESSY. THERE ISN'T GONNA BE TIME TO BE CRACKIN' WISE.
YOU MIGHT WANT TO SIT THIS ONE OUT.
I APPRECIATE YOU LOOKING OUT FOR ME AND ALL--
--BUT I ACTUALLY TAKE MY RESPONSIBILITIES AS AN *AVENGER* SERIOUSLY.
IT'S YER FUNERAL...
Y'KNOW, YOU MIGHT WANT TO WORK ON OUR LITTLE PEP TALKS...

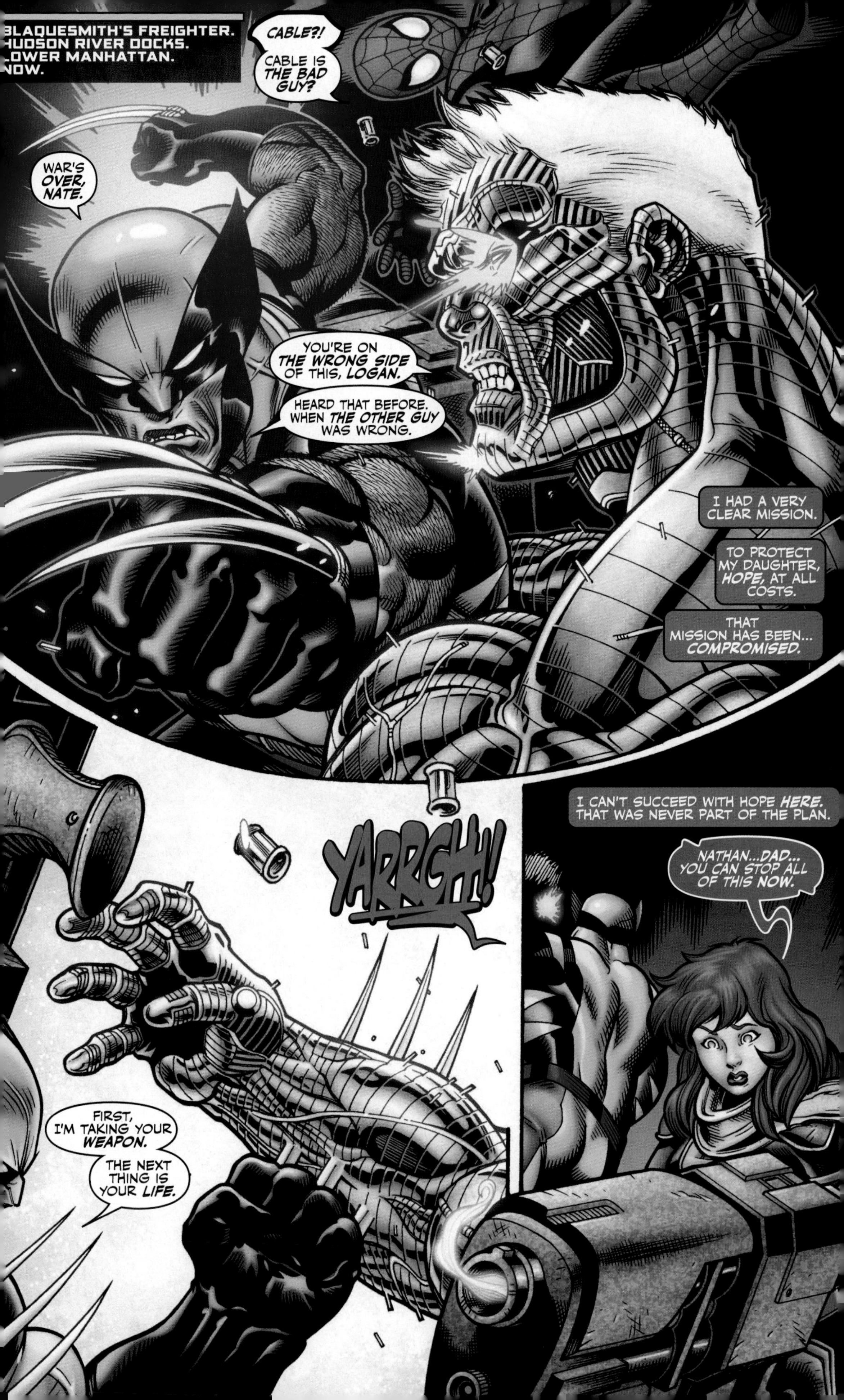

BLAQUESMITH'S FREIGHTER. HUDSON RIVER DOCKS. LOWER MANHATTAN. NOW.
CABLE?!
CABLE IS THE BAD GUY?
WAR'S OVER, NATE.
YOU'RE ON THE WRONG SIDE OF THIS, LOGAN.
HEARD THAT BEFORE. WHEN THE OTHER GUY WAS WRONG.
I HAD A VERY CLEAR MISSION.
TO PROTECT MY DAUGHTER, HOPE, AT ALL COSTS.
THAT MISSION HAS BEEN... COMPROMISED.
YARRGH!
FIRST, I'M TAKING YOUR WEAPON.
THE NEXT THING IS YOUR LIFE.
I CAN'T SUCCEED WITH HOPE HERE. THAT WAS NEVER PART OF THE PLAN.
NATHAN...DAD... YOU CAN STOP ALL OF THIS NOW.

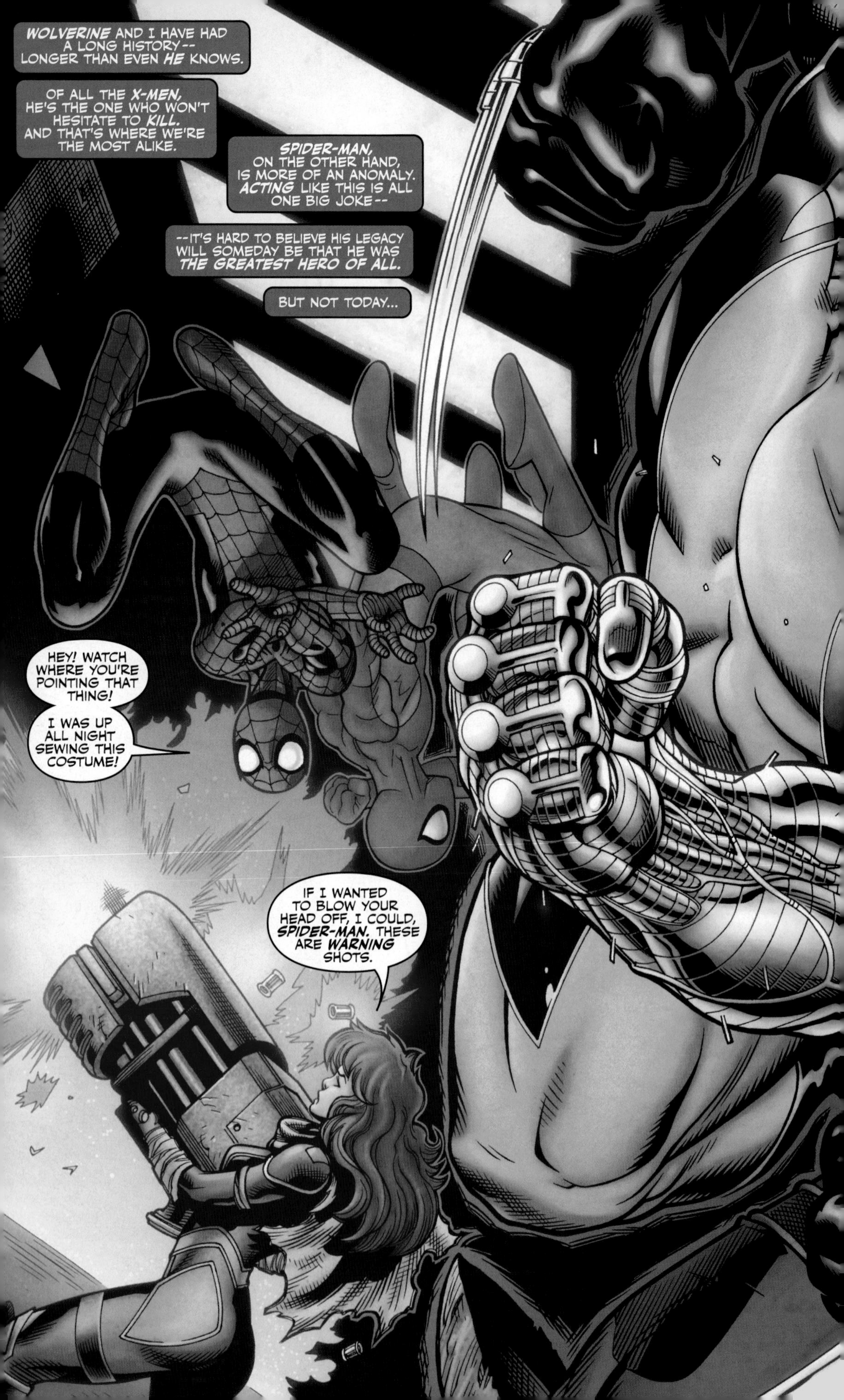

WOLVERINE AND I HAVE HAD A LONG HISTORY-- LONGER THAN EVEN HE KNOWS.
OF ALL THE X-MEN, HE'S THE ONE WHO WON'T HESITATE TO KILL. AND THAT'S WHERE WE'RE THE MOST ALIKE.
SPIDER-MAN, ON THE OTHER HAND, IS MORE OF AN ANOMALY. ACTING LIKE THIS IS ALL ONE BIG JOKE--
--IT'S HARD TO BELIEVE HIS LEGACY WILL SOMEDAY BE THAT HE WAS THE GREATEST HERO OF ALL.
BUT NOT TODAY...
HEY! WATCH WHERE YOU'RE POINTING THAT THING!
I WAS UP ALL NIGHT SEWING THIS COSTUME!
IF I WANTED TO BLOW YOUR HEAD OFF, I COULD, SPIDER-MAN. THESE ARE WARNING SHOTS.

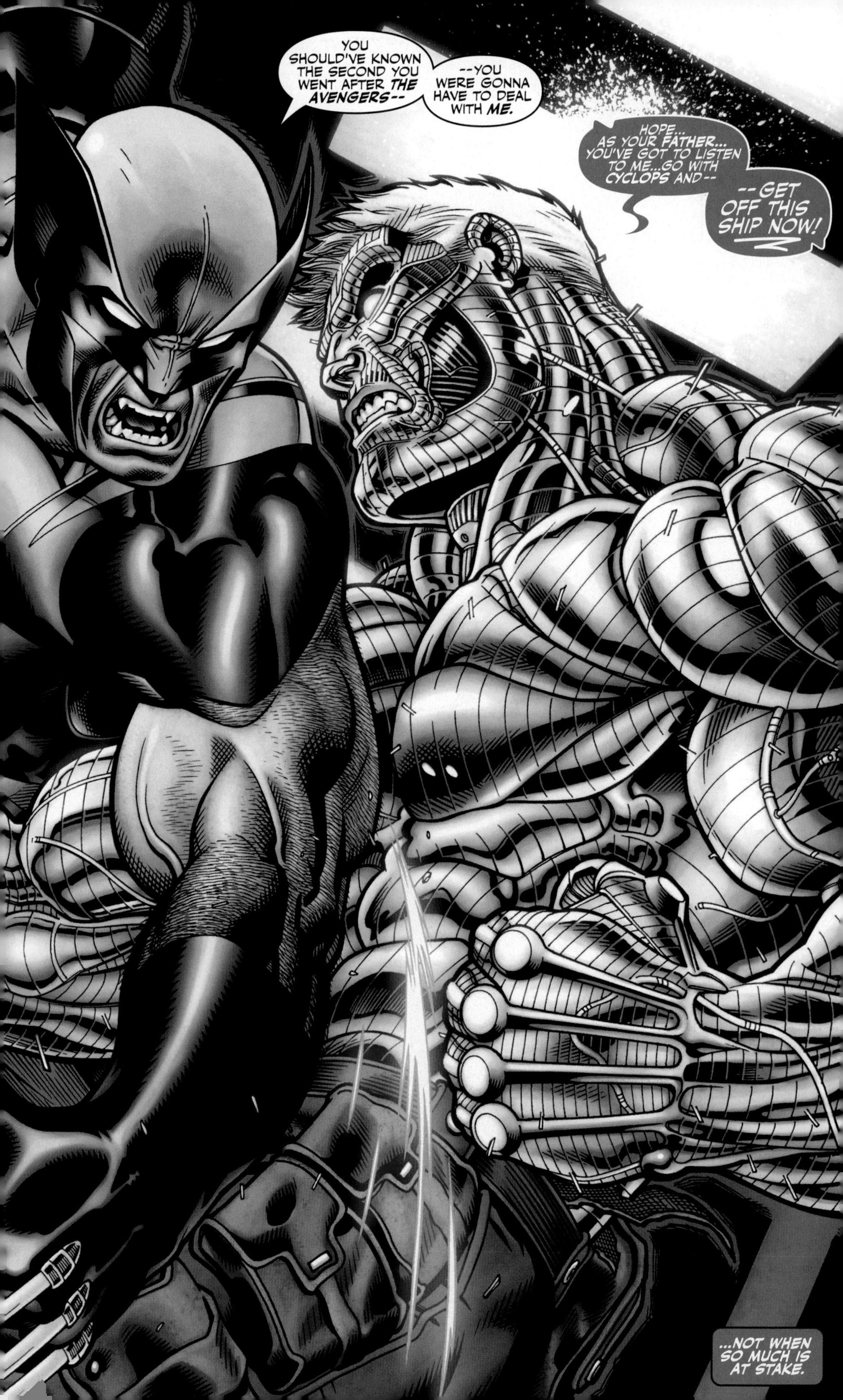
YOU SHOULD'VE KNOWN THE SECOND YOU WENT AFTER THE AVENGERS--
--YOU WERE GONNA HAVE TO DEAL WITH ME.
HOPE... AS YOUR FATHER... YOU'VE GOT TO LISTEN TO ME...GO WITH CYCLOPS AND--
--GET OFF THIS SHIP NOW!
...NOT WHEN SO MUCH IS AT STAKE.

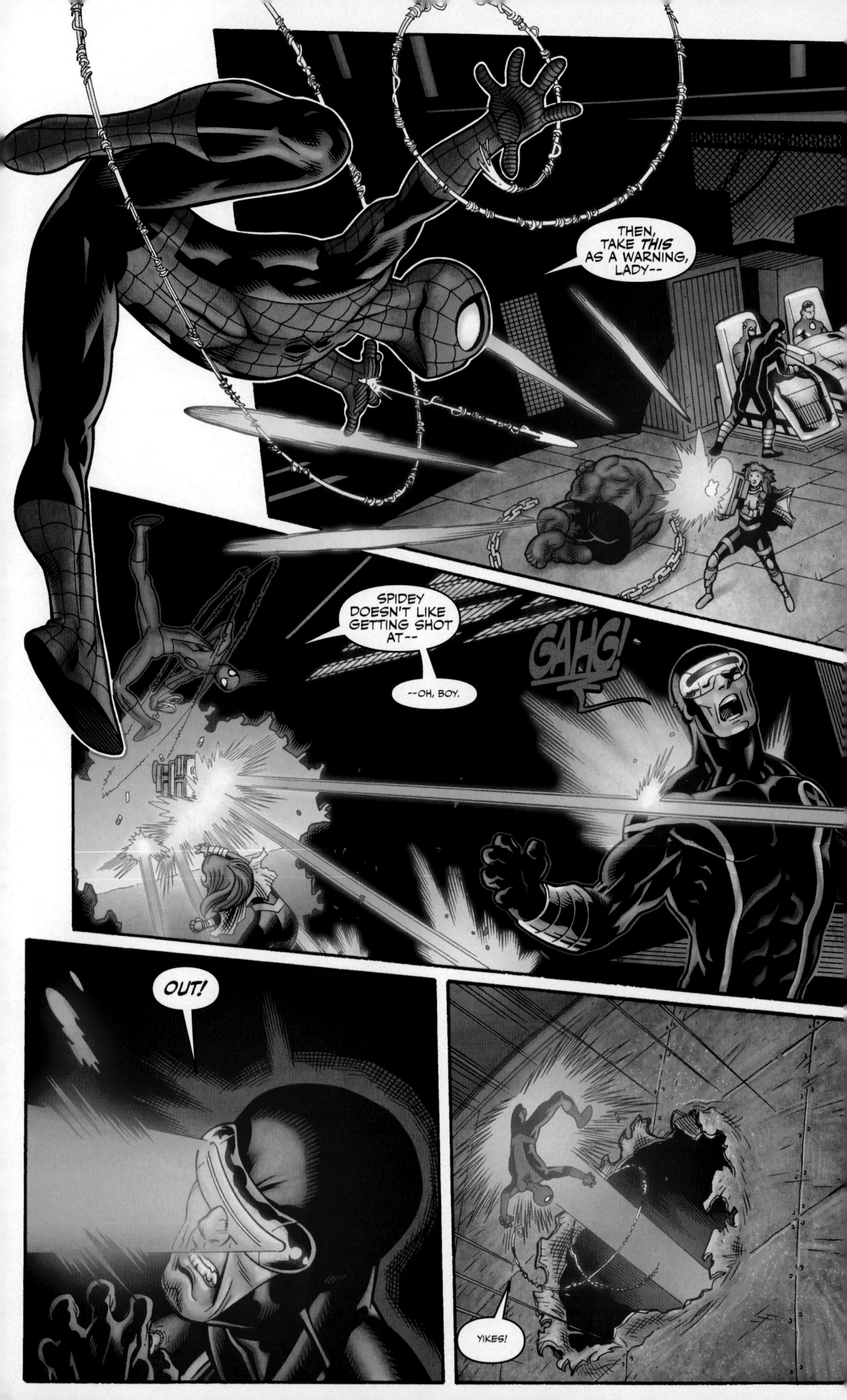
THEN, TAKE THIS AS A WARNING, LADY--
SPIDEY DOESN'T LIKE GETTING SHOT AT--
--OH, BOY.
GAHG!
OUT!
YIKES!

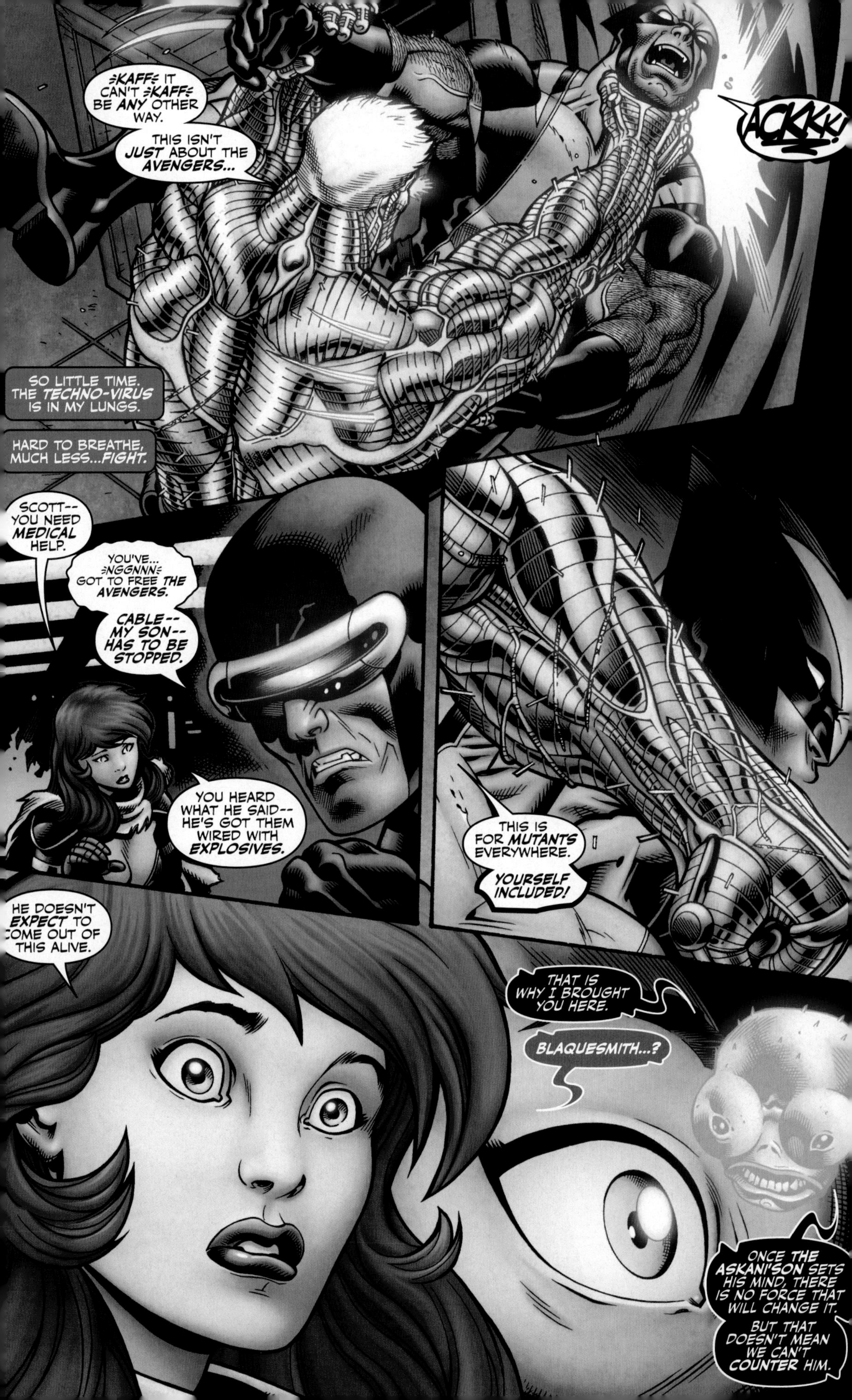

=KAFF= IT CAN'T =KAFF= BE ANY OTHER WAY.
THIS ISN'T JUST ABOUT THE AVENGERS...
ACKKK!
SO LITTLE TIME. THE TECHNO-VIRUS IS IN MY LUNGS.
HARD TO BREATHE, MUCH LESS...FIGHT.
SCOTT-- YOU NEED MEDICAL HELP.
YOU'VE... =NGGNNN= GOT TO FREE THE AVENGERS.
CABLE-- MY SON-- HAS TO BE STOPPED.
YOU HEARD WHAT HE SAID-- HE'S GOT THEM WIRED WITH EXPLOSIVES.
THIS IS FOR MUTANTS EVERYWHERE.
YOURSELF INCLUDED!
HE DOESN'T EXPECT TO COME OUT OF THIS ALIVE.
THAT IS WHY I BROUGHT YOU HERE.
BLAQUESMITH...?
ONCE THE ASKANI'SON SETS HIS MIND, THERE IS NO FORCE THAT WILL CHANGE IT.
BUT THAT DOESN'T MEAN WE CAN'T COUNTER HIM.

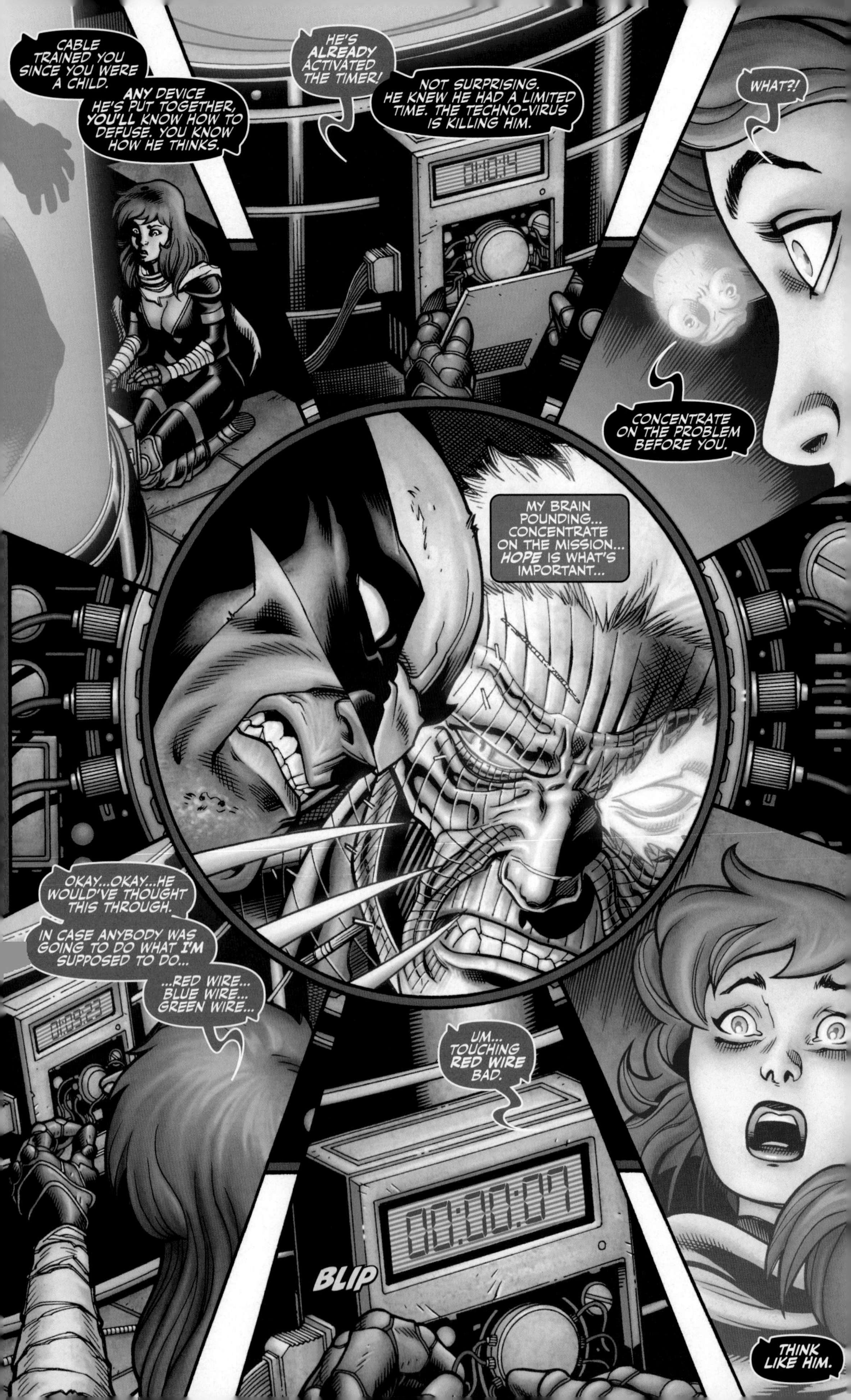

CABLE TRAINED YOU SINCE YOU WERE A CHILD.
ANY DEVICE HE'S PUT TOGETHER, YOU'LL KNOW HOW TO DEFUSE. YOU KNOW HOW HE THINKS.
HE'S ALREADY ACTIVATED THE TIMER!
NOT SURPRISING. HE KNEW HE HAD A LIMITED TIME. THE TECHNO-VIRUS IS KILLING HIM.
WHAT?!
CONCENTRATE ON THE PROBLEM BEFORE YOU.
MY BRAIN POUNDING... CONCENTRATE ON THE MISSION... HOPE IS WHAT'S IMPORTANT...
OKAY...OKAY...HE WOULD'VE THOUGHT THIS THROUGH.
IN CASE ANYBODY WAS GOING TO DO WHAT I'M SUPPOSED TO DO...
...RED WIRE... BLUE WIRE... GREEN WIRE...
UM... TOUCHING RED WIRE BAD.
BLIP
THINK LIKE HIM.

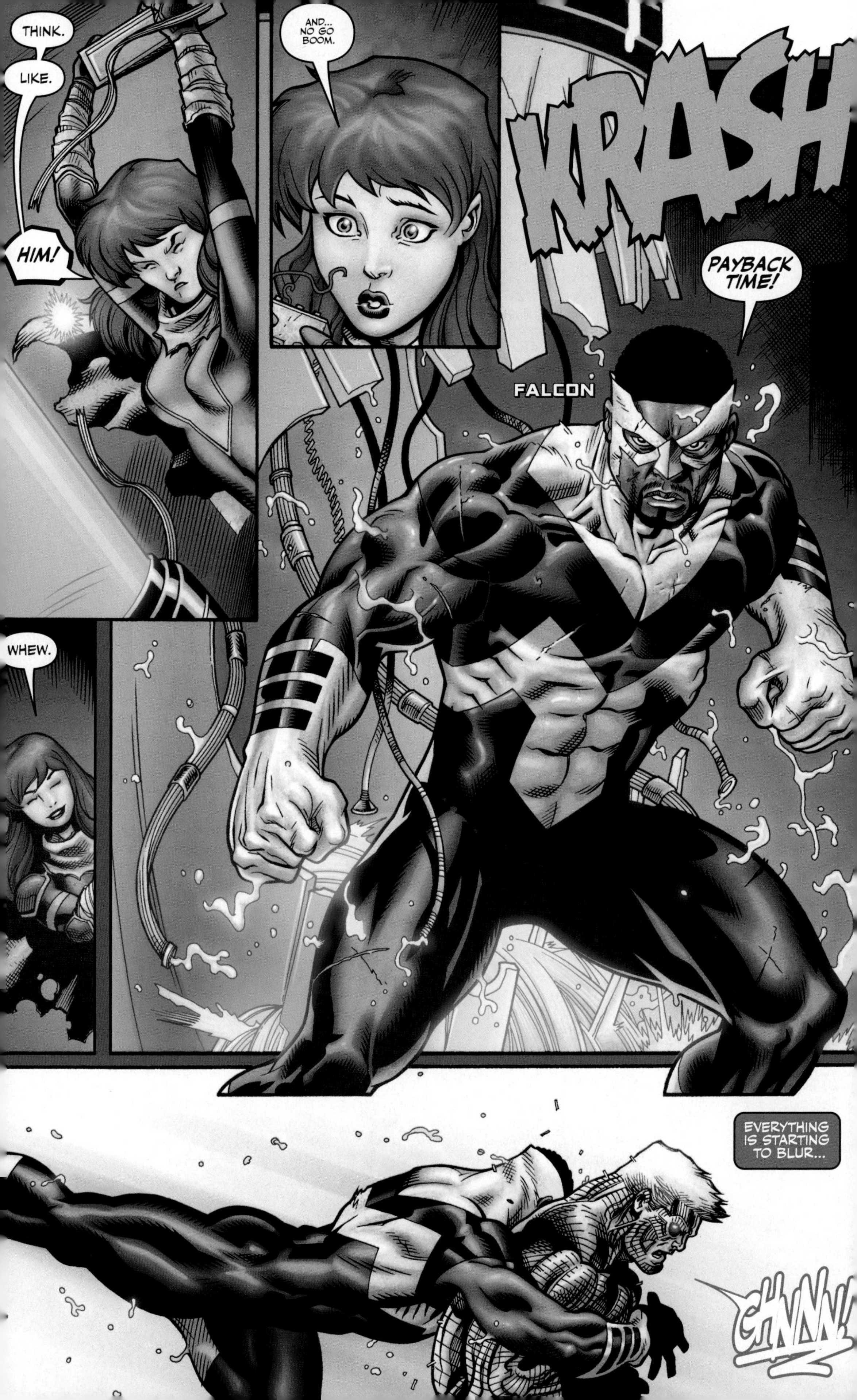
THINK.
LIKE.
HIM!
AND... NO GO BOOM.
KRASH
PAYBACK TIME!
FALCON
WHEW.
EVERYTHING IS STARTING TO BLUR...
GHNN!

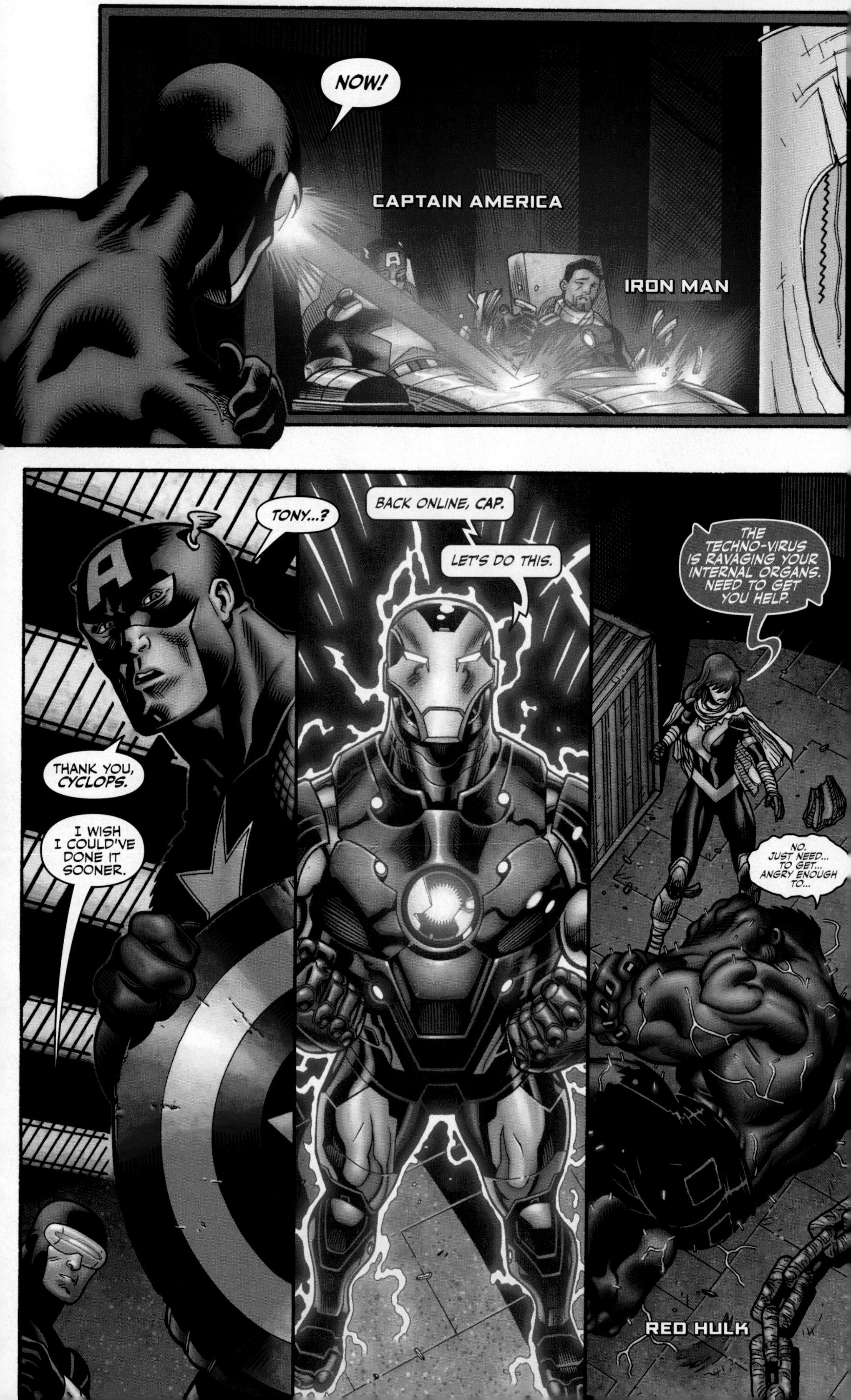
NOW!
CAPTAIN AMERICA
IRON MAN
TONY...?
BACK ONLINE, CAP.
LET'S DO THIS.
THE TECHNO-VIRUS IS RAVAGING YOUR INTERNAL ORGANS. NEED TO GET YOU HELP.
THANK YOU, CYCLOPS.
I WISH I COULD'VE DONE IT SOONER.
NO. JUST NEED... TO GET... ANGRY ENOUGH TO...
RED HULK

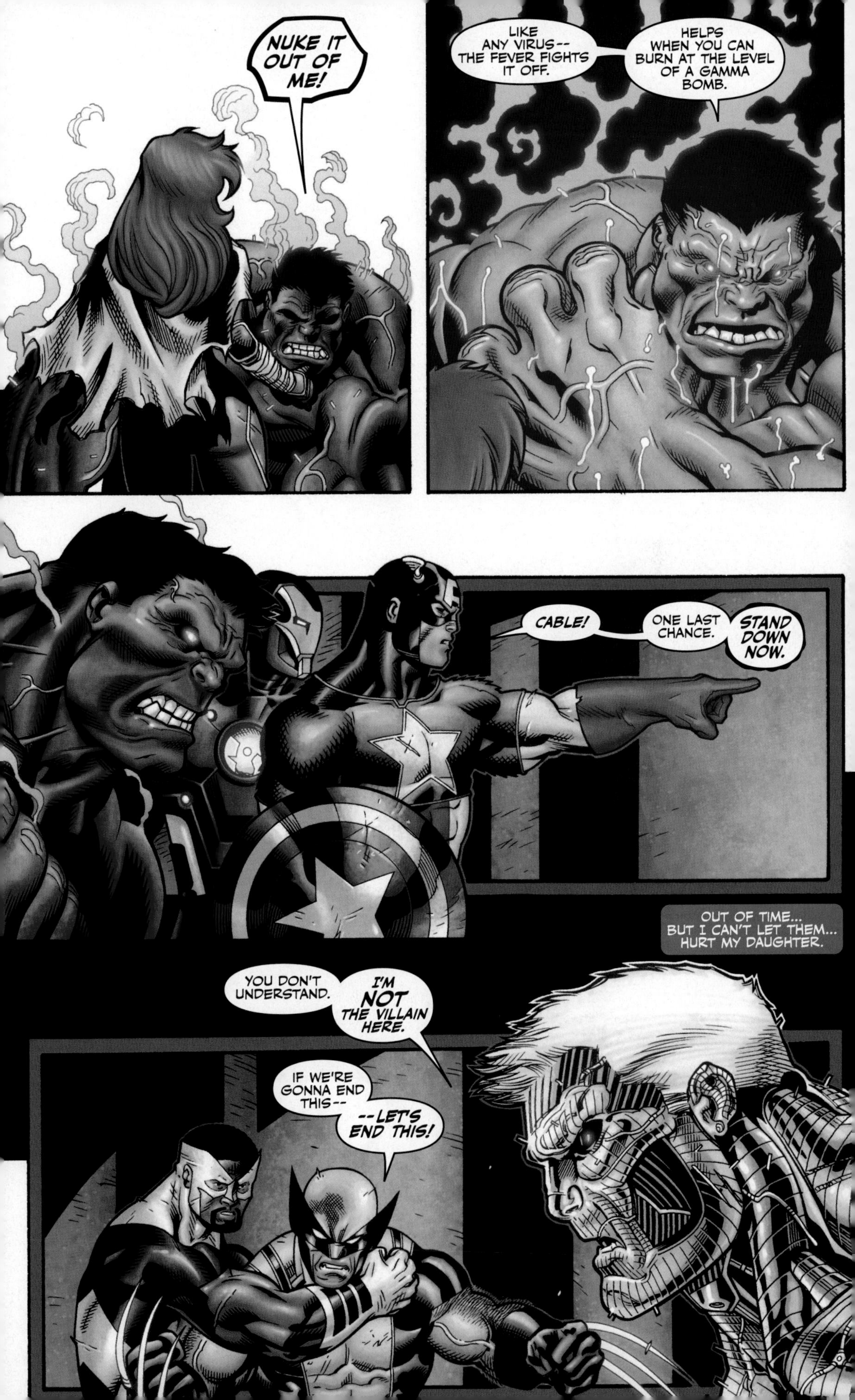

NUKE IT OUT OF ME!
LIKE ANY VIRUS-- THE FEVER FIGHTS IT OFF.
HELPS WHEN YOU CAN BURN AT THE LEVEL OF A GAMMA BOMB.
CABLE!
ONE LAST CHANCE.
STAND DOWN NOW.
OUT OF TIME... BUT I CAN'T LET THEM... HURT MY DAUGHTER.
YOU DON'T UNDERSTAND.
I'M NOT THE VILLAIN HERE.
IF WE'RE GONNA END THIS--
--LET'S END THIS!

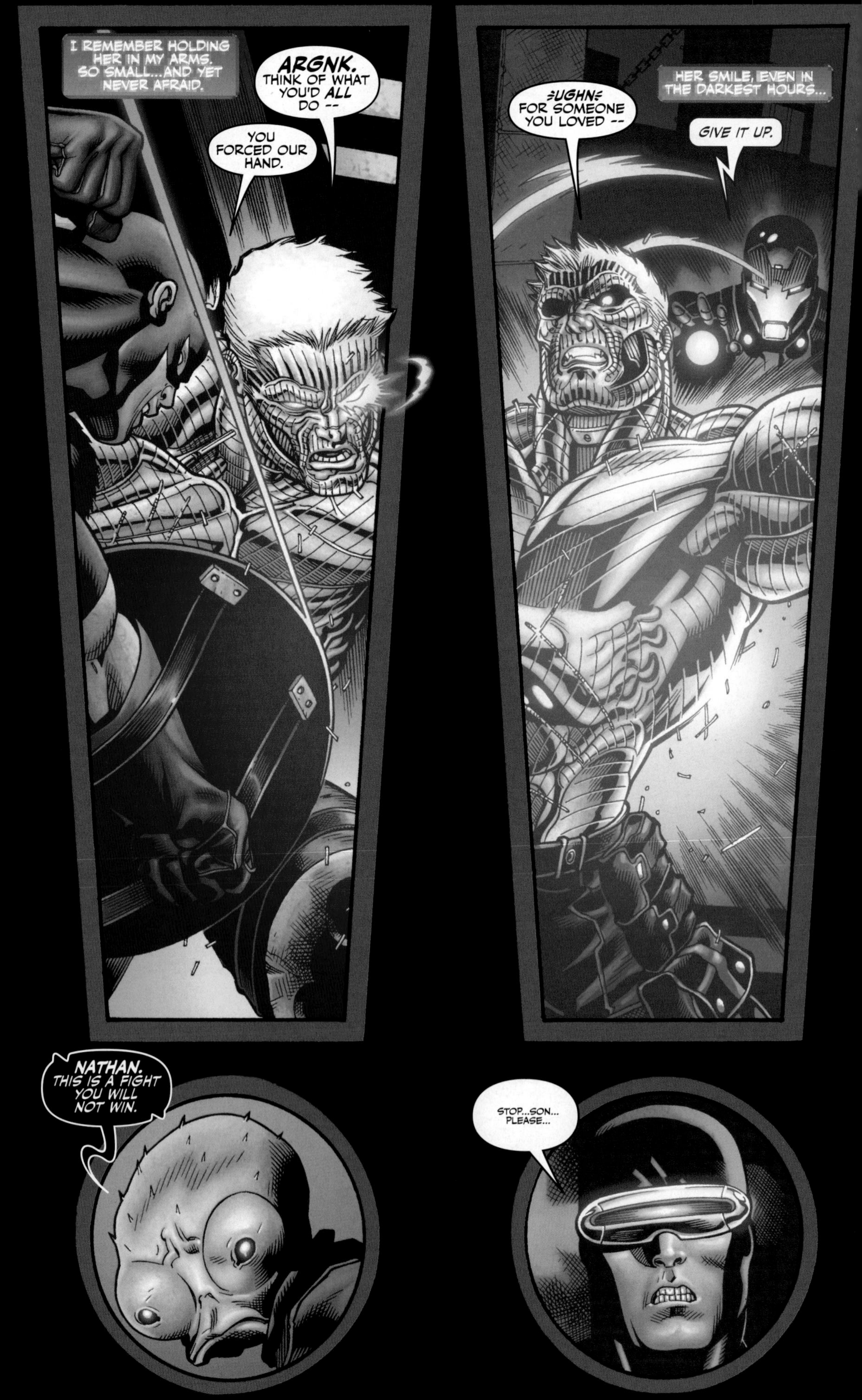
I REMEMBER HOLDING HER IN MY ARMS. SO SMALL...AND YET NEVER AFRAID.
ARGNK. THINK OF WHAT YOU'D ALL DO --
YOU FORCED OUR HAND.
HER SMILE, EVEN IN THE DARKEST HOURS...
UGHN FOR SOMEONE YOU LOVED --
GIVE IT UP.
NATHAN. THIS IS A FIGHT YOU WILL NOT WIN.
STOP...SON... PLEASE...

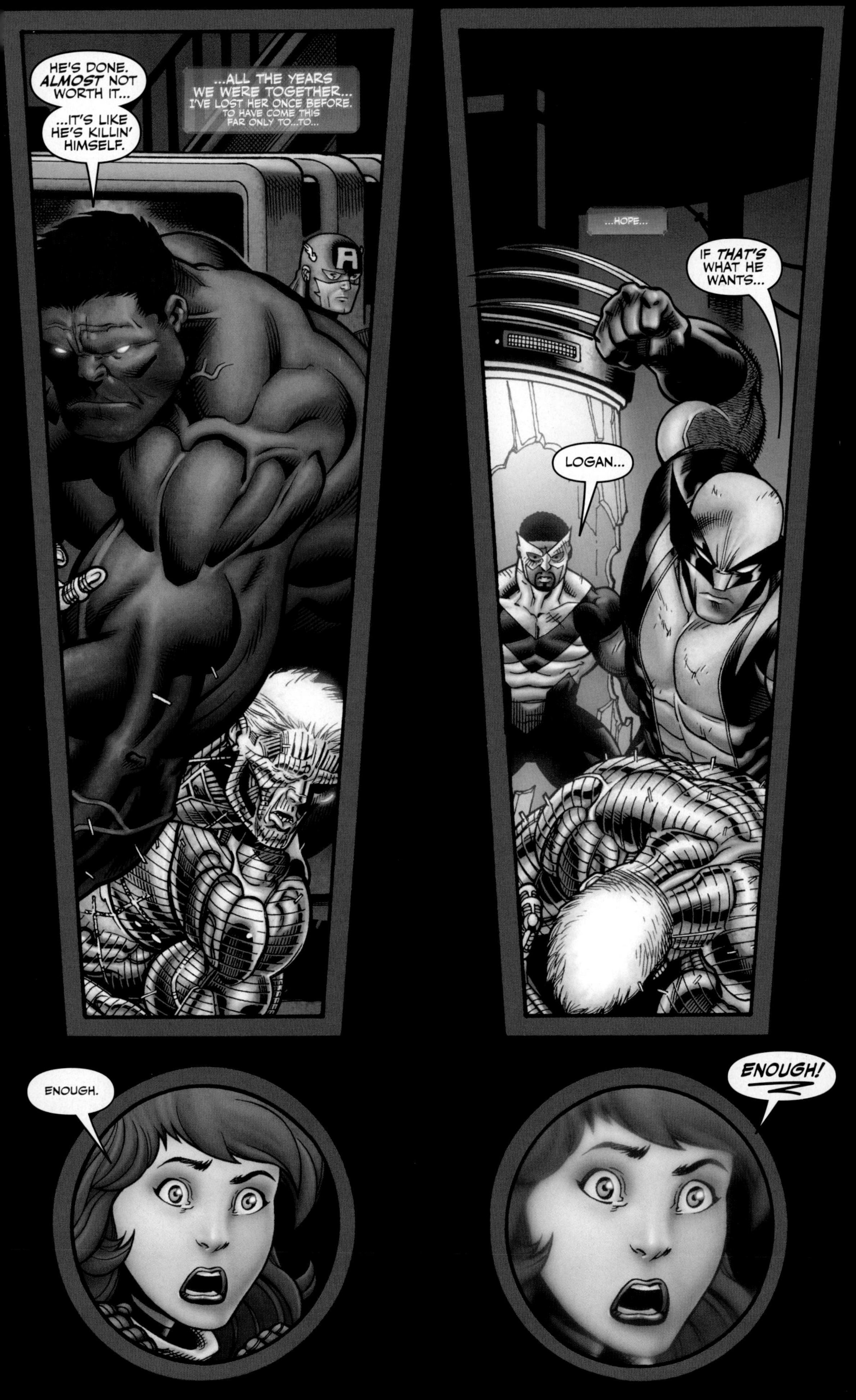
HE'S DONE. ALMOST NOT WORTH IT...
...IT'S LIKE HE'S KILLIN' HIMSELF.
...ALL THE YEARS WE WERE TOGETHER... I'VE LOST HER ONCE BEFORE. TO HAVE COME THIS FAR ONLY TO...TO...
...HOPE...
IF THAT'S WHAT HE WANTS...
LOGAN...
ENOUGH.
ENOUGH!

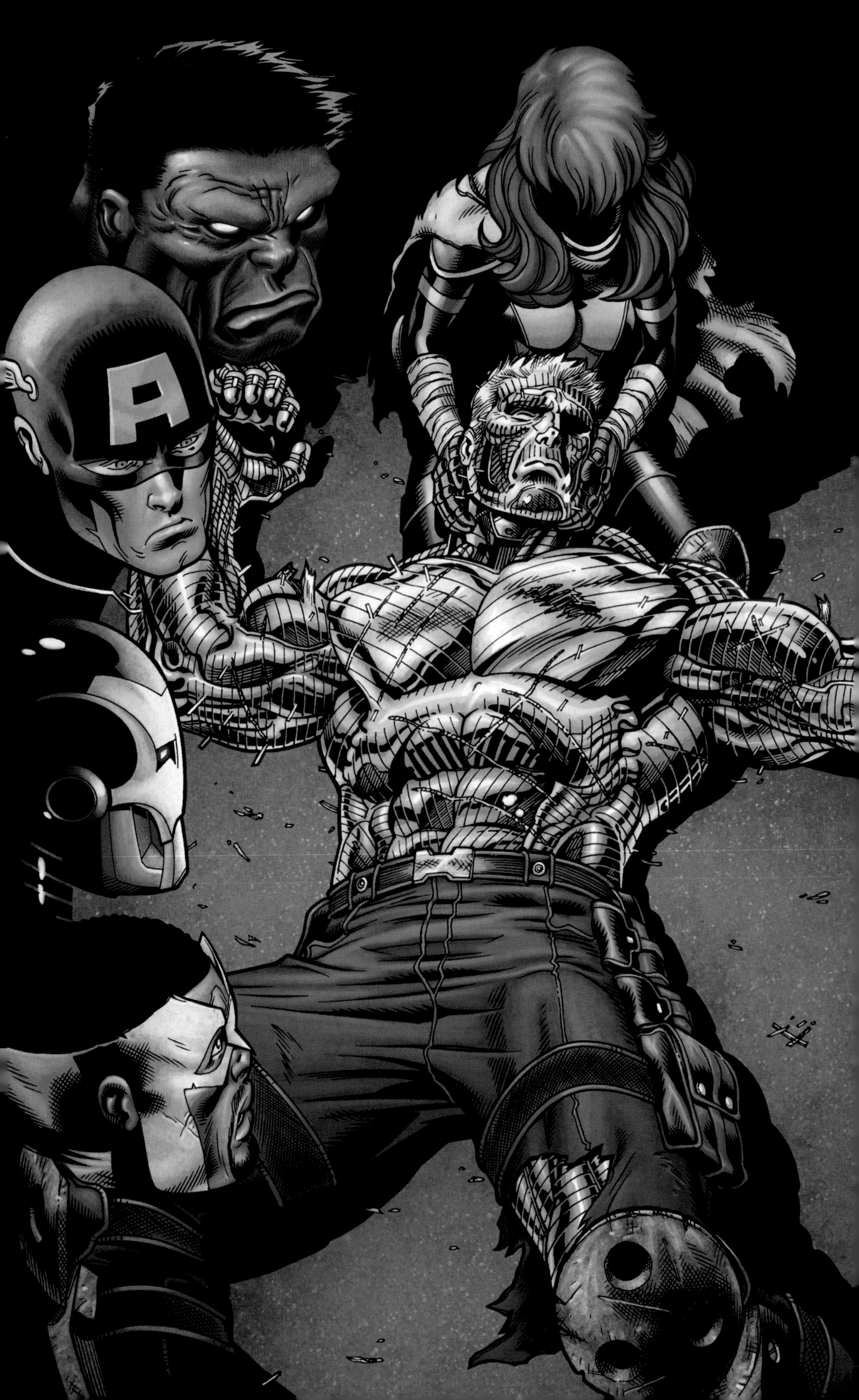

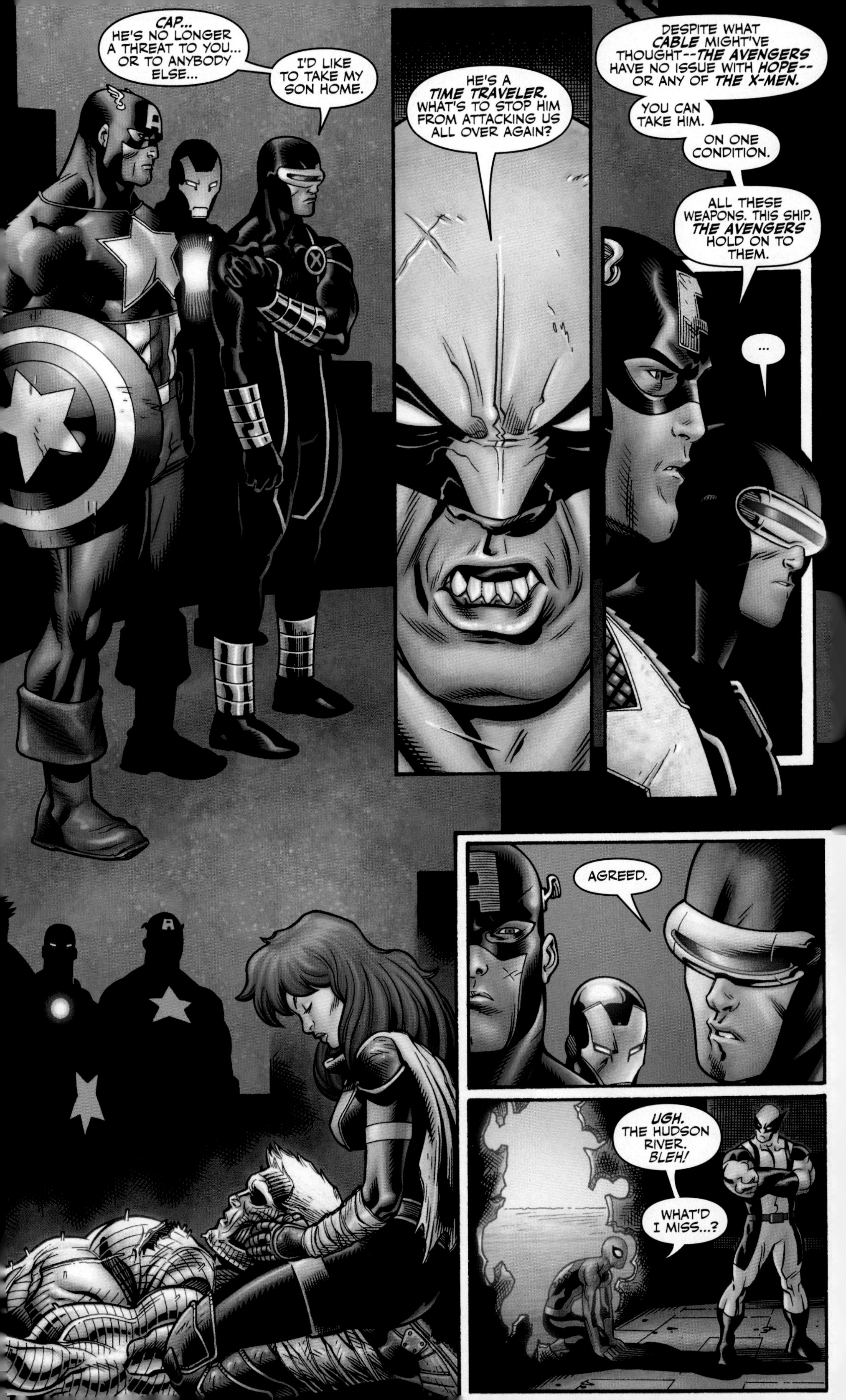
CAP... HE'S NO LONGER A THREAT TO YOU... OR TO ANYBODY ELSE...
I'D LIKE TO TAKE MY SON HOME.
HE'S A TIME TRAVELER. WHAT'S TO STOP HIM FROM ATTACKING US ALL OVER AGAIN?
DESPITE WHAT CABLE MIGHT'VE THOUGHT--THE AVENGERS HAVE NO ISSUE WITH HOPE--OR ANY OF THE X-MEN.
YOU CAN TAKE HIM.
ON ONE CONDITION.
ALL THESE WEAPONS. THIS SHIP. THE AVENGERS HOLD ON TO THEM.
...
AGREED.
UGH. THE HUDSON RIVER. BLEH!
WHAT'D I MISS...?

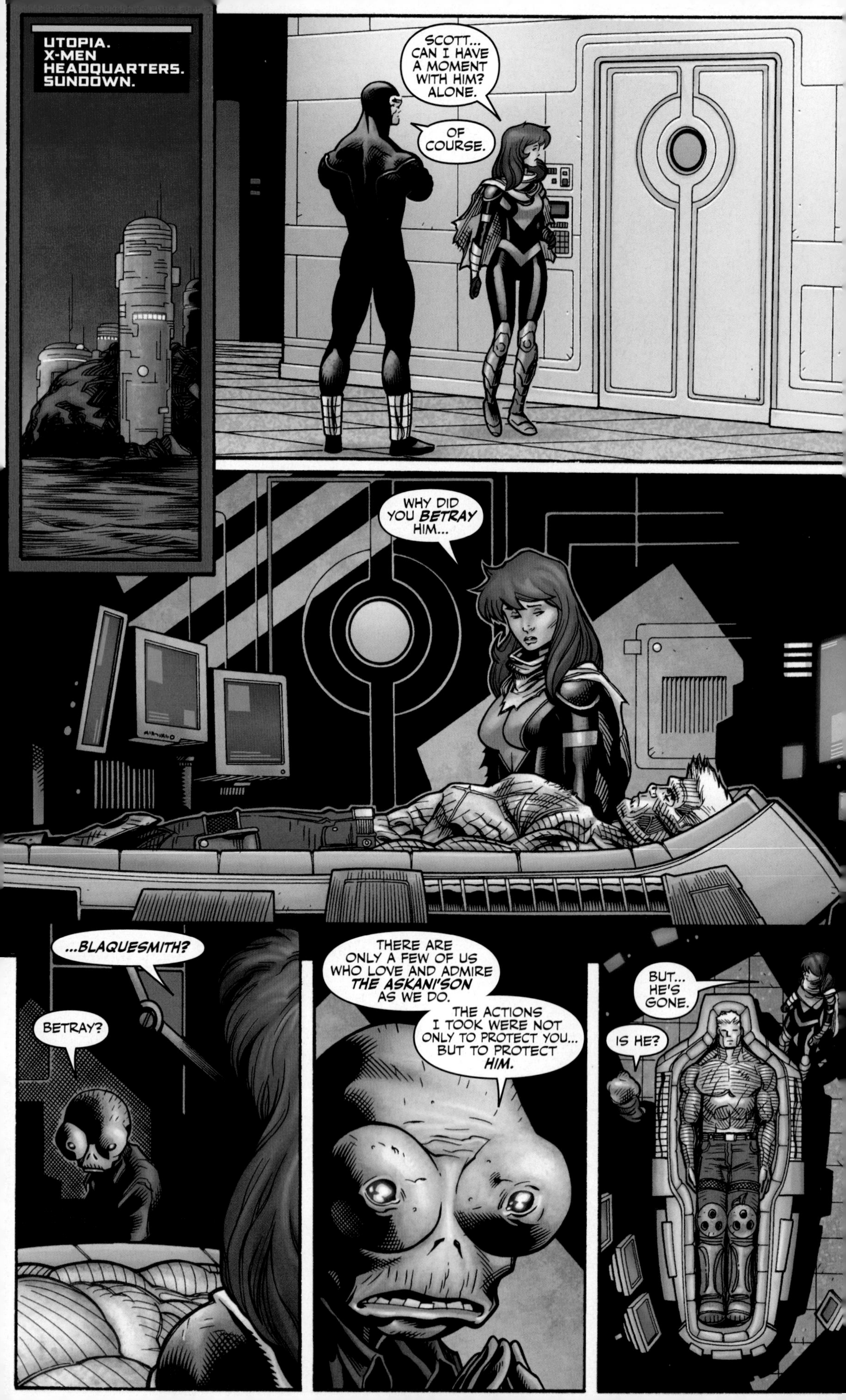
UTOPIA. X-MEN HEADQUARTERS. SUNDOWN.
SCOTT... CAN I HAVE A MOMENT WITH HIM? ALONE.
OF COURSE.
WHY DID YOU BETRAY HIM...
...BLAQUESMITH?
BETRAY?
THERE ARE ONLY A FEW OF US WHO LOVE AND ADMIRE THE ASKANI'SON AS WE DO.
THE ACTIONS I TOOK WERE NOT ONLY TO PROTECT YOU... BUT TO PROTECT HIM.
BUT... HE'S GONE.
IS HE?

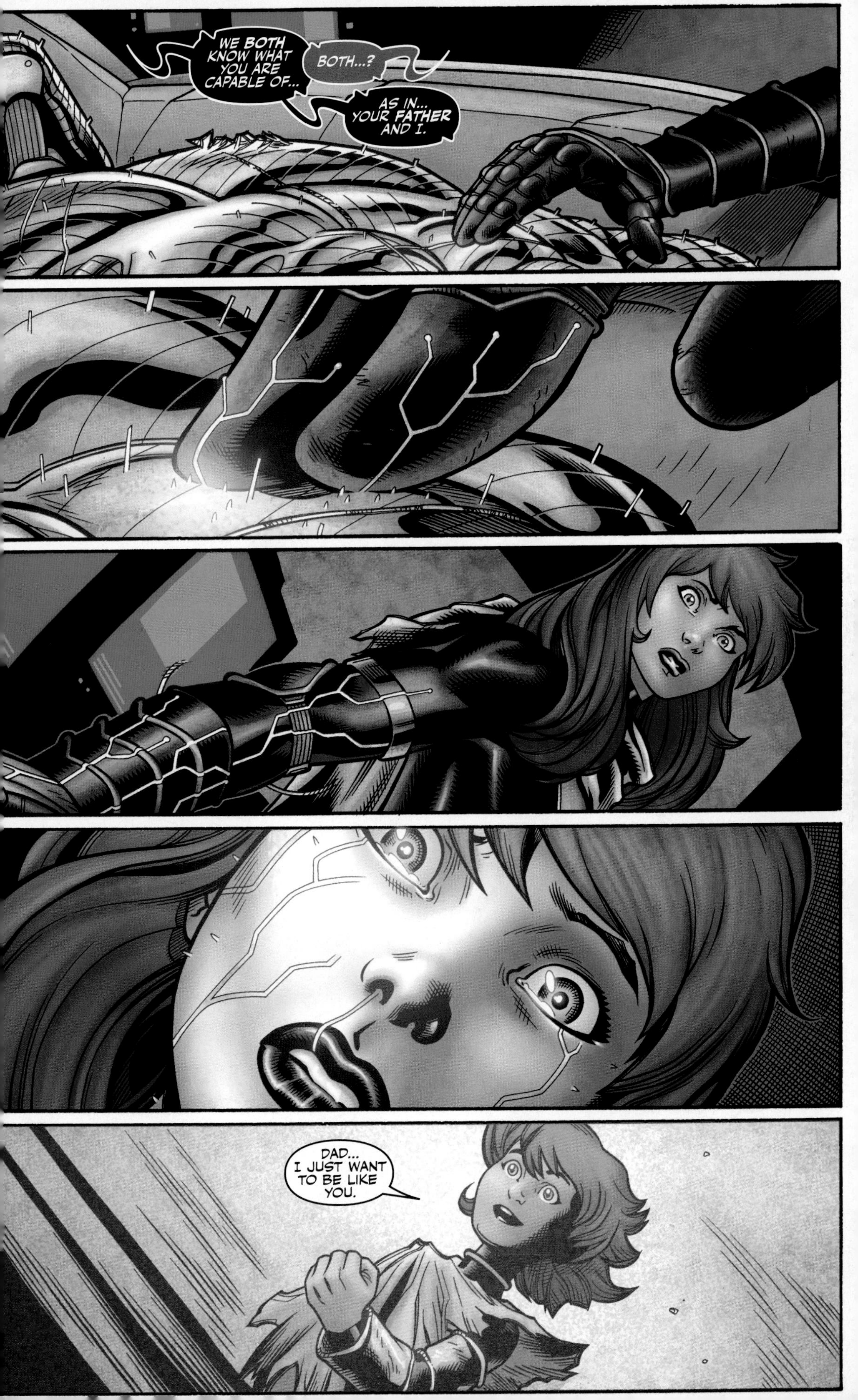
WE BOTH KNOW WHAT YOU ARE CAPABLE OF...
BOTH...?
AS IN... YOUR FATHER AND I.
DAD... I JUST WANT TO BE LIKE YOU.

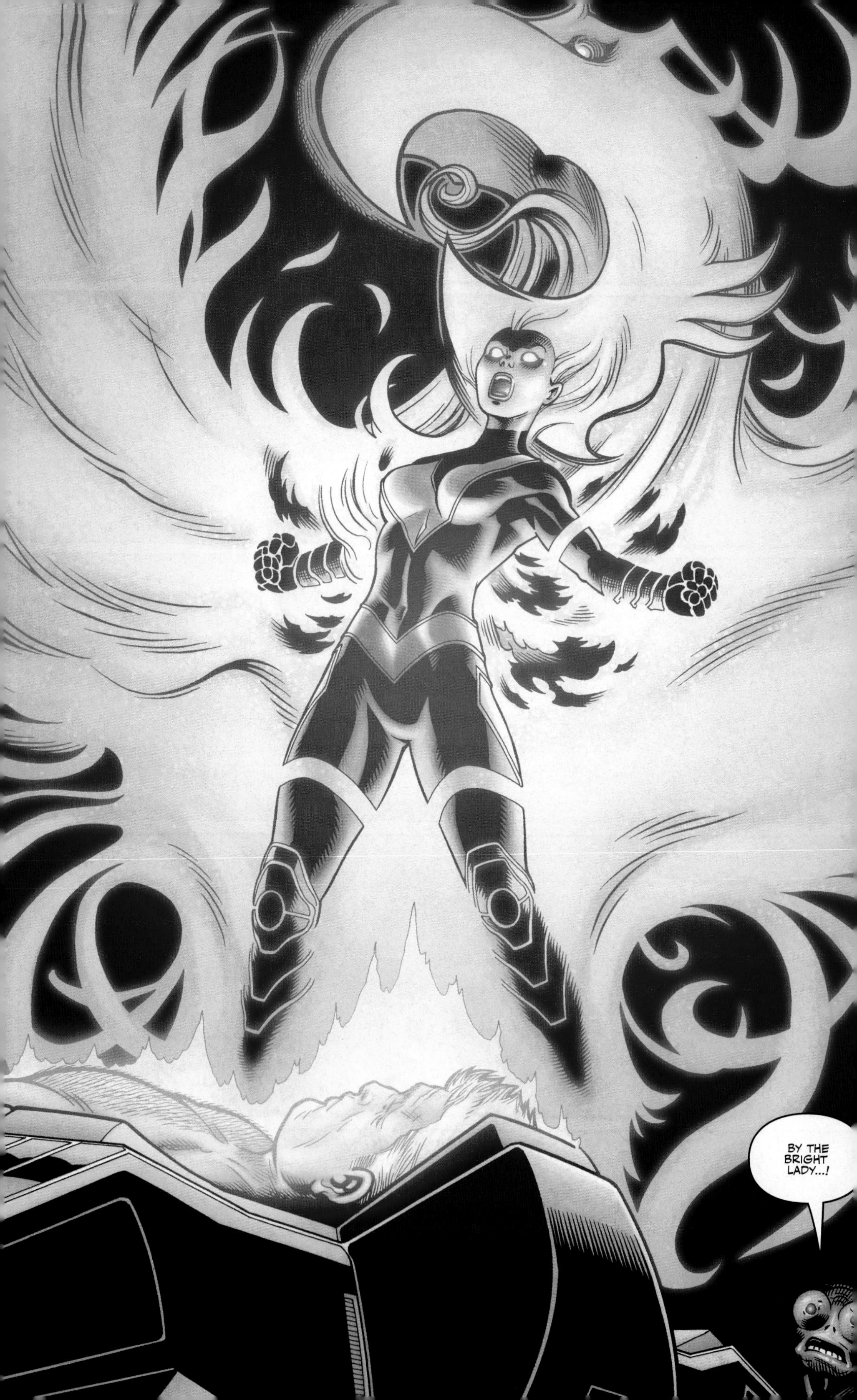
BY THE BRIGHT LADY...!

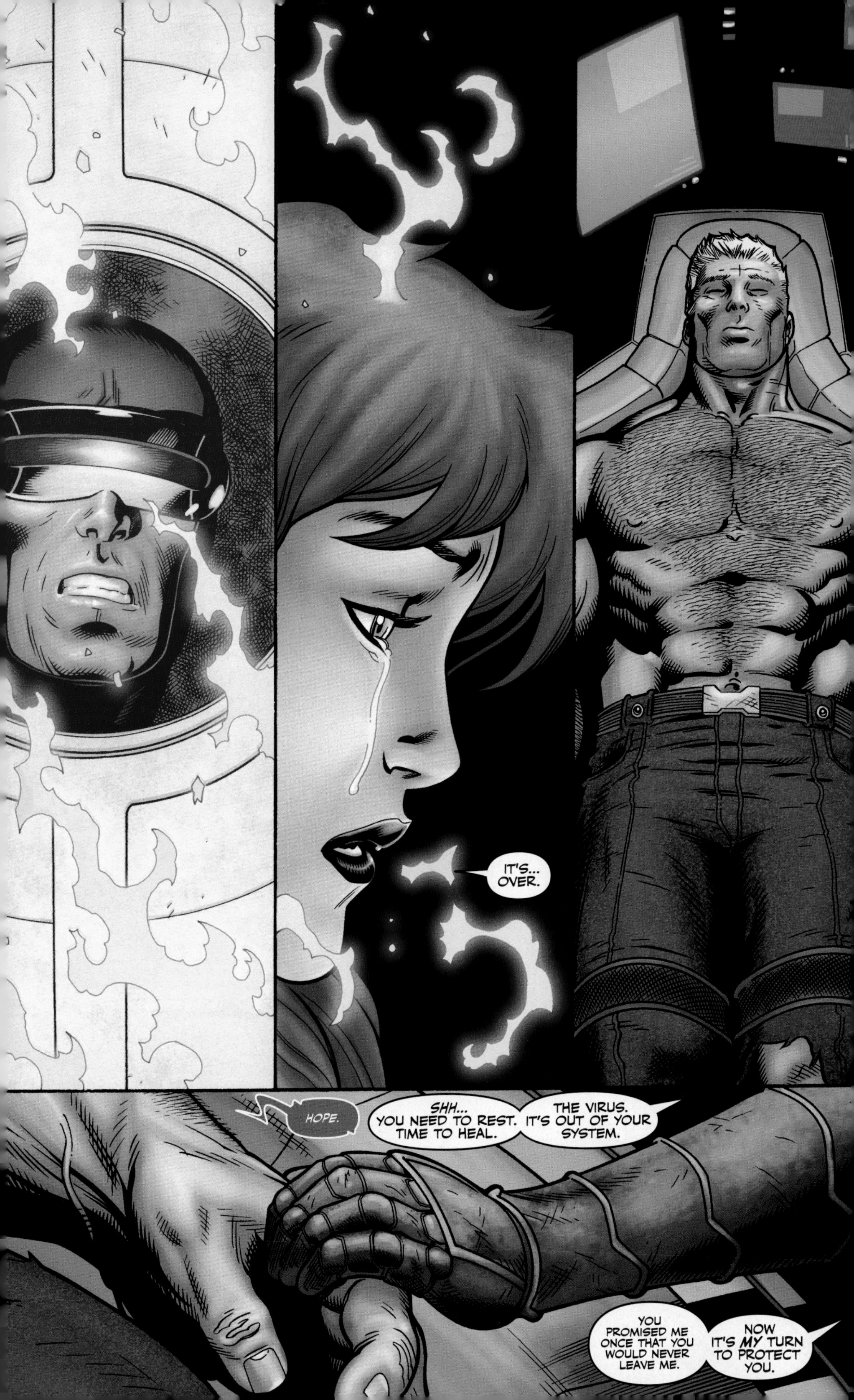
IT'S... OVER.
HOPE.
SHH... YOU NEED TO REST. TIME TO HEAL.
THE VIRUS. IT'S OUT OF YOUR SYSTEM.
YOU PROMISED ME ONCE THAT YOU WOULD NEVER LEAVE ME.
NOW IT'S MY TURN TO PROTECT YOU.

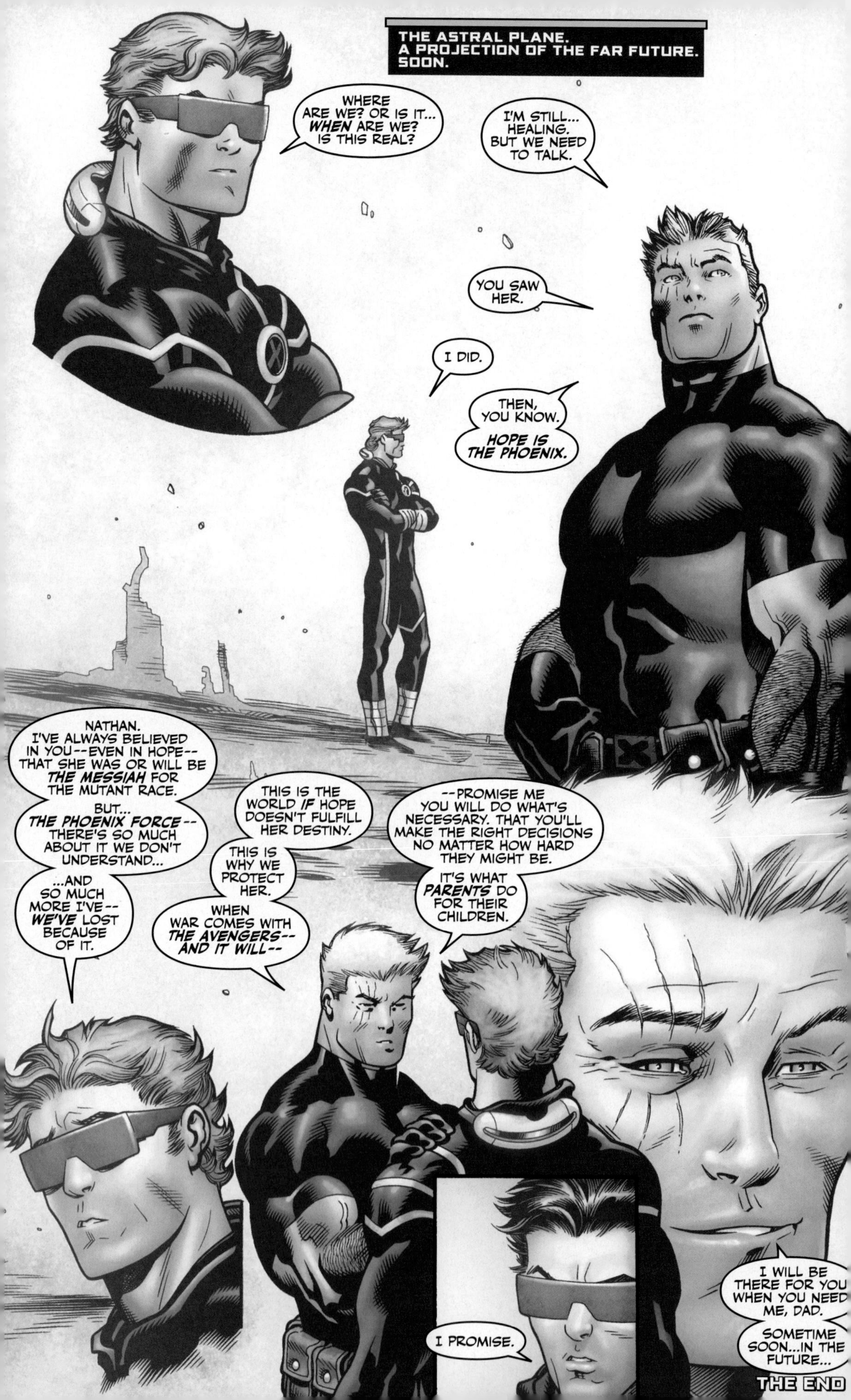
THE ASTRAL PLANE. A PROJECTION OF THE FAR FUTURE. SOON.
WHERE ARE WE? OR IS IT... WHEN ARE WE? IS THIS REAL?
I'M STILL... HEALING. BUT WE NEED TO TALK.
YOU SAW HER.
I DID.
THEN, YOU KNOW.
HOPE IS THE PHOENIX.
NATHAN. I'VE ALWAYS BELIEVED IN YOU--EVEN IN HOPE--THAT SHE WAS OR WILL BE THE MESSIAH FOR THE MUTANT RACE.
BUT... THE PHOENIX FORCE--THERE'S SO MUCH ABOUT IT WE DON'T UNDERSTAND...
...AND SO MUCH MORE I'VE--WE'VE LOST BECAUSE OF IT.
THIS IS THE WORLD IF HOPE DOESN'T FULFILL HER DESTINY.
THIS IS WHY WE PROTECT HER.
WHEN WAR COMES WITH THE AVENGERS--AND IT WILL--
--PROMISE ME YOU WILL DO WHAT'S NECESSARY. THAT YOU'LL MAKE THE RIGHT DECISIONS NO MATTER HOW HARD THEY MIGHT BE.
IT'S WHAT PARENTS DO FOR THEIR CHILDREN.
I PROMISE.
I WILL BE THERE FOR YOU WHEN YOU NEED ME, DAD.
SOMETIME SOON...IN THE FUTURE...
THE END

GALLERY

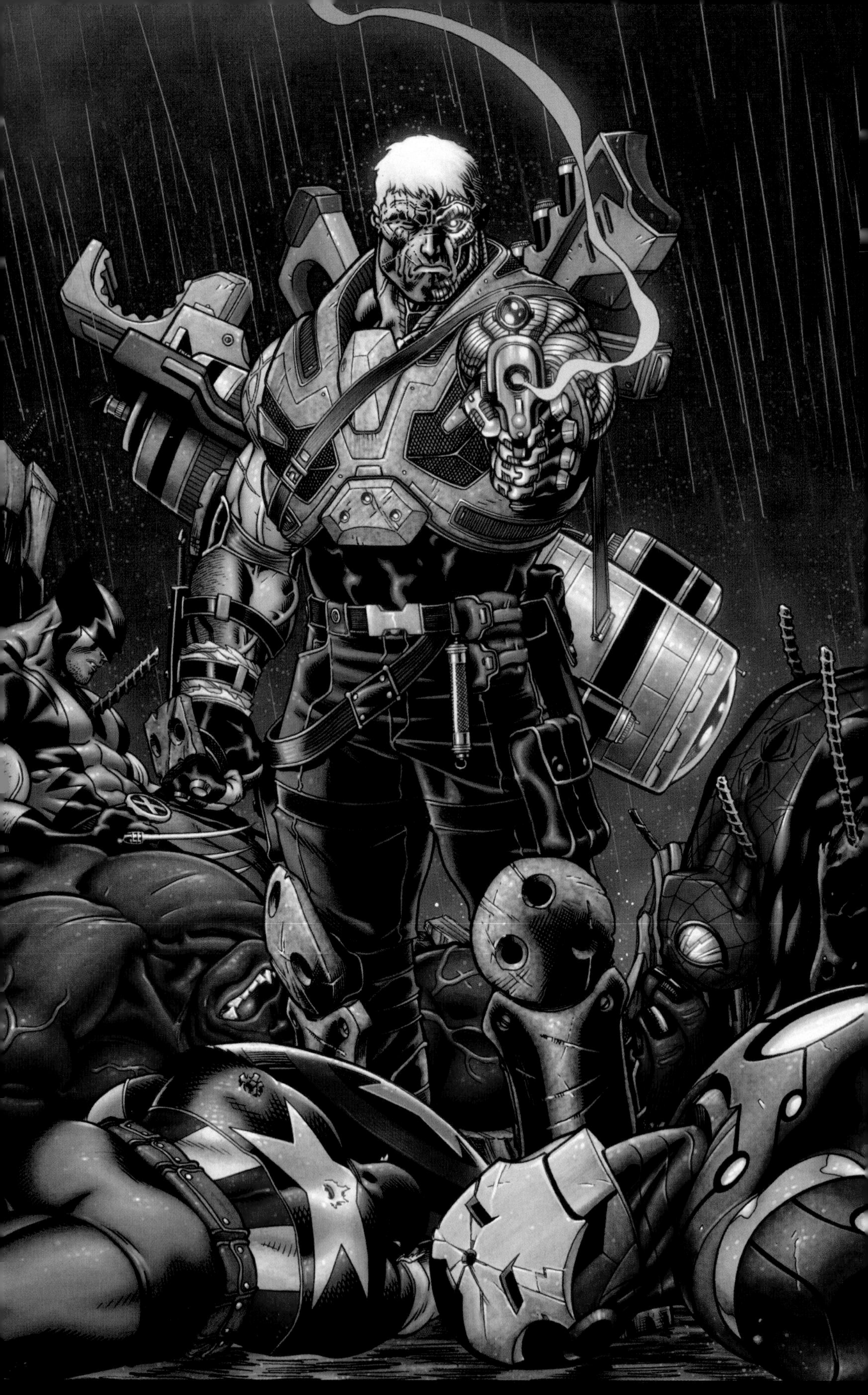

ISSUE 1 VARIANT COVER › McGUINNESS/VINES/HOLLOWELL

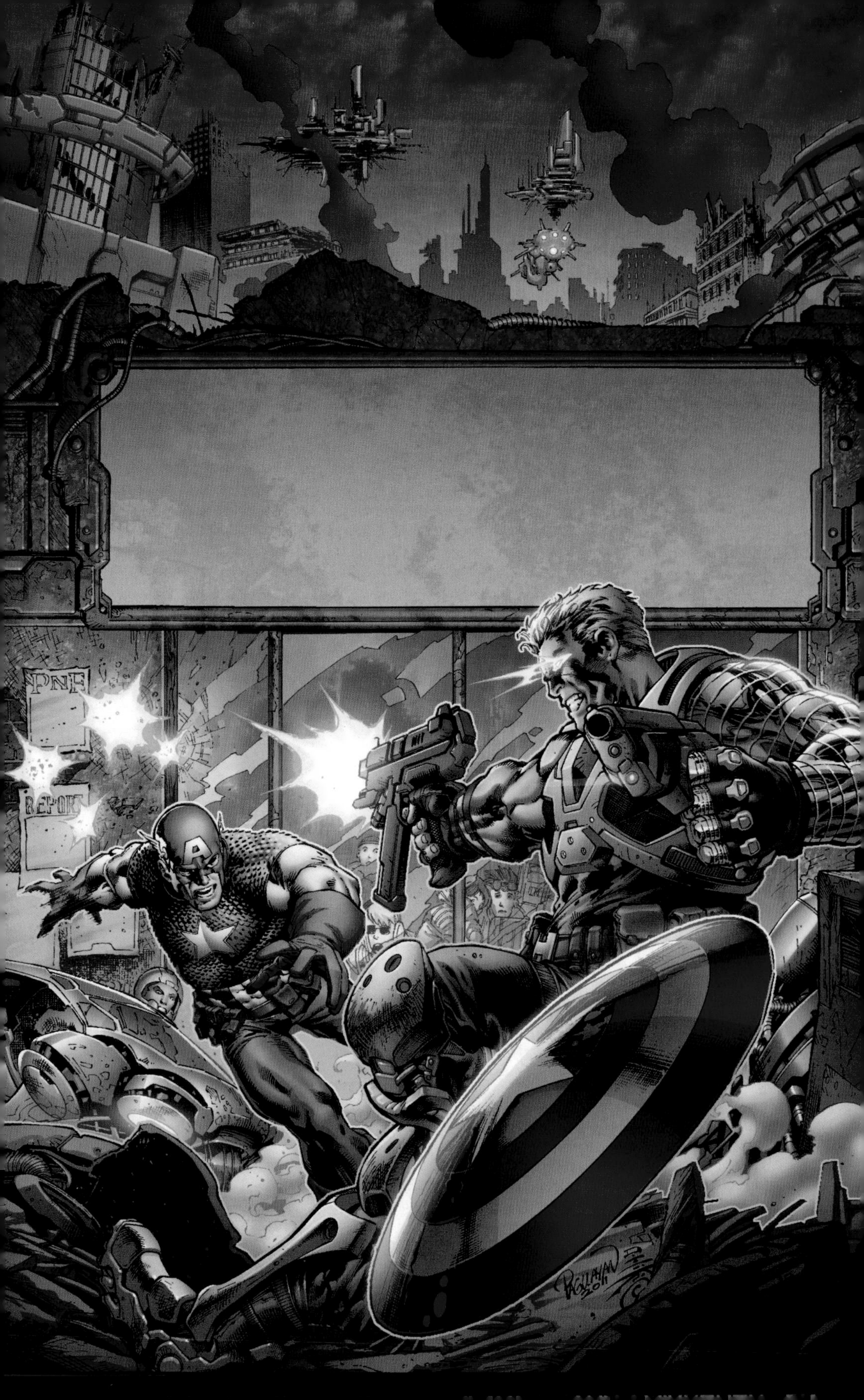
PNF
REPORT

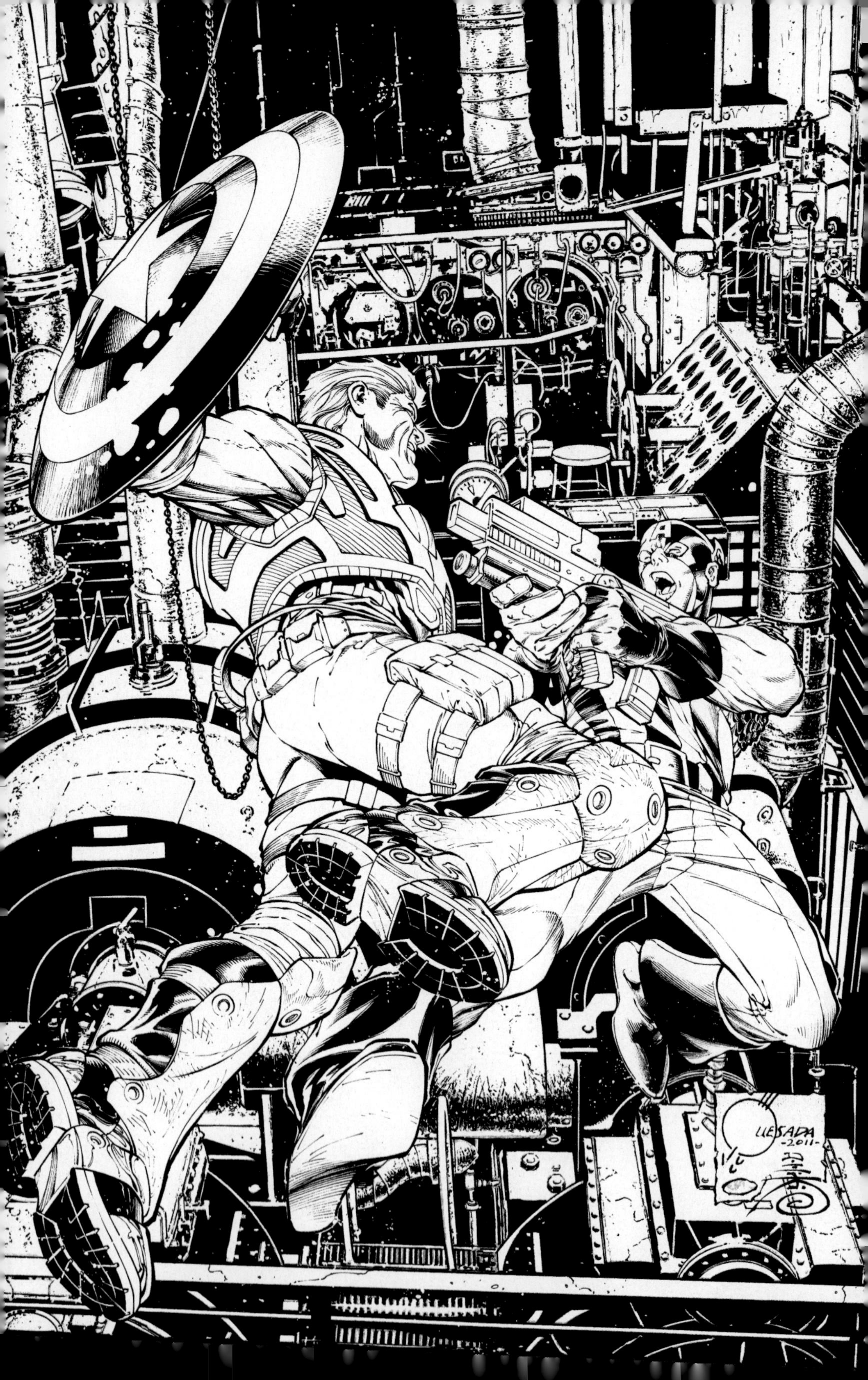
QUESADA
-2011-

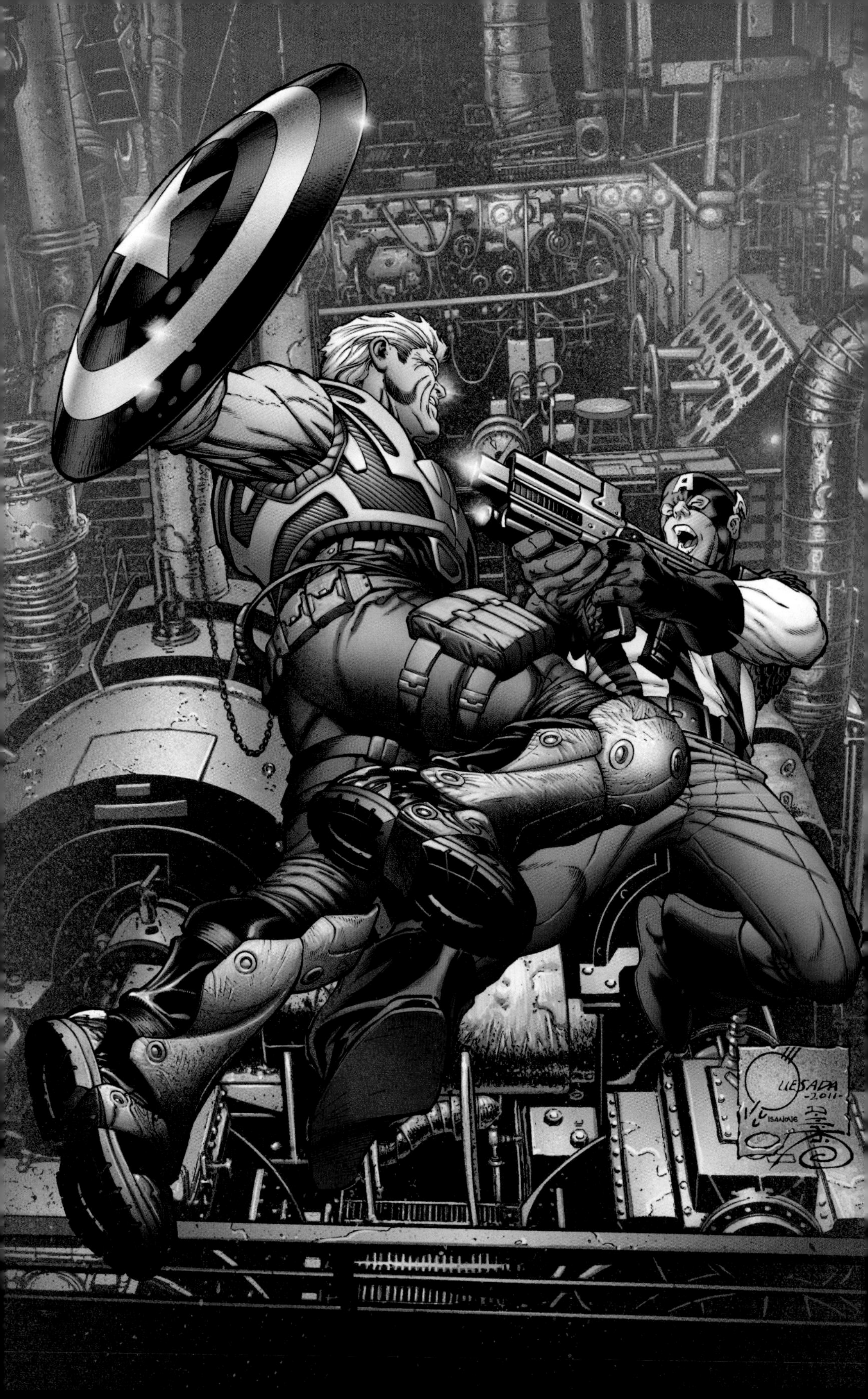
QUESADA
-2011-
ISANOVE

ISSUE 1 VARIANT COVERS > JOE QUESADA/DANNY MIKI/RICHARD ISANOVE

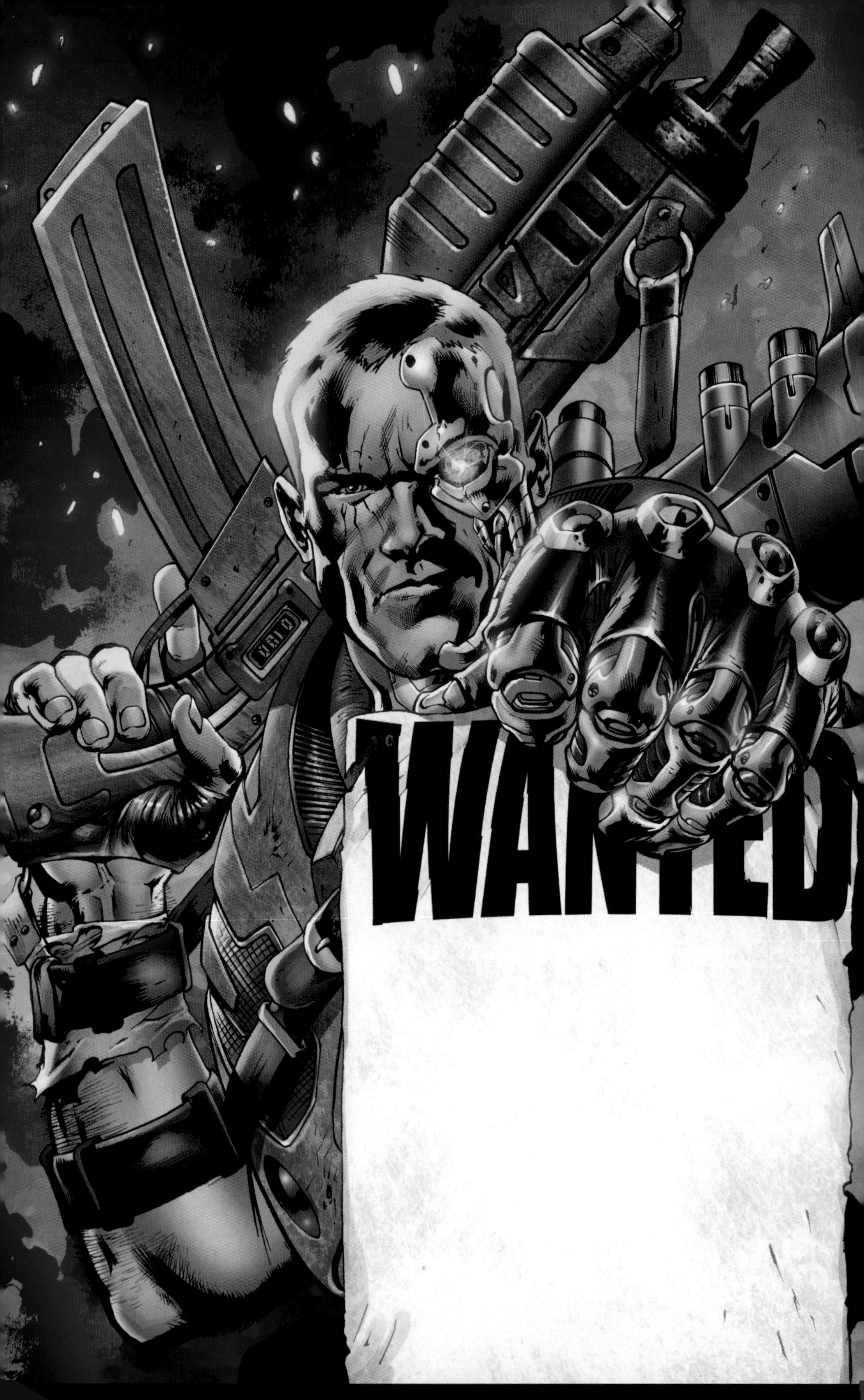
WANTED

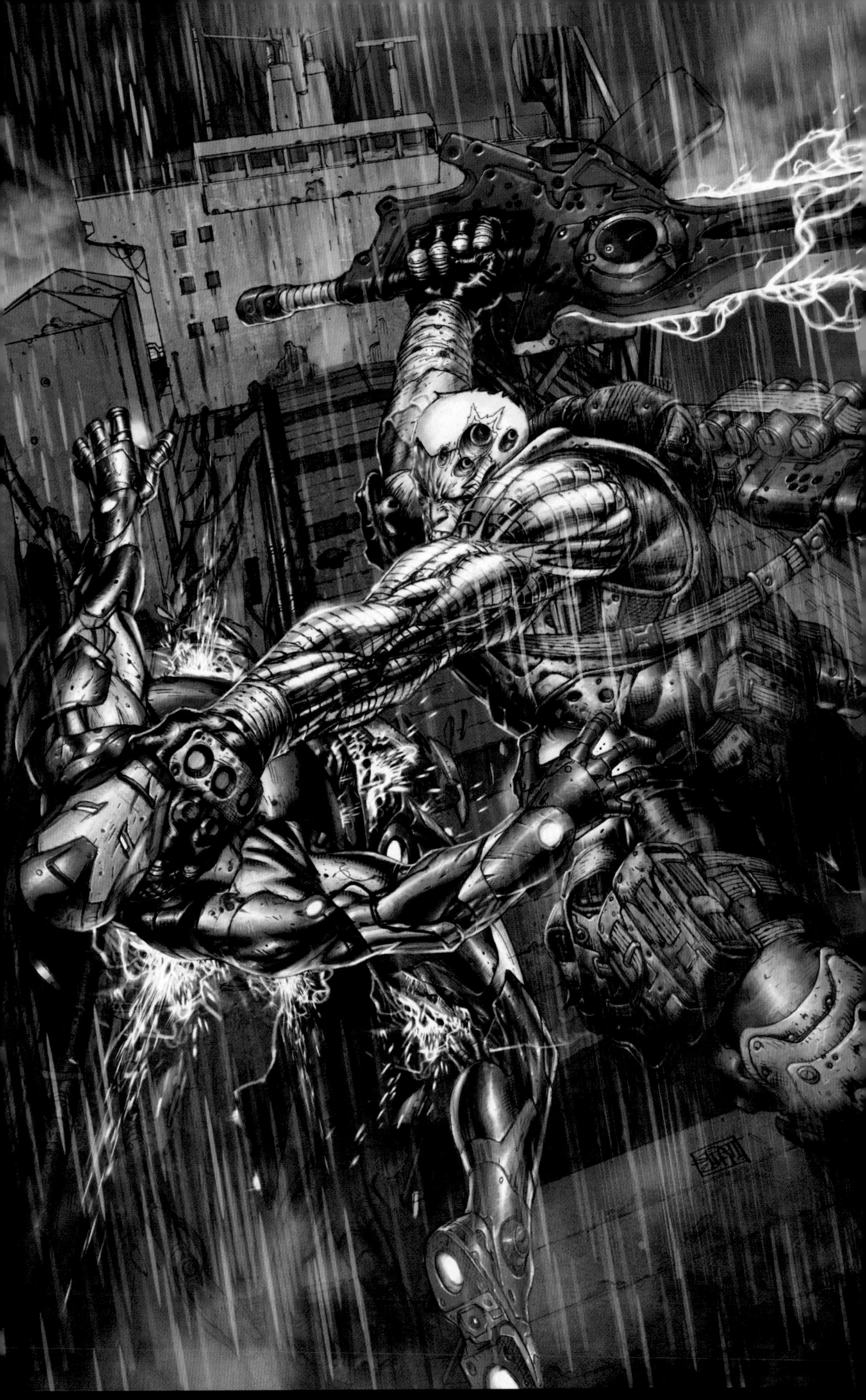

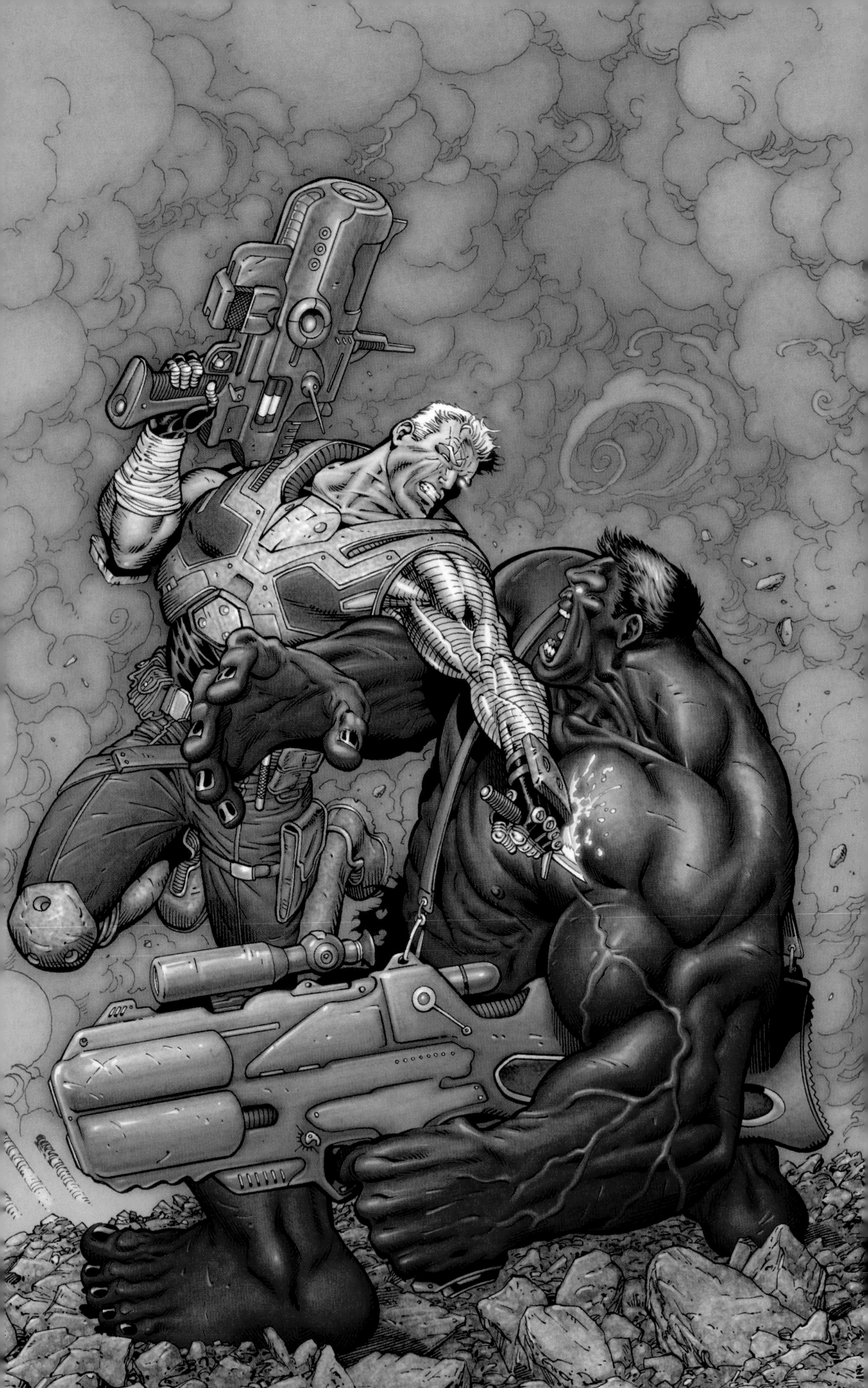

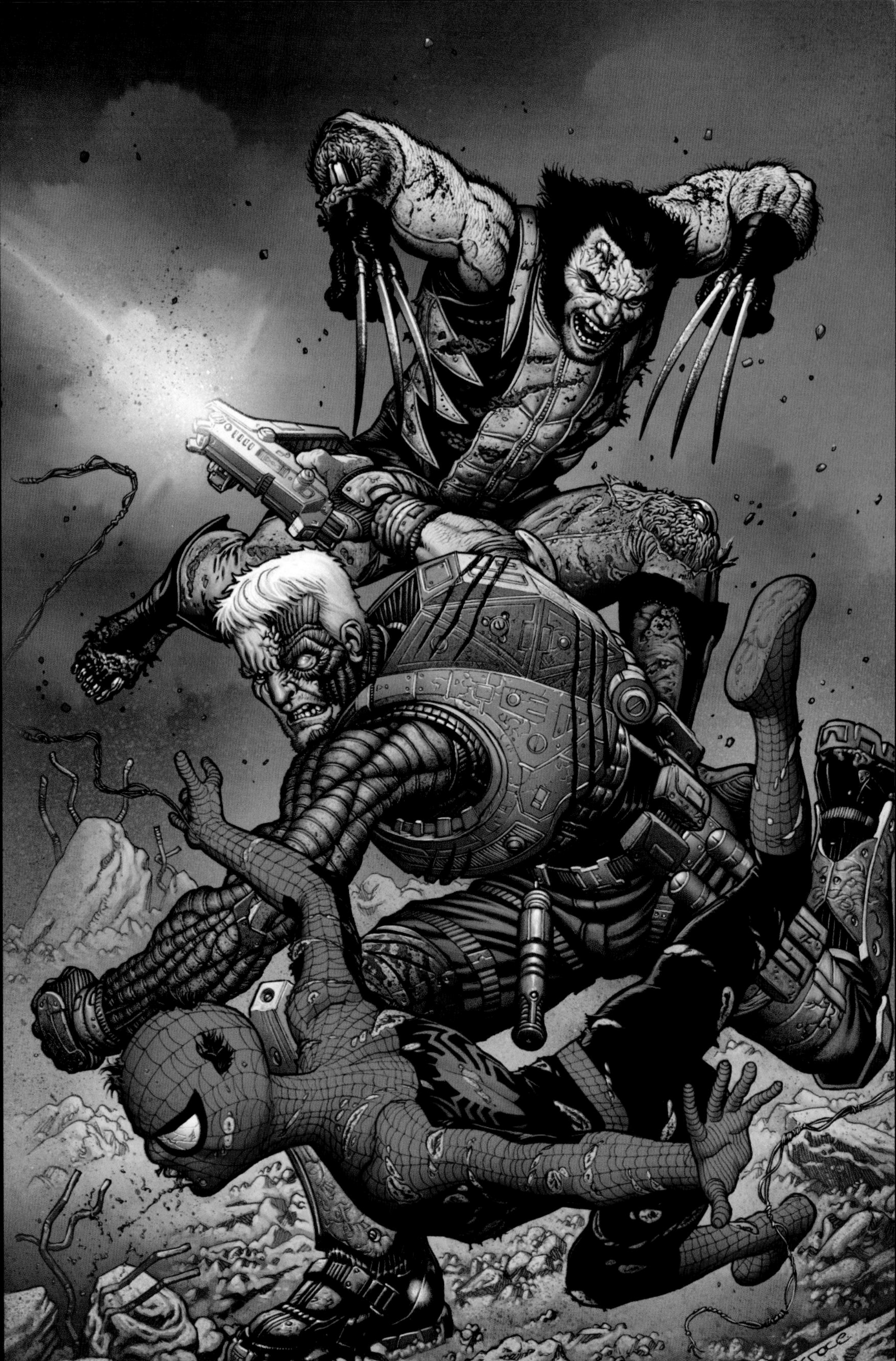

ISSUE 4 VARIANT COVER > STEVE SKROCE/RICHARD ISANOVE

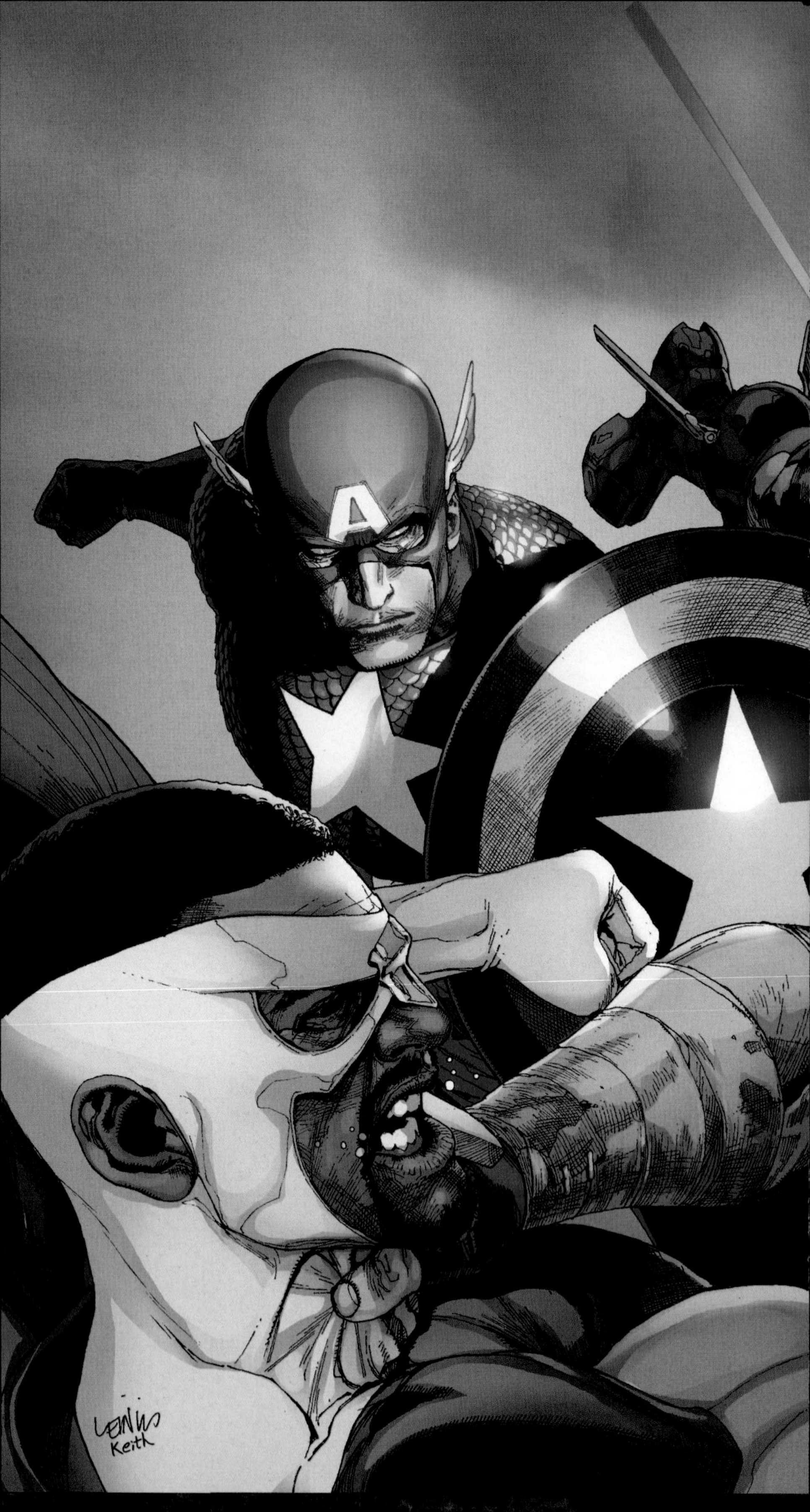
Keith

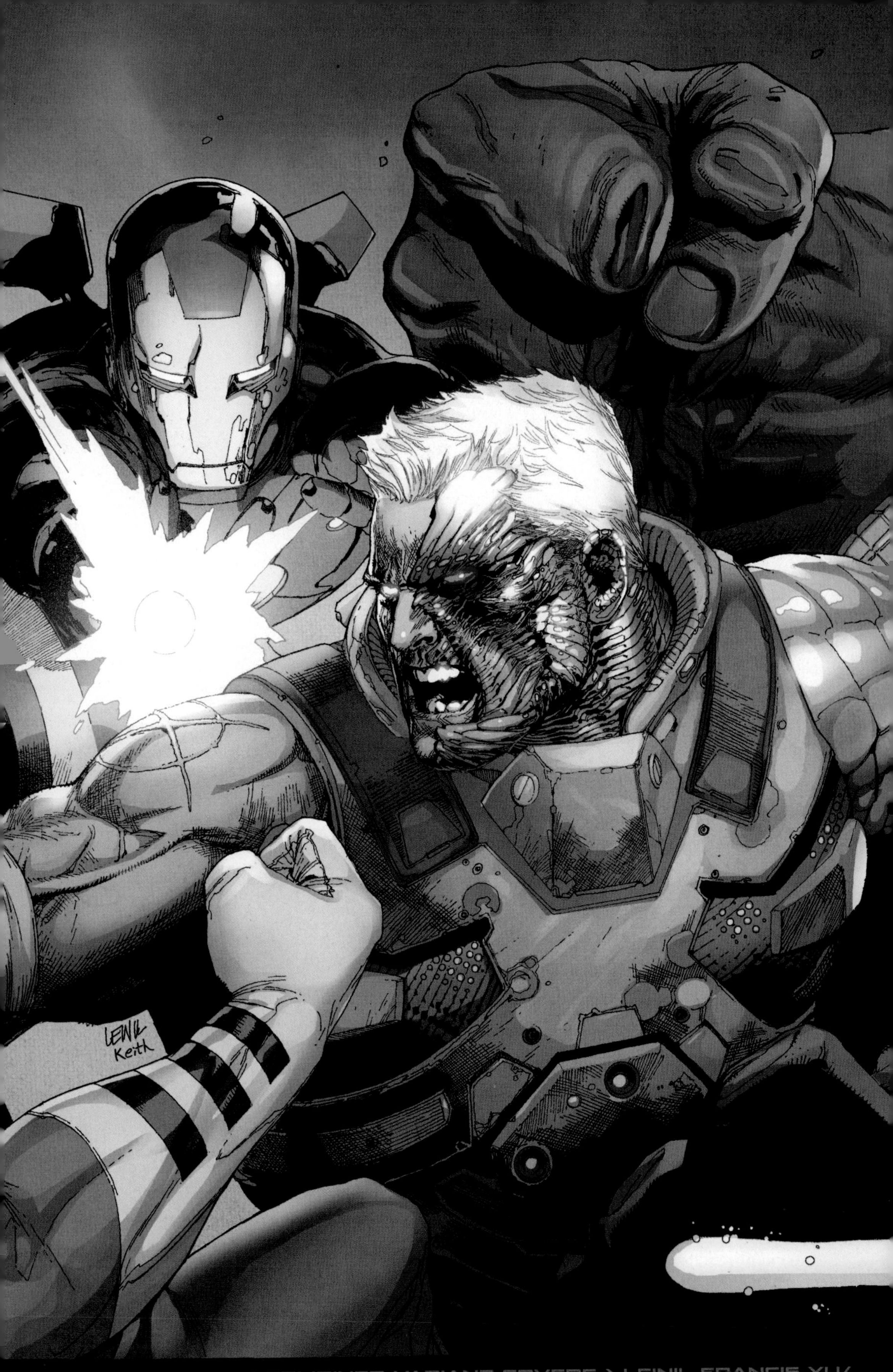
LEINIL
Keith

ISSUES 1-4 COMBINED VARIANT COVERS > LEINIL FRANCIS YU

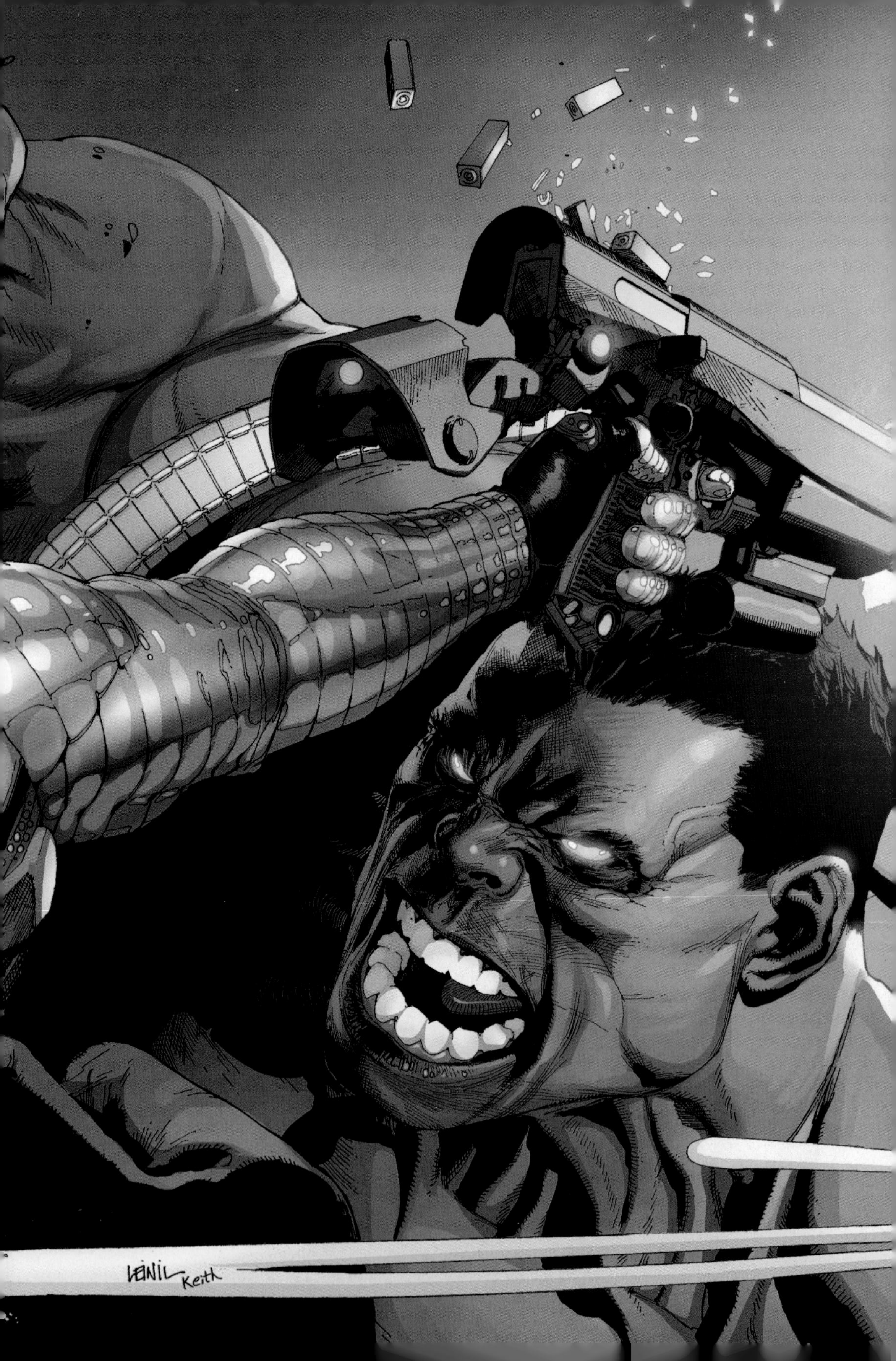
LEINIL
Keith

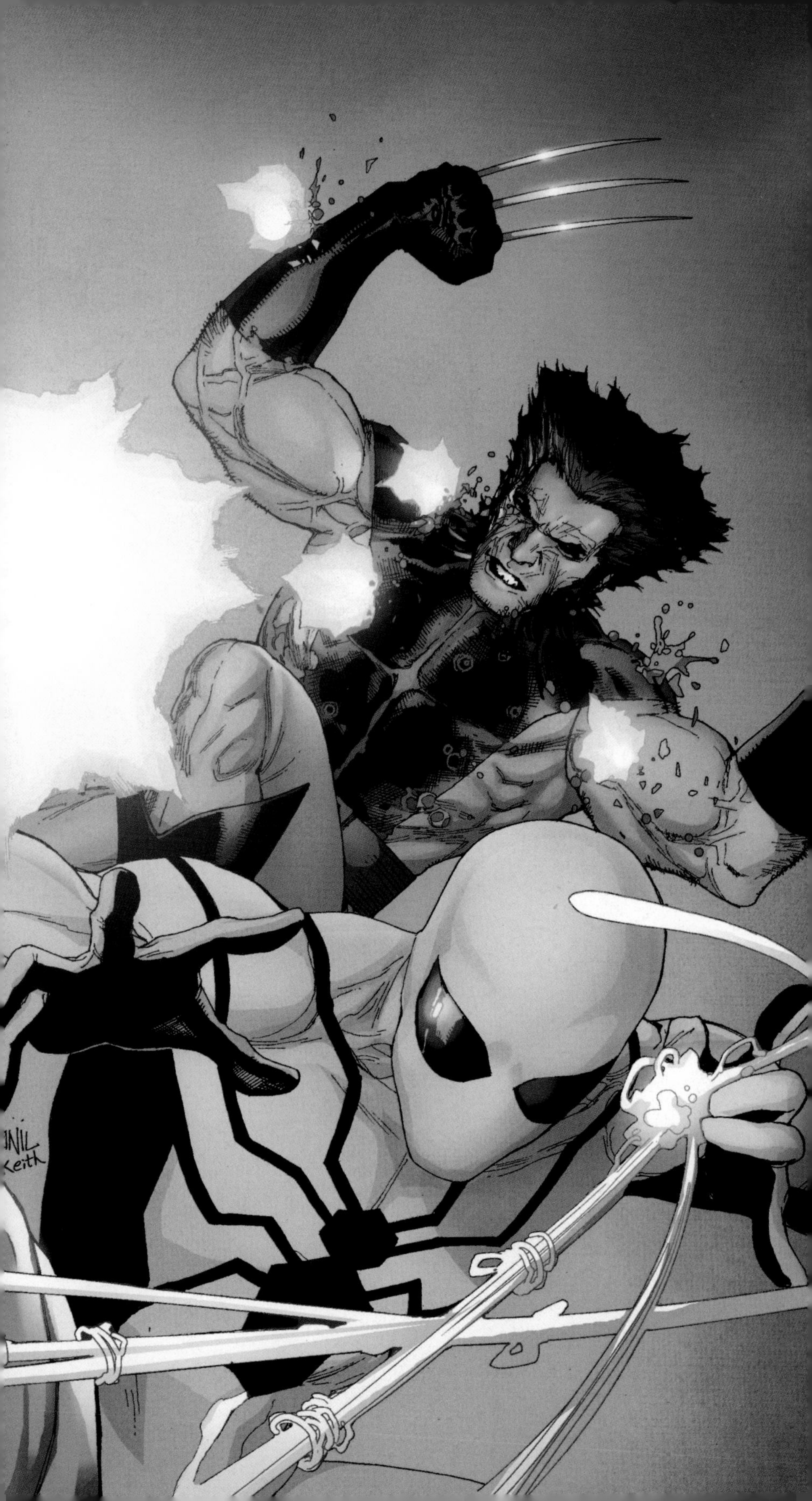

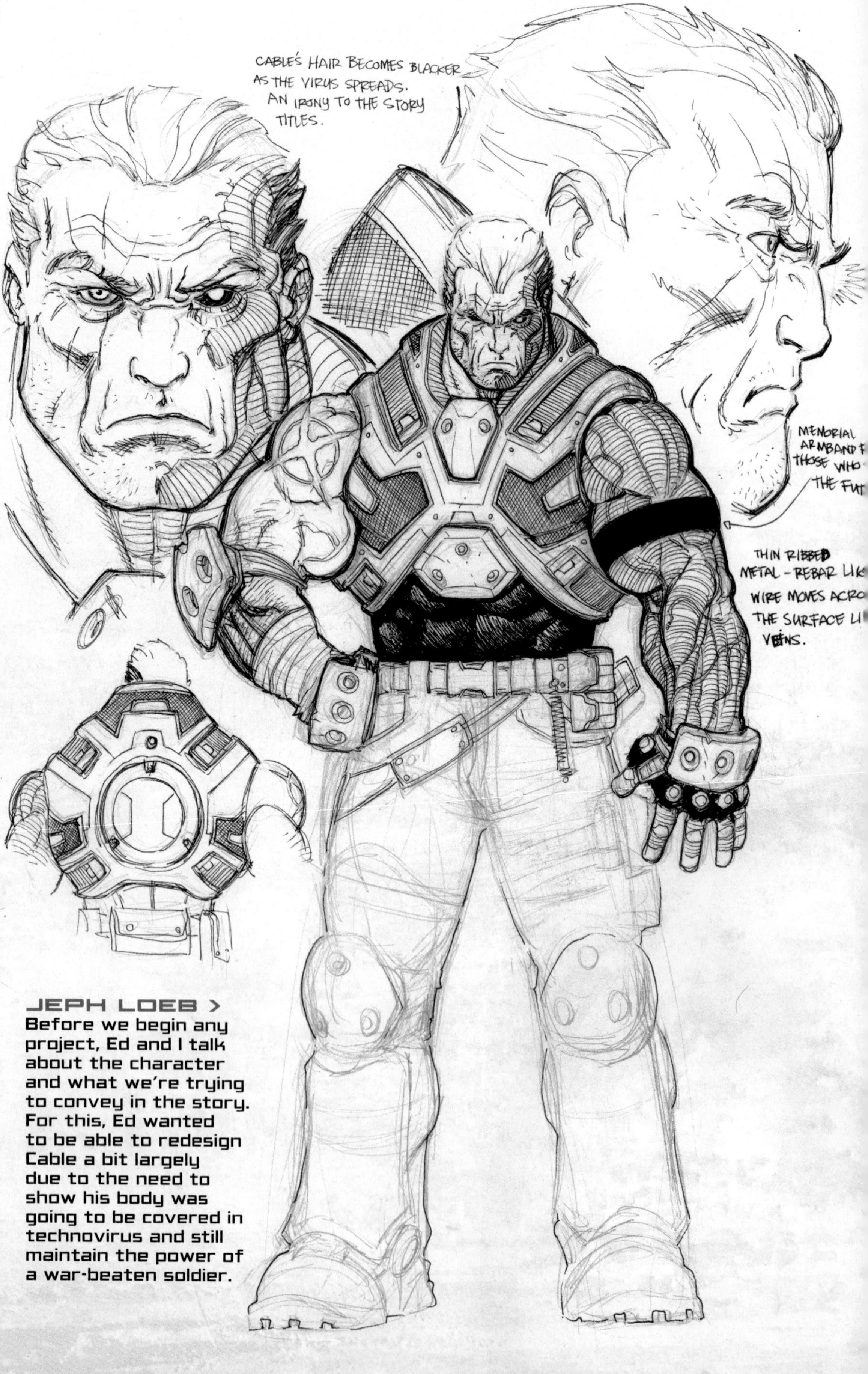
CABLE'S HAIR BECOMES BLACKER AS THE VIRUS SPREADS. AN IRONY TO THE STORY TITLES.
MEMORIAL
ARMBAND
THOSE WHO
THE
THIN RIBBED
METAL - REBAR
WIRE MOVES
THE SURFACE
VEINS.

JEPH LOEB >

Before we begin any project, Ed and I talk about the character and what we're trying to convey in the story. For this, Ed wanted to be able to redesign Cable a bit largely due to the need to show his body was going to be covered in technovirus and still maintain the power of a war-beaten soldier.

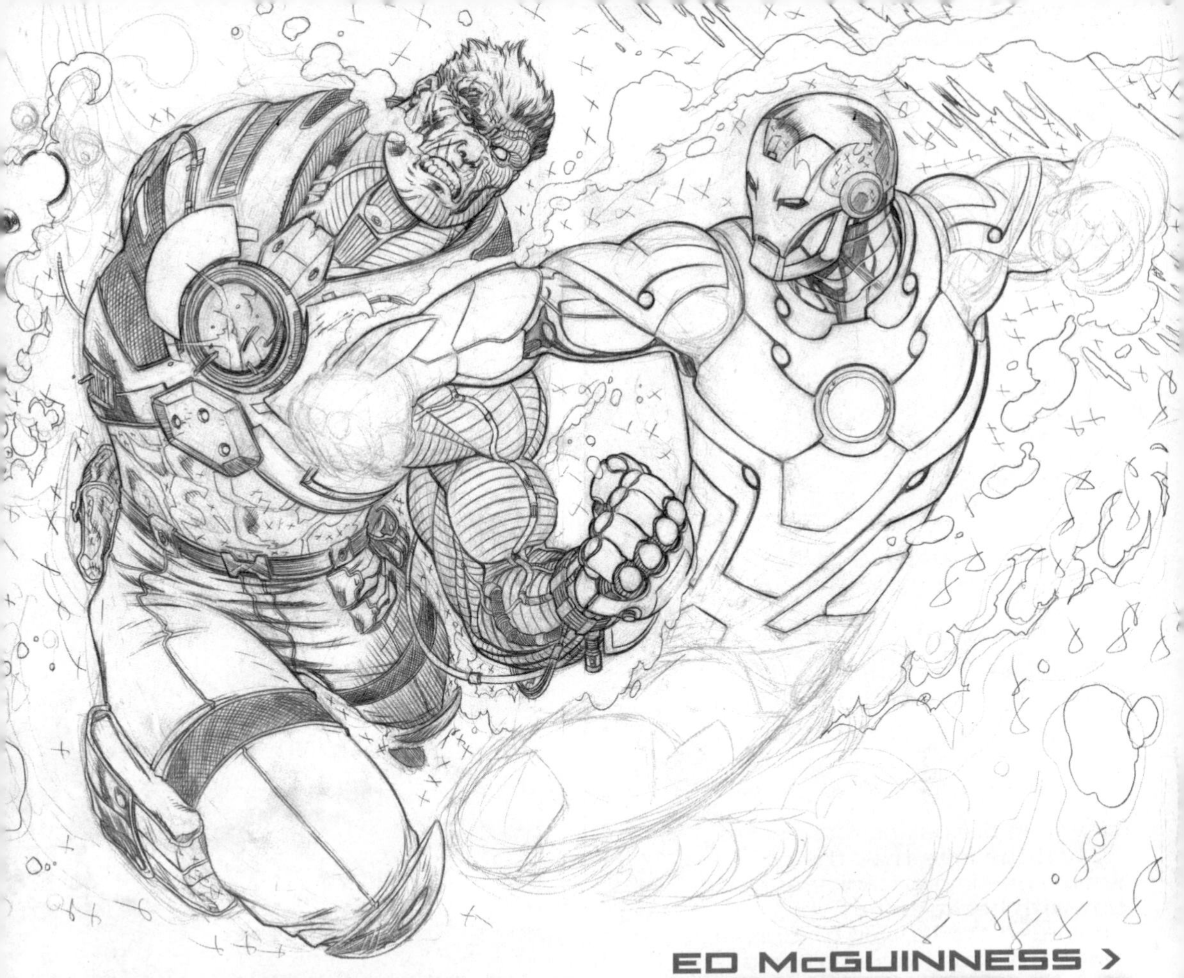

ED McGUINNESS >

SKETCHBOOK

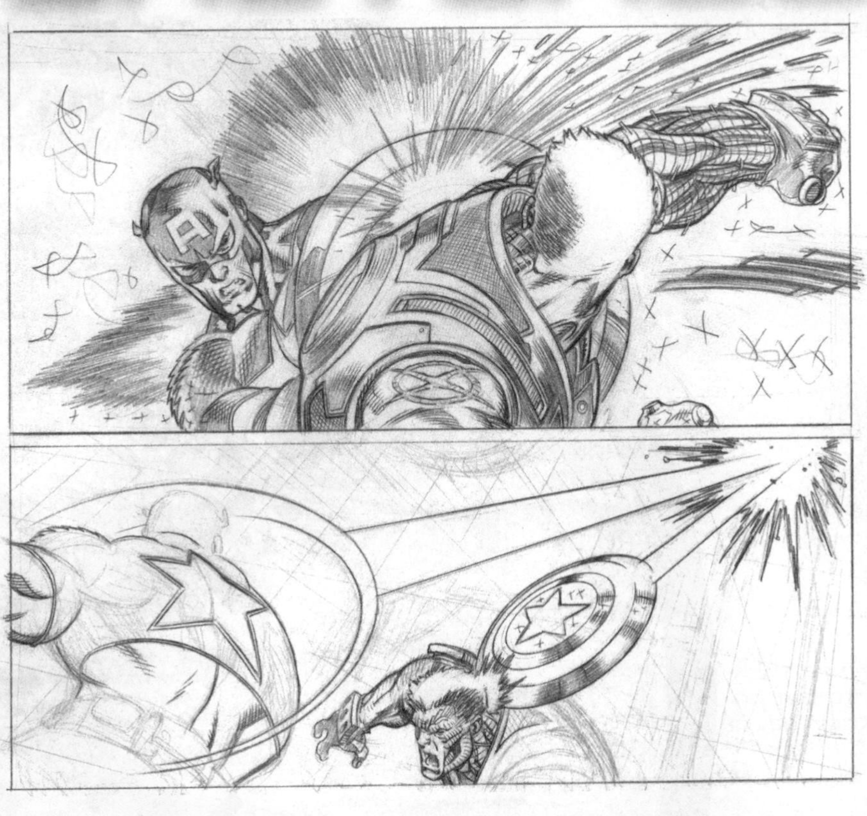

JL > One of the many joys of working with Ed is that he has that distinctive Marvel DNA in his blood. He draws pages with so much action that it can't be contain to the page -- you think that Cap's Shield is going to come bouncing out of the comic itself and hit YOU!

MOON

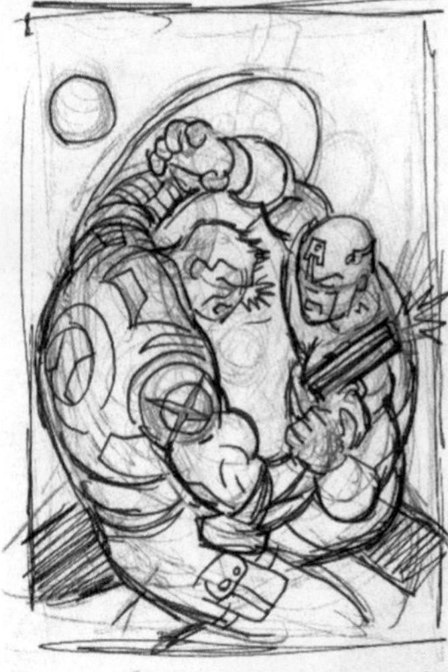

SUNRISE

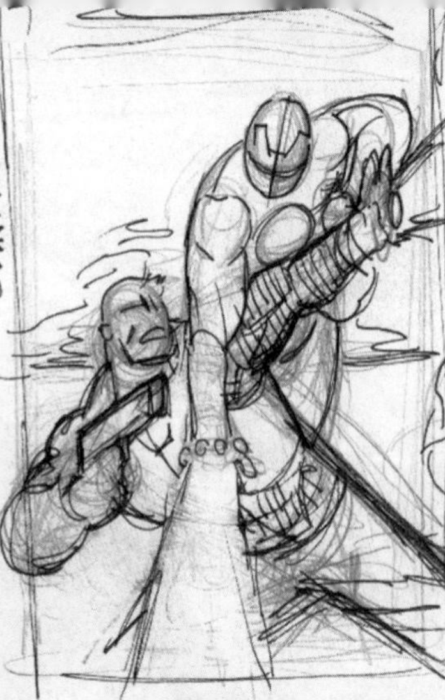

NOON

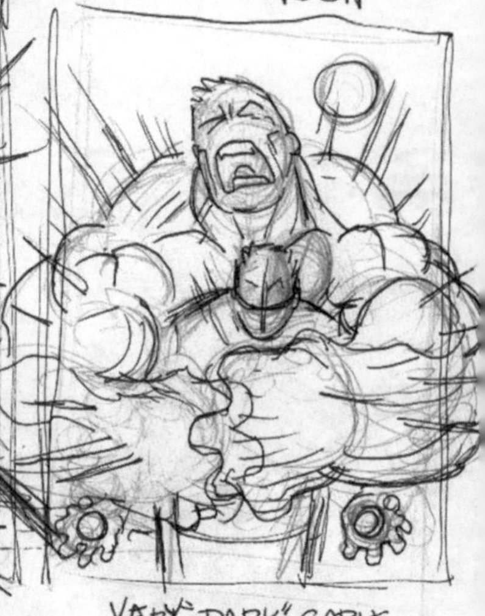

- CABLE GRABBING CAP'S SHIELD ARM
- CAP GRABBING CABLE'S GUN ARM AS A SHOT GOES OFF

NOT TOO MUCH OF CABLE'S CONDITION REVEALED.

CABLE AND IRONMAN EXCHANGING REPULSOR RAYS

VERY "DARK" CABLE IMPALING RED WITH HUNDREDS OF T-O VIRUS NEEDLES

GLOWING REPULSOR'S LEFT OVER FROM I.M. FIGHT

JL > In discussing the covers, Ed had the idea that they should be simple, iconic battles but with backgrounds that conveyed the lapsing of time since the story takes place over 18-24 hours. So we needed a horizon line, one way or the other to show night, dawn, noon and sunset. Morey Hollowell our astonishing colorist brought the fire to every one of them.

VERY DARK, SHADOWY, SCARY CABLE

HARD RAIN!

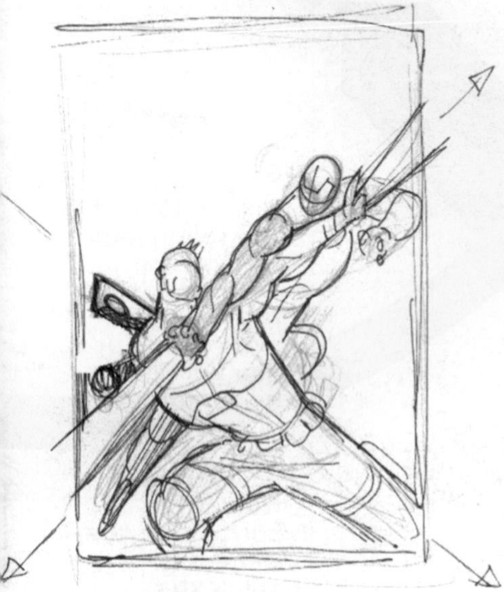

WOLVIE IMPALED IN SHADOW

RULK'S MOUTH SMOKING

BULLET HOLES IN CAP'S ARMOR

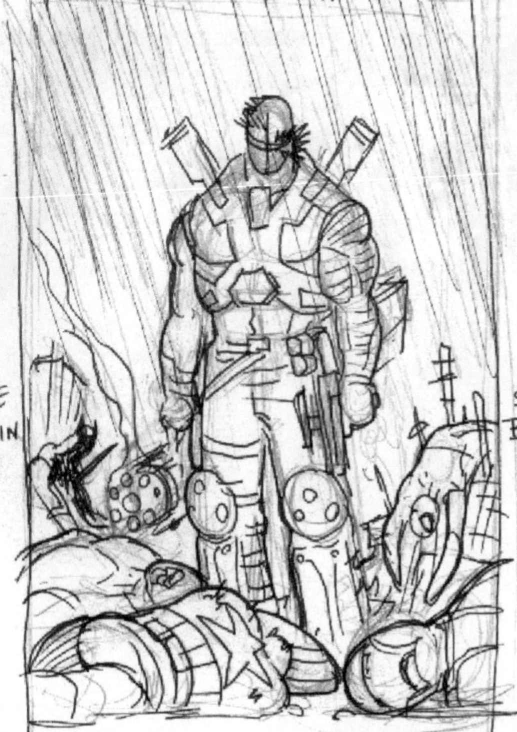

SPID... BRO...

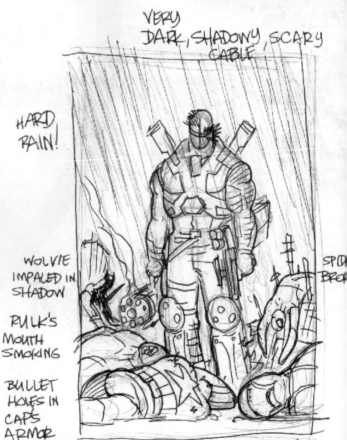

JL > Ed reconceived the cover of issue #2 to put on the subtle "X" in their battle -- it's stuff like that where Ed's designs skills shine.

IRON MAN'S HEAD TWISTED BACKWARDS.

E. I THINK THIS SHOULD FEEL BRUTAL W/OUT GORE!

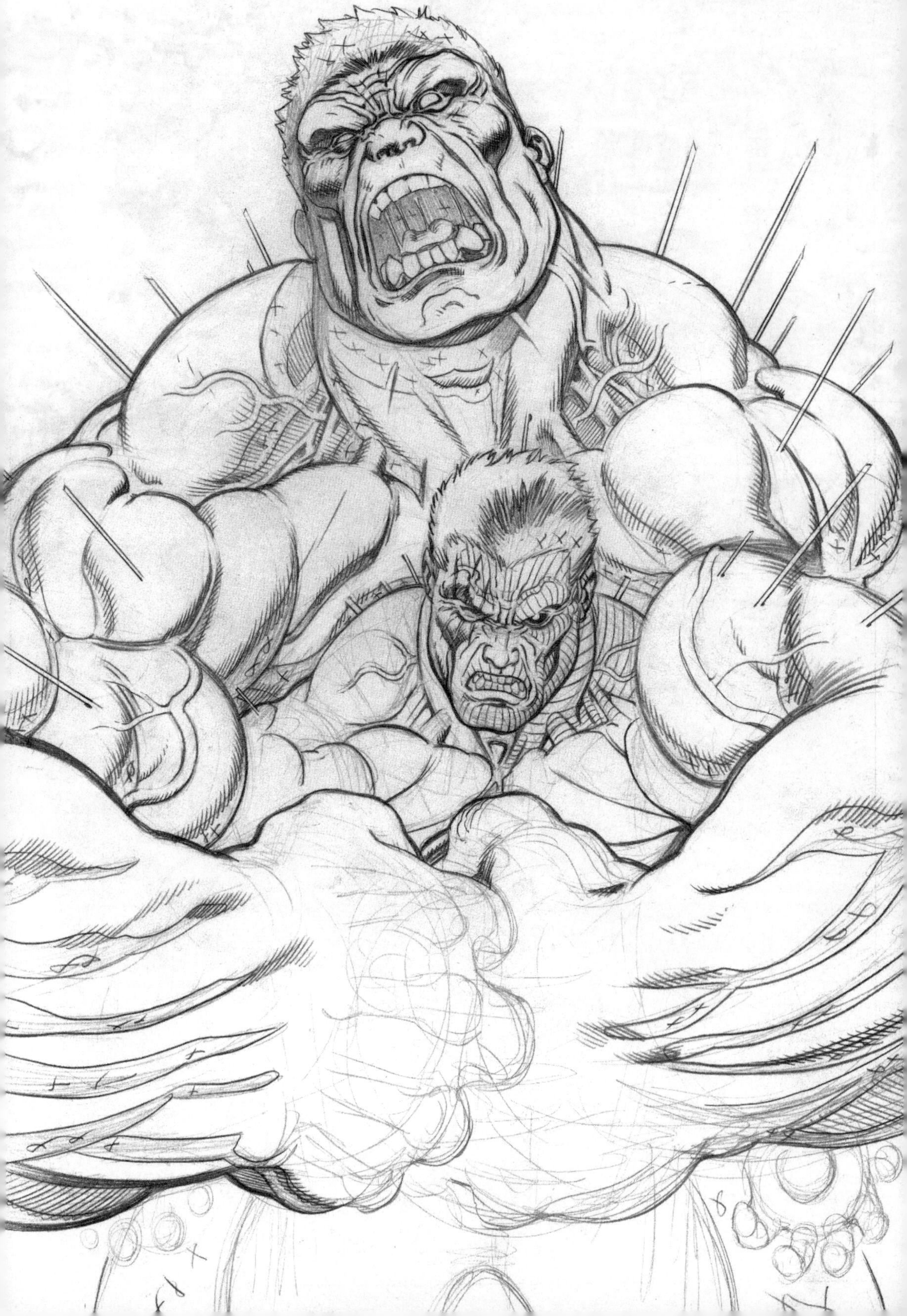

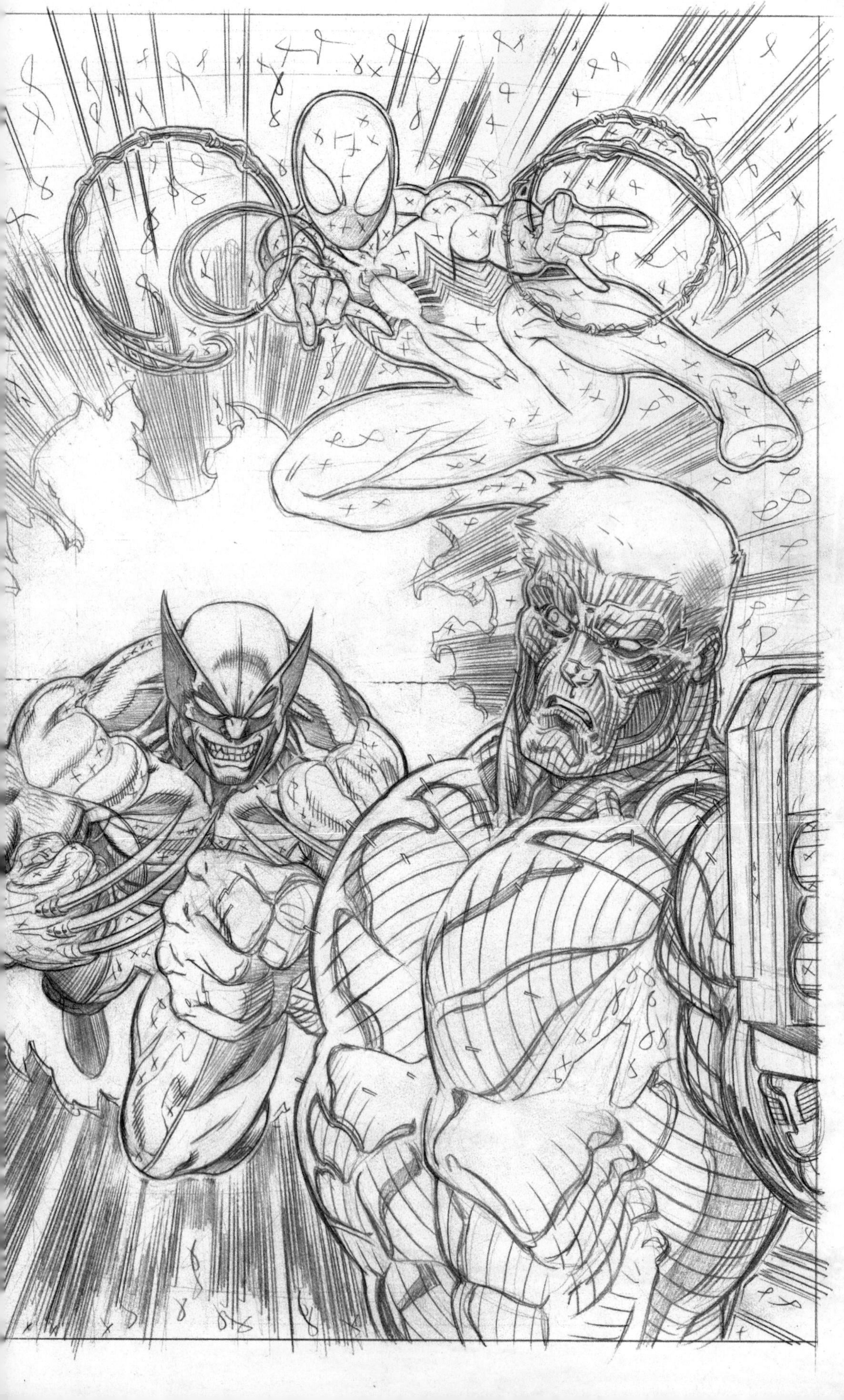

JL > On the left is one those pages you rarely get to see. From the very beginning, Ed had wanted to get Wolverine into his X-Force costume and Spidey into the black costume -- for no other reason other than he loves those designs. I tried my best to make it work within the story -- even so much as to write the final page of Issue 3 with them changed. But when I started the script for Issue 4, this plot thread kept dangling and it was going to take away from the urgency of the story. The Avengers have been kidnapped, the clock is ticking, but these two heroes have time to change costume?

Finally, I talked to Ed and he agreed, but then he had to redraw the last page of Issue #3, which fortunately had not been inked yet. The cover for Issue 4, on the other hand, was already done and solicited, so that couldn't be changed.

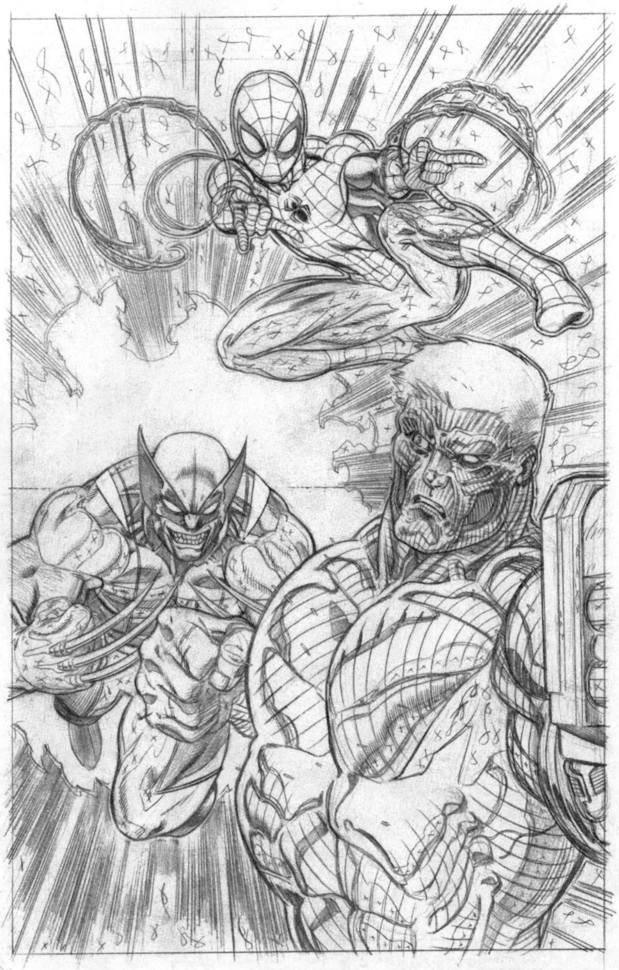

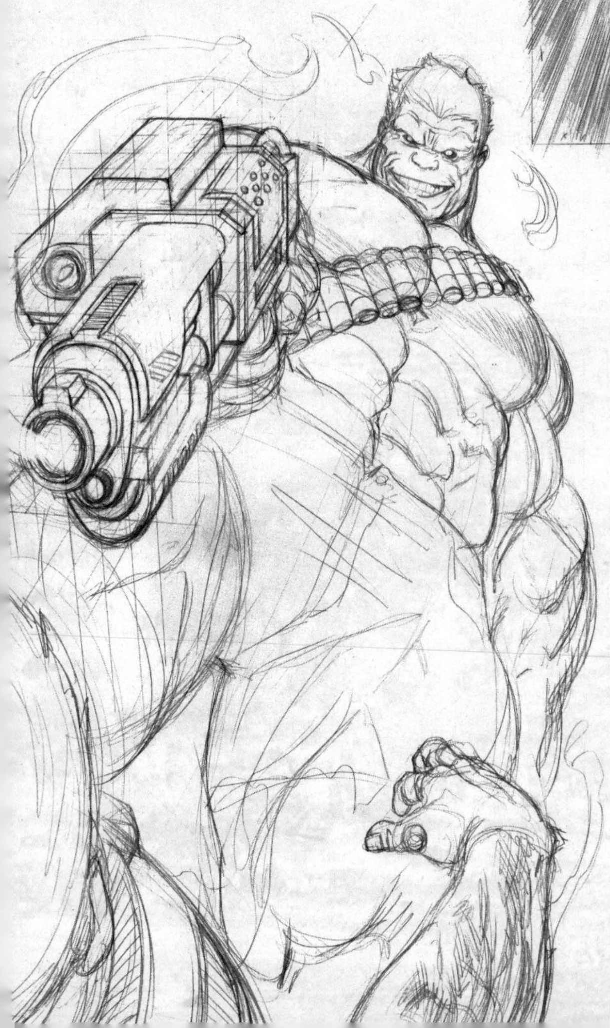

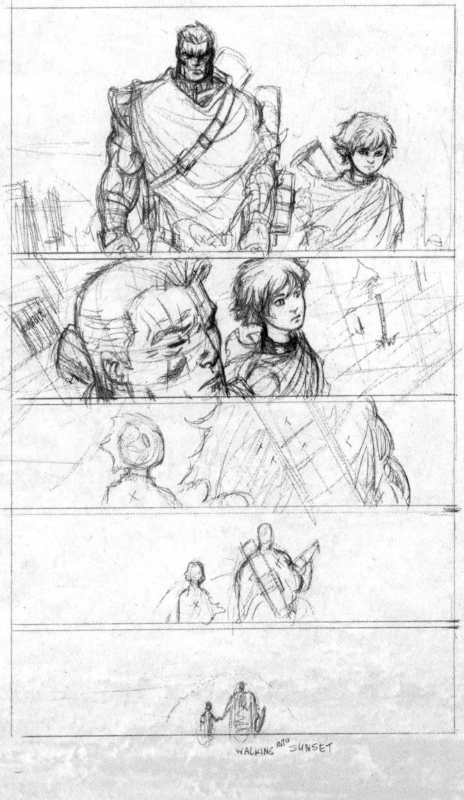
WALKING INTO SUNSET